The Failure of Independent Liberalism

1930–1941

by R. Alan Lawson

Capricorn Books, New York

For my father and mother

Herman and Norma Lawson

Acknowledgments

This study depended upon many persons. I wish first to acknowledge the indispensable aid and criticism given by John Higham, under whom it was my good fortune to study at the University of Michigan. Others at Michigan also gave wisdom and good advice that I greatly appreciate: Sidney Fine, a man of awesome knowledge about the 1930's, Connie Bassil, Robert Sklar, and the political scientist Norman Thomas.

My friends at the University of California, Irvine, made that a happy time in which to continue my efforts. Among many from whom I learned, Keith Nelson and Spencer Olin were especially helpful for their close reading of the text.

At Smith I have received intelligent criticism from Daniel Aaron, Mark Aldrich, David Allmendinger, Allen Weinstein, and Mira Wilkins. And Kenneth Porter of the University of Oregon gave me the benefit of his wide knowledge in several useful suggestions.

Thanks also are due to Peter Herman and Michael Krisman, who helped with the research, and to Hilda MacArthur and Catherine Smith for their typing and insightful comments.

Finally, I would like to thank several principals of my story for graciously consenting to interviews:

Thomas Amlie	Horace Kallen
Thurman Arnold	Harry Laidler
Roger Baldwin	Corliss Lamont
Alfred Bingham	Lewis Lorwin
Frances Browne	Robert MacIver
James Burnham	Archibald MacLeish
John Chamberlain	Carey McWilliams
Stuart Chase	Gorham Munson
Malcolm Cowley	Dorothy Norman
David Cushman Coyle	Edward Norman
Paul Douglas	George Soule
Waldo Frank	Ordway Tead
Arthur Holcombe	Donald Young
Matthew Josephson	

All these persons helped me avoid many more errors than the ones I have assuredly committed to print. Equally important, they have enhanced the pleasure and the illumination that should come with such an effort to understand.

Contents

I hail with joy the oceanic, variegated, intense practical energy, the demand for facts, even the business materialism of the current age, our States. But woe to the age and land in which these things, movements, stopping at themselves, do not tend to ideas. As fuel to flame, and flame to the heavens, so must wealth, science, materialism—even this democracy of which we make so much— unerringly feed the highest mind, the soul.

—WALT WHITMAN, *Democratic Vistas*, 1871

Let us perfect ourselves within, and in due season changes in society will come of themselves, is the teaching. And while saints are engaged in introspection, burly sinners run the world.

—JOHN DEWEY, *Reconstruction in Philosophy*, 1920

John Dewey has emphasized, quite rightly, the fact that thought which does not ultimately guide action is incomplete. But the reverse of Dewey's dictum is likewise true. Action that does not, in turn, lead to reflection, is perhaps even more gravely incomplete. For one person who is lost so completely in reverie or abstract thought that he forfeits the capacity to act, there are now a hundred so closely committed to action or routine that they have lost the capacity for rational insight and contemplative reconstruction: therefore they have lost the very possibility of reformation and self-direction.

—LEWIS MUMFORD, *The Conduct of Life*, 1951

Preface

This book attempts to explain a significant but as yet only lightly explored segment of American reform during the Depression. I have chosen to term the persons involved "independent liberals" because they charted several independent courses mostly between organized Marxism on the left and the New Deal on the right. From their efforts emerged two major reform impulses directed at replacing the old capitalist order with a more cooperatively organized society.

The first of these impulses, for which the term "pragmatic rationalism" seems apt, attracted many who stressed experimental reason rather than organic social ties or historical precedents. They were much influenced by John Dewey's instrumentalism and Thorstein Veblen's concept of an engineered society designed to end arrogant wastefulness. In their ranks stood such notable economists and social critics as Stuart Chase, George Soule, Paul Douglas, and Alfred Bingham. And at the fore was Dewey himself, more active in social affairs during the thirties than ever.

The second expression of independent liberalism argued for social cohesion through a humane regard for tradition and environment. Its proponents advocated two specific programs in addition to a pervasive respect for the accumulated wisdom of Western civilization and of nature.

Regionalism, in which Lewis Mumford, Howard Odum, and various refugees from the Southern Agrarian school were especially prominent, proposed organization of the country into cohesive units as an antidote to the rootlessness of mass society. The regionalists emphasized tradition and cooperation as the bases of a new society that would place high value on esthetic and spiritual ends. Their belief in shared wisdom and a sense of communal responsibility sought to replace the social vision of Horatio Alger with the older lessons of Emerson.

Cultural pluralism, the second of the traditionalist platforms, also

13

stressed local unity within national diversity. But it insisted that the most valuable of the ties binding men together were not regional but ethnic and held that the unique value of American life depended on preserving harmony between distinct ethnic cultures, rather than subjecting all to assimilation within a single national standard.

Independent liberalism enlisted many of the most intelligent American social critics. In designating them liberal I act on the conviction that there is no necessary distinction between "radical" and "liberal." When the term "liberalism" appeared first in ravaged nineteenth-century Europe, it was used to describe all attitudes with some degree of open-mindedness that existed between the extremes of disruption on the left and tradition on the right. A liberal is one who seeks solutions without resorting to inflexible dogma. Depending on the needs of the moment, he may act moderately or he may turn to radical action, even revolution. In the American context what has most consistently characterized the changeable liberal has been his bias toward progressive reform. During the 1930's some persons of liberal temper supported the New Deal. Others who felt the need for more radical action remained outside the New Deal at the same time that they exercised their liberal aversion to dogma by avoiding commitments to the Marxists.

In describing the efforts of the latter group, the independents, as a "failure" I speak in distinctly limited terms. The independents analyzed cogently, often profoundly, and were not discredited by events. But they failed to gain power or to persuade others to enact their essential programs.

That failure reveals an ancient strain in America between ideas and power. Social critics of every era and the historians who have followed have puzzled inconclusively over how much they should value ideas according to their intrinsic merit and how much according to their practical outcomes. In some cases the issue could be avoided. Those with esthetic or other-worldly motives could say with Emily Dickinson that "the soul selects her own society. Then shuts the door." But reformers have had to face the demands of society outside. In the United States, complex and moralistic at the same time, there exists a tension between being good and doing well. Clear-cut ideologies have not flourished in such an atmosphere; but reform programs that attempt to mediate between diverse interests have sometimes had success. Thus it was that when the New Deal sought to cope with the great reform needs of the 1930's through a many-sided appeal to interest groups, it could make a plausible case that it was following the American tradition of trying to do the best possible job under the circumstances. Most historians have tended to agree. Their reformist sensibilities, taken together with their respect for power as the chief determinant of historical significance, have naturally led to a view of the thirties as the Age of Roosevelt.

But the urgings of the independents for something better deserve attention not simply because their leaders included men of greater mental force than could be found within the New Deal, but also because the New Deal did not succeed in curing the major social ills it confronted. The argument of practicality—that those in government service had political savvy and those outside were mostly naïve or perverse—has rung increasingly hollow over time. Practicality can be treacherous. It urges compromise but may be used against compromise by deeming some evils too firmly rooted for practical reform to touch. It may insulate society against the foolish hope of heaven on earth, and in so doing leave victims of tolerated evils little but Dr. Faustus' bitter wisdom, that all places shall be hell that are not heaven.

We have, finally, the present malaise to ponder. America has not become happy. The decline of independent liberalism at the end of the 1930's was followed by a steadily deepening pessimism. That depression of the spirit coincided with the establishment of a moderate political consensus that has kept ideology and utopia at bay and pleas for radical change a disaffected and seldom heeded rumble from below.

Introduction

The Channeling of Reform

The rich variety of reform thought that gained prominence during the Depression did not simply spring out of the wreckage of the old capitalist order. It bore the marks of a struggle against the malfunctionings of the industrial economy stretching back to the end of the Civil War. Major problems persisted during those many years: an unfair return to farmers, ugly factory conditions, and inequitable treatment of ethnic and racial minorities. Pervading those issues was an anxiety that America was ending its career as a frontier nation and entering an era in which individual opportunities would be ever more restricted. The new situation seemed to call for consolidation of interests into groups that could successfully compete with one another.

Farmers in the Populist Party sounded the loudest cry for solidarity in the late nineteenth century: "In the North, in the South, everywhere," a spokesman declared, "the farmers are organizing. They are adopting systems of trade and studying questions of political economy as they never did before. . . . With flying banners and an irresistible force they are moving . . . that their mission may be accomplished, and peace, prosperity and happiness may be the inheritance which they bequeath to future generations."[1]

Labor, too, was organizing. Not inclined to accept the Populist offer to join in common cause, or the socialist appeal to form a labor party, most workers who favored unionization came together on the basis of their common skills. Samuel Gompers' American Federation of Labor was a "pure and simple" union, reminiscent of the old guilds and a model for the new form of interest grouping.

In the professions the same guild tendency was pronounced. Between the end of the Civil War and 1900, all the major professions formed organizations to control standards and improve resources. The middle class, which was the locus for the growing professional groups, expanded

19

more rapidly than any other. But while that trend bespoke rising affluence, the gap between rich and poor widened and became more galling as improved communication made it better known. In 1890 Jacob Riis impressed a wide audience with his description of the wretched New York poor in *How the Other Half Lives*. That same year Ward McAllister, inspirer of the Social Register, bowed to the stylish rich in *Society as I Found It*. His book complemented the new villas that loomed over the tenements and were later endorsed in the new city of Chicago by the Columbian Exposition of 1893. Massive colonnaded buildings announced a sumptuary Roman style to grace a nation of expanding wealth and power.

Such graphic evidence of a dynamic society prompted systematic study of American life. When the Russell Sage Foundation conducted the famous Pittsburgh Survey (1907–9), it set the model for proliferating factual reports with thorough detail and the hopeful premise that knowledge is power or, at least, the prelude to the sensible exercise of power.

These studies helped illuminate a crucial imbalance between private and public life. As the private sphere underwent a steady consolidation, politics suffered from disorganization and loss of respect. Laments over the decline of political quality, which had filled the nineteenth century since the defeat of the intellectual aristocrat John Quincy Adams, grew louder after the Civil War. The amassing of great fortunes and the welding together of American enterprise into colossal trusts during those years were done under the aegis of laissez-faire, which produced clusters of special interests and undermined the older communities based on locale and common beliefs. The stress on free-enterprise individualism led, thus, to a great massing of things and the isolation of persons. Reformers had a choice of responses. Either they could accept the disintegration of community and strive for a fair balance between fragmented groups and interests, or they could seek a principle or common program that would fuse the scattered elements of culture into a new whole.

The strategy of balancing appealed most to those reformers who intended to work through politics and practical private agencies. Progressive reformers stressed regulatory commissions and antitrust legislation with a vigor that ultimately established a pluralism of power blocs as the dominant style in American public life. So far did the pluralist ideal of give and take, share and placate, penetrate the national psyche that a recent critic could sensibly quip that American hero worship shifted after the turn of the century from Andrew Carnegie to Dale Carnegie![2] As early as 1908 Arthur Bentley, a social analyst of uncommon ability, concluded that government itself had become one more interest group among many heaped upon the national balance.[3] From that followed the great achievement of the New Deal. Franklin Roosevelt's great coalition often staggered, but it had the force to reverse the nineteenth-century trend of private interest supremacy and establish the national political interest group as the dominant power broker.

A related form of pluralism guided the settlement house movement. Hull House, begun by Jane Addams in 1889 from a conviction of obligation to do something useful and to share with the less fortunate, set dual aims for the settlements. First, they were to serve as "outposts in the slums," to provide information about city life, especially as it affected the motley variety of immigrants; second, the settlement workers were to assume the responsibility for pressing their new wisdom toward reform in a way that would not compromise the integrity of separate groups. Thus, they became tutors to those who did not comprehend the growing diversity of society. They promoted the pluralist virtues of tolerance and breadth of vision and worked on a wide array of concrete reforms.

Labor was similarly preoccupied with balancing. The American Federation of Labor desired simply to increase its share of the nation's goods by pitting its collective strength against that of management. No plan for revolution or systematic reformation came from its counsels. It was the despair of its militant rivals—Marxists, Socialists, and even Populists—who wished to use the labor value of production to establish the preeminence of the working class. But the AFL became the dominant union force because of its clear understanding of how society was developing.

The competing goal of reform through a principle of unity had a more grandiose cast to it than pluralism and attracted the bulk of critical theorists. On one articulate fringe were visionaries typified by Edward Bellamy and Henry George. In his novel, *Looking Backward*, Bellamy dramatized the hopefulness residing in the antique American belief in a Governing Design of providence. Bellamy maintained that history's victims would pass through all obstacles and arrive at a harmonious society. In a letter to the Boston *Transcript* in 1888, reproving them for finding his book too fantastic in its depiction of a perfectly mechanized Utopia, Bellamy spoke confidently of the "stream of tendency" setting toward a vastly more efficient and moral society, a stream fed by "every sigh of poverty, every tear of pity, every human impulse, every generous enthusiasm, every true religious feeling, every act by which men have given effect to their mutual sympathy." The golden shore lay dead ahead. "Our children will surely see it, and we, too, who are already men and women, if we deserve it by our faith and by our works."[4]

The self-taught economist Henry George wished to leave less to inexorable forces. His approach was more in the American tradition of the surefire formula than in that of the Grand Design. Indeed, he advertised his famous *Progress and Poverty* (1879) as having "The Remedy" —a single-tax plan by which any rise in the value of land ownership would be returned by taxation to the communities whose use of the products of that land made its value possible. George worked out his formula ingeniously and dramatically. While Tolstoy overstated the case in declaring that "people don't argue with George's teaching: they simply don't know it," George's theory did not receive the careful consideration owed it by the community of orthodox economists and men of influence who dismissed it out of hand as crank or seditious. George, in turn, rejected traditional economics in words that marked him as one of the more absolutist unifiers: "Whoever considers the political and social problems that confront us must see that they center in the problem of the distribution of wealth, and he must also see that, though their solution may be simple, it must be radical." Attempts to balance contrasting interests and sentiments would not do. "Our charities, our penal laws, our restrictions and prohibitions, by which, with so little avail, we endeavor to assuage poverty and check crime, what are they, at the very best, but the device of the clown who, having put the whole burden of his ass into one pannier, sought to enable the poor animal to walk straight by loading up the other pannier with stones?"[5]

Certain of the Socialists, especially those within the American Utopian tradition, had similar absolutist and millennial visions. And as with Bellamy the beauty of the vision made them seem imminent to their authors. Upton Sinclair, for example, who was finally to emerge in the 1930's as a bona fide politician, prophesied in 1907 that a revolution establishing an industrial republic run by workers would take place within one year after the 1912 election. Sinclair's great unifying principle was social evolution, a favorite of that Darwinian day, which would generate "forces . . . by a process as natural and as inevitable as that by which a chick breaks out of its shell or a child comes forth from the womb at the proper hour."[6] At the time Sinclair, always one to base his life on his beliefs, was presiding over Helicon Hall, a commune he hoped would prefigure the reformation soon to come. But the hall burned down—and World War I, not Utopia, followed 1912.

Other Socialist critics, predominantly Marxists and Fabian Socialists, operated within a more earthbound frame of reference. They anticipated a long campaign of education to root out myths and ignorance. Many of them sought applications of the psychological theories then on the rise—dominated by Freud, Jung, the behaviorists like Stanley Hall and Edward Thorndike and the lesser known William McDougall, whose insistence on the importance of instinct found a direct and influential echo in the writings of Thorstein Veblen. No Socialist critic was more in the early twentieth-century air than H. G. Wells. His discussions of community gave a place to psychic factors that extended Socialism far beyond its original economic and political base. One should conclude, Wells asserted in 1909, that:

> Socialism is a moral and intellectual process. . . . Only secondarily and incidentally does it sway the world of politics. It is not a political movement; it may engender political movements, but it can never become a political movement; any political body, and organization whatever, that professes to stand for Socialism, makes an altogether too presumptuous claim.

And then Wells presented the sort of appeal for organic unity and growth that was coming into vogue: "The whole is greater than the part, the will than the instrument. There can be no official nor pontifical Socialism; the theory lives and grows. It springs out of the common sanity of mankind."[7]

More precisely indebted to psychological theories were the Englishman Graham Wallas and his precocious student at Harvard, Walter Lippmann. Both critics stressed the tidal pull of irrational impulses and hoped that enough could be learned about motivation to make intelligent social management possible.[8] But they were not anxiously seeking a psychology of adjustment. Their "great society" was not huddled on a placid mid-ground. Rather they wished to have psychological forces understood so that an elite of talent could move toward the limits of its creative potential and inspire the remainder of society to reach a far higher pitch of life than would otherwise be possible. Thus might the routine dullness that cursed machine society be offset. An analogy described what the "great society" would be like:

> If I try to make for myself a visual picture of the social system which I should desire for England and America [mused Wallas] there comes before me a recollection of those Norwegian towns and villages where everyone, the shopkeepers and the artisans, the schoolmaster, the boy who drove the post-ponies, and the student daughter of the innkeeper who took round the potatoes, seemed to respect themselves, to be capable of Happiness as well as of pleasure and excitement, because they were near the Mean in the employment of all their faculties. . . . I recollect that the very salt and savour of Norwegian life depends on the fact that poets and artists and statesmen have worked in Norway with a devotion which was not directed by any formula of moderation. When I talk to a New Zealander about the future of his country, and about the example which she is creating of a society based upon the avoidance both of destitution and superfluity, I sometimes feel that she may have still to learn that the Extreme as a personal ideal for those who are called by it is a necessary complement of the Mean in public policy.

Clearly, to speak on such a scale carried one beyond strict psychological analysis, as Wallas recognized. Here, he cautioned:

> We reach the point where our examination of the condition of Happiness, and, indeed, the whole method of psychological analysis, ceases to be a sufficient guide to life. It is rather through Philosophy than Psychology, rather through a general interpretation of the universe, than through a detailed study of so small a part of it as our own minds, that the call of the Extreme makes itself most clearly heard.[9]

In the end it was the same for all the critics who sought the unification of society on behalf of reform. Beyond information and technique they needed a wholehearted program of ideas and sentiments—a workable faith.

The problems of devising a reform program in the face of rapid change caused some analysts to sink back into reaction or despair. With ingeniously novel pessimism the historian and scion of a famous family, Henry Adams, warned about dimly perceived laws of force.

Since the age of science began, he noted, man had confidently sought to accommodate the rising flood of knowledge. But he had loosed a fearsome spiral that was accelerating toward doomsday. "As the mind of man enlarged its range," Adams wrote, "it enlarged the field of complexity, and must continue to do so, even into chaos, until the reservoirs of sensuous or supersensuous energies are exhausted, or cease to affect him, or until he succumbs to their excess."[10] The issue Adams raised persisted throughout the century with growing force as science increased its social control and destructiveness.

A different concern about disorder occupied the New Humanists. Led by Irving Babbitt of Harvard and Paul Elmer More, literary critic of the *Nation*, the New Humanists advocated rigid standards of thought based on classical and Renaissance models, and an equally rigid "inner check" to maintain moral control over bestial instincts. It was a static concept. Opposed to modern literature and social reform experiments, the New Humanists dragged their crusted sea anchor astern, but they hardly slowed the voyage. They remained few in number and served mainly during the twenties to deepen the scholarship of cultural history and to provide a foil for progressives.

Most critical thinkers after 1900 were optimistic reformers seeking a principle of unity. In their search they divided between those who relied most heavily on science and efficiency and those who looked to philosophy and the force of intuition.

Enthusiasts for science and technology included evangelical members of the business community who wore rather loosely the mantle of reform. Thomas Edison and Henry Ford, for example, were great innovators who symbolized progress to their generation. But though they often spoke in appropriately progressive terms, they did little directly to reshape social and political institutions. Their mechanical creations inadvertently wrought the great change.

A businessman who came closer to inspiring conscious reform was Frederick Winslow Taylor, the early leader of the efficiency movement. His *Scientific Management in Business* (1911) outlined ways to increase production by gearing the motions of workers more precisely to their tasks. But Taylor also sensed implications for social welfare. If expertise could be applied to the working efficiency of man, why not to his well-being and intellectual improvement as well? After Taylor's death in 1915, Harlow S. Person tried to lead the Taylor Society toward reform.

That effort sparked the great continuous struggle within the scientific management movement between reform-minded social engineers and businessmen whose chief ardor was for profits.

Industrial psychology, which arose alongside scientific management, was always more firmly under business control. In theory, however, it was neutral. Hugo Munsterberg's *Psychology and Industrial Efficiency* (1913) and *Business Psychology* (1915) provided the early key arguments for neutrality. But neither Munsterberg nor his successors explained how neutrality could be maintained when management hired the psychologists and set the industrial goals.

The most important support for reform through social engineering came from an outsider who scorned conventional economics and business. Thorstein Veblen irritated other economists by attacking classical theory and by wandering through many obscurely related fields of inquiry to gather the evidence for his case. Veblen returned the antagonism. His famous gibe at the orthodox economic conception of man as a "homogeneous globule of desire," existing "self-imposed in elemental space," expressed his view of the foolishness of trying to understand economic behavior without giving attention to surrounding institutions and customs. These, Veblen concluded, were far more than the products of calculation or external pressures; they came from instinct or its distortion. Since Veblen believed the basic instinctive drive was toward "workmanship," skill and efficiency and the beauty they created were to him natural human aims. The principle of hedonism, on which classical economics had built its foundations, seemed a perversion of the ideal of purposeful effort. Veblen allied himself with the great English critics of utilitarianism, John Ruskin and William Morris, and the anarchist Peter Kropotkin in celebrating the benefits to be gained from the proverbial "labors of love." The issue was concisely drawn by the contrast between Benthamite opposition to the "pain" of work and Veblen's praise of those who fulfill themselves because, as he was fond of saying, they "take pains." Where Veblen departed importantly from Ruskin and Morris, however, was in his optimism—of which there was more than gruff appearances indicated—that large mechanized industry could be bent to the service of workmanship. From that conviction followed the analysis that was of such provocative force to the economic planners who came to the fore in the 1930's, shortly after Veblen's death. Veblen argued a basic distinction between the captains of business and the technicians in a way that granted moral precedence to the latter and provided a non-Marxian principle of radical change:

> The realities of the technician's world are mechanistic realities [he declared], matters of material fact. And the responsibilities of the technician, as such, are responsibilities of workmanship only; in the last resort responsibility to his own sense of workmanlike performance, which might well be called the engineer's conscience. On the other hand the arts of business are arts of bargaining, effrontery, salesmanship, make-believe, and are directed to the gain of the business man at the cost of the community, at large and in detail. Neither tangible performance nor the common good is a business proposition.[11]

Seeing matters so, Veblen was able to speak in favor of a soviet of engineers, justified on both moral and technological grounds. By extending the counsels of science and efficiency that far, Veblen became the most radical as well, perhaps, as the most intellectually exciting prophet of the pragmatic reformers.

The case for reform rooted in philosophy and intuition had powerful spokesmen as well, though often far from the center of popular debate. Charles Sanders Peirce, the great iconoclast among American philosophers, sketched an eidolon of love at a future time when knowledge had been perfected enough to establish truths to which all would feel bound.[12] Peirce's Utopian logic existed only as an undertone to his rigorous analytic thought, but it suggested how the desire to reform had touched the profoundest depths. More accessible, and almost equally impressive for the power of the philosophic mind that shone through it, was the concept of binding loyalty that Josiah Royce presented. Royce touched old religious chords in speaking for the Absolute, the moral center, from which all moral claims must stem and toward which all just relationships or loyalties must ultimately converge.[13] Royce spoke in theological tones at a time when the secular tide was running against him. Moreover, he had little of the popular touch. He was a speculative man who let his thoughts soar as they would. The brilliant essayist John Jay Chapman remembered one night of conversation in Cambridge when Royce and Judge Oliver Wendell Holmes argued out a point:

> Royce won, of course—somewhat after the manner of Gladstone— by involving the subject in such adamantine cobwebs of voluminous rolling speculation that no one could regain his sense thereafter. He

not only cut the ground from under everyone's feet; but he pulled
down the sun and moon, and raised up the ocean, and everyone was
shipwrecked and took to small planks and cups of tea.[14]

But Royce's prayer for a Beloved Community did finally gain wide
consideration in the altered form given it by the literary historian Van
Wyck Brooks. Confessing little aptitude for philosophy or contact with
Royce while a student at Harvard, Brooks yet spoke of the Beloved
Community, governed by a passion for excellence in the arts and joy
in useful labor to be gained by daring to follow intuition out of the
Sargasso Sea of American commercialism. Brooks began as a solemn
young man of twenty-two with *The Wine of the Puritans* (1908), a
critical study of American culture. He found Puritan "wine" to be of
sour vintage, brewed out of a dyspeptic drive for material success. Yet
there was a redeeming side. The wine gave off an aroma of mystical
idealism that welled up from the Puritans' religious convictions. A few
American heroes—Whitman, Hawthorne, Melville, and the Transcendentalists foremost among them—had used that idealism to infuse the
common life with beauty and wisdom. In *America's Coming of Age*
(1915) Brooks refined his thesis by adding the useful terms "highbrow"
and "lowbrow" to identify the false division usually made between
idealism and practical life. Commonly, Brooks noted, Americans were
brought up in a resolutely highbrow moral atmosphere, their schooling
fixed on the pure and noble, never the earthy or practical. Afterward
they were thrown out into an arena of material striving that no other
nation could match in intensity. Dismay and a kind of creeping schizo-
phrenia were all but inevitable. Brooks saw the need for middle ground
where a socialist transformation could combine the best aspects of highbrow and lowbrow culture.

Brooks's finely wrought pleas came at an opportune moment. He was
one of those "fiddles tuning up all over America" that William Butler
Yeats spoke of in 1915. In that year Brooks met another of the critical
spokesmen for a new generation, Randolph Bourne, and was impressed
by him partly for the same fortuitous reasons that touched others. For
Bourne, a humpbacked dwarf—"twisted" but "unscarred," as Dos
Passos remembered him—presented a strong, luminous mind in contrast
to his pathetic body. Just as he had transcended his own physical weakness, Bourne insisted that the new generation was capable of curing a

deformed America. It required the resolute will to go beyond the disposition of earlier reformers to compromise away moral and artistic
integrity. Bourne was ready for an elitism further reaching than Lippmann's. During World War I, which he found destructive of all true
values, Bourne wrote to Brooks that the effort by themselves—"we
fearless ones"—to create a new literary leadership was the only cause
to which one "could give one's allegiance at the present time, with any
confidence of attaining any goal or rescuing anything of value from the
engulfing blackness."[15] Brooks agreed and asserted after his friend's
premature death in 1918, at the age of thirty-two, that:

> [Bourne] revealed us to ourselves, he intensified and at the same
> time corroborated our desires; above all, he showed us what we had in
> common and what new increments of life might arise out of the friction
> of our differences. . . . He was a wanderer, the child of some nation
> yet unborn, smitten with an inappeasable nostalgia for the Beloved
> Community on the far side of socialism. . . .[16]

The fiber of that Beloved Community remained vague—as perhaps
so highly intuitive a concept was bound to be. It was sufficient to work
toward a heightened appreciation of the artist as a definer of community.
The first task of the artist was to inspire public confidence in his perception. Consequently, neither Brooks nor his allies, Lewis Mumford
and Waldo Frank chief among them, engaged much in direct political
action. But they labored earnestly on the faith that their writings might
make a difference profound enough to affect society in all its aspects.

Ideas for a new reform ethic found their greatest outlet just before
World War I in the *New Republic*. A wealthy banker, Willard Straight,
founded the journal in 1914 to replace the muckraking magazines of a
few years earlier. The original intellectual keynote for the *New Republic*
was provided by its editor, Herbert Croly. His highly influential book,
The Promise of American Life (1909), outlined a program to increase
political effectiveness by placing more responsibility in the hands of
experts and "so simplifying [government] that only decisive decisions
and choices are submitted to the voter." [17] Here was another variant of
the call for a principle of unity to be administered by an elite. In Croly's
case the appeal was laced with a streak of mysticism and moral ardor
that he drew partly from the teachings of Royce and George Santayana

that he had absorbed at Harvard. He declared that "the principle of democracy *is* virtue!" And since awareness of the ways of virtue came slowly even to highly attuned natures, "the cost of government in time, ability, training, and energy should fall not upon the followers but upon the leaders" who qualify by their understanding of the moral charge.[18] Predictably, Theodore Roosevelt—the "virtuous demagogue," as John Jay Chapman described him—was impressed by Croly's book to the point where he adopted Croly's phrase "New Nationalism" to describe his 1912 Presidential platform. Fired by the powerful editorial collaboration of Croly, Walter Lippmann, and Walter Weyl, and by the reformist tension of the times, the *New Republic* seemed in a position to connect elective politics and reform thought. When Woodrow Wilson's "New Freedom," which the *New Republic* had criticized for its archaic individualism, shifted toward the unifying program of Roosevelt's "New Nationalism," the *New Republic* felt that it might have had influence and looked to the possibility of becoming the house organ for a new era of social reconstruction.

The *New Republic*'s appeal showed importantly in John Dewey's decision to use it as the vehicle for his emergence, late in his career, as a social commentator. That development was anticipated by the educational reform work Dewey carried on in his Laboratory School at the University of Chicago at the beginning of the century. There Dewey established important liaison with a group of reformers and teachers, especially Jane Addams and the superintendent of Chicago schools Ella Flagg Young. He admired their natural insights into the problems with which his instrumental philosophy abstractly wrestled, for their "translation of philosophical conceptions into their empirical equivalents."[19] Their careers were graceful segments of the wide struggle to improve American life. Yet Dewey looked beyond the practical accomplishments of his friends. As early as 1891, in an essay on Matthew Arnold and Robert Browning, Dewey had defined "our problem" as the need to "bridge this gap of poetry from science."[20] Despite Dewey's respect for the piecemeal reforms of Jane Addams and other progressives, he set out on a comprehensive quest for "reconciliation of the scientific view of the universe with the claims of the moral life."[21] The rightful scope of critical thinking seemed to him large and exhilarating:

> The value of research for social progress; the bearing of psychology upon educational procedure; the mutual relations of fine and industrial

art; the question of the extent and nature of specialization in science in comparison with the claims of applied science; the adjustment of religious aspirations to scientific statements; the justification of a refined culture for a few in face of economic insufficiency for the mass—such are a few of the many social questions whose *final* answer depends upon the possession and use of a general logic of experience as a method of inquiry and interpretation.[22]

Dewey's efforts at fusion almost joined the two wings of the unifying reformers—those advocating science and efficiency and those who relied upon philosophy and intuition. But World War I proved fatal to the merger. Once America had entered the war, Dewey supported it on grounds that amounted to the homely old view that one should make the best of a bad thing. Pacifists—or passivists, as Dewey tartly called them—advanced a position that amounted to "a sort of oriental absolutism" in advocating nonresistance to all forms of force.

> I can but think [he lectured] that if pacifists in war and in penal matters would change their tune from the intrinsic immorality of the use of coercive force to the comparative inefficiency and stupidity of existing methods of using force, their good intentions would be more fruitful.[23]

The argument permanently alienated many whose acceptance of pragmatism had been subordinate to certain inviolable moral positions. And as a practical matter, Bourne insisted, regardless of how willing one might be to try to use the barbarities of war for good ends, efficiency and rational discrimination in the use of force are just the sorts of things that the chaos of war does not permit. Bourne called upon his alliance with the intuitiveness of Van Wyck Brooks to make the case and thereby helped cast off the fragile lines instrumentalism had extended to hold the pragmatic and intuitive reform movements together:

> In the crisis, this philosophy of intelligent control just does not measure up to our needs. What is the root of this inadequacy that is felt so keenly by our restless minds? . . . Is there something in these realistic attitudes that works actually against poetic vision, against concern for the quality of life as above machinery of life? Apparently there is.[24]

Then Bourne distilled the controversy and indicated the separate tracks reform critics were to follow henceforth: "It is the creative desire more than the creative intelligence that we shall need if we are ever to fly."[25]

Dewey later regretted his support for World War I because it obviously did not make the world safe for democracy. He also regretted the early death of Bourne in one of his few references to the most celebrated of his adversaries. Expressed late in life in rather avuncular tones, Dewey's regret emphasized the lost opportunity for Bourne to mellow and be available for reconciliation. But, if it was more than wishful thinking that Bourne would have stepped back onto the bridge, reconciliation was not acceptable for Brooks, Mumford, and others who followed in Bourne's wake. They rigidified their differences with Dewey and his method of "creative intelligence," preferring instead to intensify their search for a liberal tradition—the "usable past" that Brooks spoke of so eloquently during World War I.[26]

The twenties were inhospitable to activist reformers. Yet critics did not lack the will or opportunity to work. They had witnessed a great creative insurgence during the prewar period that certainly did not die out with the change to conservative Republican administration and the failure to attain a stable peace. Moreover, reform thinkers had so much to do in working out the plans they had begun devising before 1917 that an enforced lull in action was not a tragic blow. Indeed, they could even benefit, in the tradition of the wandering exile leader, by a freedom from urgent pressures to act that allowed time to reflect and prepare for whatever crises might come.

Dewey's career during those years exemplified the possibilities of dissociation from power. Though the twenties were the years when he most fully expanded his critique of American society, he spent much of that time away from home—a peripatetic philosopher on a global scale. He lectured at the Imperial University of Tokyo in 1919 and then at the national universities of Peking and Nanking from 1919 to 1921; from there he moved on to do a series of educational surveys of Turkey in 1924, Mexico in 1926 and the Soviet Union in 1928; finally he closed a decade's travels by delivering the Gifford Lectures at the University of Edinburgh in 1929. Dewey's Tokyo lectures appeared in 1920 as *Reconstruction in Philosophy* and established for a wide public the theme of all his ensuing discussions on the application of the method of intelligence to social concerns. Almost thirty years later in a new preface to the book, he reiterated his steadfast purpose, changed only by a deepened sense of urgency that it be enacted:

> In short, the problem of reconstruction in philosophy, from whatever angle it is approached, turns out to have its inception in the endeavor to discover how the new movements in science and in the industrial and political human conditions which have issued from it, that are as yet only inchoate and confused, shall be carried to completion.[27]

A series of books by Dewey set out to fulfill the mission: *Human Nature and Conduct* (1922); *Experience and Nature* (1925) in which Dewey extensively considered the place of art in life for the first time; *The Public and Its Problems* (1927), which presented Dewey's crucial concept that the basic public was a face-to-face community out of which the logic of larger communities should stem; and *The Quest for Certainty* (1929), wherein Dewey surveyed the damage absolute religious dogmas (and by implication other sorts of dogmas) do to the experimental reason needed to maintain a humane community.

Dewey's progress was paralleled by the growth of movements that stressed pragmatic efficiency—though not necessarily in the spirit of liberal concern for social welfare that permeated Dewey's works. For them the war had a distinctly beneficial side. Even as it struck violently at optimism, it provided an inspiring lesson in how America could mobilize resources when she chose. Under the direction of Bernard Baruch, who was to close his many days as a kind of talisman called upon by political leaders to ward off trouble, the War Industries Board engaged the services of numerous economists and planners who characteristically looked back on the experience as a great experiment in social planning. Some of them sought to carry on the work elsewhere. Alvin Johnson led the way by presiding over the founding of the New School for Social Research in New York, dedicated to the purpose of using social science study for progressive reform and planning. The concept elicited enthusiastic support from Dewey. And the iconoclastic Thorstein Veblen found a congenial place there that ended a long, embittering search for an academic home.

Similar hopes for large-scale research and planning moved Wesley Mitchell, another economist with the WIB, to start the National Bureau of Economic Research, destined to become the nation's greatest depot of economic information. True to the spirit of deferred ends that marked the twenties, Mitchell held the bureau aloof from struggles for political power but expressed a "fighting faith" that it would have an important educative influence on national affairs by supplying statistics about the nation's economic institutions.

Similarly encouraged by war planning, industrial efficiency and planning movements developed at a quickening pace. A veritable vogue of the engineer took hold. The Taylor system of scientific management gained many adherents within the factories and attention outside through the efforts of the Taylor Society. In politics the impulse expressed itself most clearly in the general admiration of Herbert Hoover, the "Great Engineer," who showed how an efficient scientific manager could serve human ends by overseeing Belgian relief during the war. Henry Ford left a somewhat different impression as the self-made engineering "genius"—everybody's Connecticut Yankee. The image was essentially nonpolitical—and not very accurate, either, since Ford had only rudimentary mechanical skills—but it was persuasive enough to get him boomed for the Presidency in 1920.

Interest in industrial psychology squared both with the industrial management movement and the growing public interest in psychology during the twenties. Freud had become widely hailed by then, and the famous Army intelligence tests provided a large bank of data along with the shocking suggestion that mental deficiencies and aberrations were widespread. That the tests were crude in their newness and geared to a native white middle-class range of experience did not dawn for several years. In the gloom of the moment observers wondered whether mankind was capable of maintaining a democracy in an increasingly complex society. Walter Lippmann in his classic *Public Opinion* (1922) grimly tightened his prewar elitism. Manipulation of passive, uncomprehending masses seemed to him inevitable. The best Lippmann felt reformers could work for was the chance to apply pressures so that the masses might be drawn along after worthy goals.

Farther to the left, the Socialists, though one of the obvious heirs to the experience in collectivism the war afforded, were in disarray as a result of the Red Scare. Unable to mount a strong political challenge of their own, Socialists joined with the revived agrarian movement. After much jostling and dispute the Farm-Labor Party of 1920 was launched, only to be discouragingly trounced by Warren Harding and "normalcy." In 1924, after the Democrats and Republicans both had chosen conservative Presidential candidates, the Farm-Labor generated a stronger challenge in the person of Robert La Follette. Though old and ailing, "Fighting Bob" was bitter enough about the Republican Party's desertion of its progressive principles to run as an independent. Again, defeat was overwhelming, and both Socialists and Farm-Laborites had to withdraw from active battle for the remainder of the decade.

Leftist disaffection led also to the founding of the League for Industrial Democracy in 1921. The LID extended a tolerant welcome to anyone who wished to work for a benevolent collectivist society. Socialist in the broadest sense, the LID grew from the Intercollegiate Socialist Society that Jack London and Upton Sinclair helped begin in 1905 and that eventually became the Students for a Democratic Society. Its members worked diligently to establish liaison with labor leaders and to provide data on social conditions in a way that proved especially important in the astute campaigns of Norman Thomas during the thirties.

Intuitive reform critics continued to look to Brooks for inspiration. But in mid-decade he suffered a mental breakdown, the climax of a permanent inner conflict between his desire to affirm his native American heritage and the harsh critiques of America he had repeatedly delivered. For the last half of the twenties Brooks was silent. The cause suffered further when many of the new creative generation Bourne had welcomed fled to Europe rather than combat evils at home, as Bourne hoped they would. Few were left to assume the burdens of reeducation. But these few were spirited and talented. A. J. Nock's *Freeman* provided a useful outlet for their commentary; and the creative vigor of the decade, both at home and abroad, helped sustain their hopes. Waldo Frank, one of the *Freeman* company, framed the decade with *Our America* (1919) and *The Rediscovery of America* (1929). In both works he echoed the call for a usable past. But he went beyond Emersonian radicalism to consider older religious traditions. Frank explored psychology for its clues to the universal; wrote novels celebrating natural impulses as against the synthetic gestures of mechanized society; and finally found his greatest kinship within Latin societies where his studies of their cultures became classics.[28]

Frank's friend Lewis Mumford was, however, the more consequential student of American life. He became the leading interpreter of the liberal tradition from the time of his study of antebellum culture, *The*

Golden Day (1926). Before then he had begun his long career as a critic of architecture and regional planning. His aim was to find organic relationship between the ways people lived and the ways they thought and felt. Ideally, that entailed widening the chances for his countrymen to express themselves. So he gladly joined Alfred Kreymborg, Brooks, and Paul Rosenfeld in 1927 to launch the *American Caravan*, a yearly compilation of the best new writers in the hinterlands the sponsors could find. The venture was hopeful and experimental: but within the prevailing mood of esthetic sophistication, and cynicism, the *Caravan* failed to survive for more than a few years. Mumford was stung by criticism that his enterprise was romantic and likely to be exploited by untalented amateurs who would play upon misguided sympathy. As the decade ended he invested much of his personal angst in a life of Herman Melville that balanced the somber last years of the nineteenth century against the sunlit aspect of *The Golden Day*. Melville's troubled life illustrated for Mumford the cost to the artist of a callous materialist society. When the Great Crash followed soon after his study appeared, Mumford was able to watch it with hardened detachment, neither surprised, nor disappointed, nor lacking in ideas for replacing what had been lost.

From the South voices of a different timbre also rose during the 1920's in traditionalist dissent to industrial life. At a time when the South was beginning its remarkable literary renaissance, a handful of young critics and writers gathered at Vanderbilt University in Nashville, Tennessee, to begin their journal, *The Fugitive* (1922–25). They, too, warned against the destructive tendencies of commercialism and offered the consolations of the old agrarian ways. "Throw out the radio and take down the fiddle from the wall" was one way of urging self-sufficiency in the arts as well as economy. Although quite different from the liberal reformers in their view of social truths, the agrarians could join them in detached readiness for the Crash. Their manifesto, *I'll Take My Stand*, announced a general rejection of industrialism. They, alongside the pragmatic rationalists with their sense of the obsolescence of laissez-faire capitalism and the liberal traditionalists with their intense feelings for the spiritual inadequacies of American life, could find a certain poetic justice in the way the twenties ended.

The Appeal to Reason

1. A Hopeful League

The gathering resolve of liberals in the late 1920's to press for major reform took definite political shape with the formation of the League for Independent Political Action in 1929. The organizers of the League believed that Hoover's New Era was destined for a fall. It could not permanently survive when its drive for profiting a few was destroying needed markets by impoverishing the masses at home and foisting impossible burdens of debt on foreign nations. But the League hopefuls were amazed and filled with a heady sense of vindication when the great stock market crash occurred in October of the same year. Suddenly a great opportunity had presented itself. In the guise of trouble, it kindled excitement and visions of fundamental change that liberals had hardly dared to conjure earlier.

Planning for the League began the month before the debacle. In September, 1929, a group of liberal intellectuals, headed by Paul Douglas, an economist at the University of Chicago, called for a meeting in Cleveland of reformers who favored an alliance to consolidate their interests in drastic change. A small but enthusiastic group convened in October and elected a slate of officers that reflected the range of reform sentiment the League wished to span. John Dewey was named chairman. The vice-chairmen included James Maurer, a trade unionist active for many years in Socialist causes; W. E. B. Du Bois, the Negro radical; and Paul Douglas. Oswald Garrison Villard, long a champion of liberal intellectuals, was elected treasurer, and the Farm radical Howard Y. Williams, who had once been a social gospel preacher and in 1928 a candidate for Congress from Minnesota on the Farm-Labor ticket, became executive secretary.

The League quickly agreed that its main goal was to be the formation of a new party to benefit farmers and wage earners. Entered into with full awareness of the dismal fate of prior third-party movements in

39

America, that ambition indicated a strong conviction that capitalism was dead and that the Democratic and Republican parties, resting upon a capitalistic base, were moribund. In that judgment the pragmatic rationalists in the League agreed with the Marxists who flourished all about them. But their distrust of hard-baked ideology, a distrust powerfully reinforced by Dewey's instrumentalism and the mordant writings of their economic mentor, Veblen, set the pragmatic rationalists unbridgeably apart from the Marxists.[1]

Paul Douglas led the efforts to create a framework for the new party. His design was to fuse the concept of a farm-labor coalition, which Progressives of the La Follette type had long held, with advanced economic doctrines that had grown out of a number of technical studies of the 1920's.[2] Populist radicals, who originated the farm-labor idea, had characteristically been suspicious of the orthodoxies of professional economists. They looked upon notions adopted from Adam Smith and Herbert Spencer as excuses for business and banking magnates to further their own interests, at the expense, it seemed, of the rest of society. When the edge of that suspicion extended to include the urban industrial world, and things new in general, it became a serious detriment, inhibiting support from labor and influential intellectuals.[3] Paul Douglas recalled that "it was in a sense both ridiculous and humiliating to have Senator La Follette dictate to the Cleveland convention which nominated him in 1924 a program which was almost entirely based upon the vanished days of small and independent business."[4]

The findings of pragmatic economists incorporated by League leaders gave promise of adding nonrural support to the farm-labor-consumer alliance idea. The National Bureau of Economic Research, begun by Wesley Mitchell in the 1920's, was especially important in providing economists with vast quantities of economic data that disputed Spencerian dogma. Mitchell himself concluded from his empirical storehouse that business cycles and related economic phenomena do not follow set patterns that can be deduced from mathematical or "natural" laws.[5] Such a conclusion fitted well with Veblen's view of the absurdity and hypocrisy of the prevailing economic orthodoxies and with the Populist suspicion of the capitalist system. It fitted equally well with the experimental temper of economists who, although independent of any party, were more politically minded than Mitchell, yet sought a similarly empirical solution to the problems of the Depression.

In his pamphlet for the League, *Why a Political Realignment?* (1930), Douglas explained that the Minnesota Farm-Labor Party would serve as the model and, with the assent of that organization, as the rallying point for the development of a new third party. Douglas was impressed by the success of the Minnesotans in electing two United States Senators and three Congressmen in the previous six years. That achievement seemed a striking contrast to the Socialist Party, which, for all its fervent appeals for collectivist reform, could show only a record of defeat, culminating in the agony of Debs' incarceration in the Atlanta Penitentiary. Beyond that failure and, as League members saw it, underlying it, was the taint of alien dogma that clung to the Socialists. Dewey answered the question posed by his article in the *New Republic* (1931), "Who Might Make a New Party?" by including professional men, white-collar workers, farmers, and laboring men as the core of the new party and excluding Socialists. Douglas felt a more charitable willingness to admit Socialists—"good" Socialists, such as Norman Thomas, who had eschewed belief in "the class struggle"—within the new party as a special auxiliary. Both Dewey and Douglas noted the fruitful service of socialism to America. But they concluded with regret that Americans had become allergic to all "isms" and—shades of Haymarket and the Red Scare!—to Marxist "isms" especially.[6]

The desire of the League for Independent Political Action for a novel radicalism, fresh-cast for the occasion, asserted itself with considerable vigor because of the feeling that the Depression, in its unprecedented blackness, called for entirely new policies if there was to be any sort of recovery at all. The heart of the crisis, as the pragmatic rationalists saw it, was the collapse of adequate provisions for meeting minimum consumer needs. Never before had the country come to such a pass. To cross it, they felt, there must be broad reforms to extend consumer control over the forces of production.

The pattern of action proposed by the League distinguished it from the main currents of reform thought. By emphasizing the interests of consumers, the League departed from customary Socialist doctrine and its wellspring, Marxism, which presented class struggle between producers and owners as the central theme of social life. The distinction between the League viewpoint and Progressivism was subtler but significant. Both Progressives and League advocates urged a cooperatist economy featuring socially controlled sharing rather than competition.

But Progressivism, despite its brief flirtation under the aegis of Theodore Roosevelt with Herbert Croly's New Nationalism, had concentrated on encouraging local cooperatives of farmers and small businessmen within the traditional frame of decentralized government and free enterprise, whereas the League emphasized national planning by a dominant federal government.[7]

Borrowing the phrase "Cooperative Commonwealth" from Edward Bellamy's romance of a collectivist Utopia, *Looking Backward* (1888), League spokesmen based their hope for a new party upon a directed economy that would ensure useful employment for all and equitable distribution of the fruits of that employment. Such a comprehensive approach could not very well adopt the Progressive sympathy of a Robert La Follette or a William Borah for traditional ties to local communities and local enterprise. The concept of a national planning administration was a distinct departure from American custom and sentiment. The pragmatic rationalists in the League could not fall back into the comforting arms of history. They could not emulate the Progressives by nostalgic appeals to "Americanism." Nor, in their enmity to formal ideology, were they able to follow the Socialist technique of invoking the "Laws of History" to explain present predicaments and predict future solutions. Rather, the pragmatic rationalists slighted history as a source of counsel and relied instead on a rational calculation of the public interest. From their point of departure only the road ahead lay open.

By 1930 the League had sufficient strength and coherence to begin planning for possible gains in the next year's election. John Dewey sent a minor ripple through the political world by asking Senator George Norris to lead insurgent Republicans out of that reactionary party into the promised land of the League's farm-labor coalition.[8] But Norris, in concert with Senators William Borah of Idaho and Smith Brookhart of Iowa, declined the invitation. Norris cited the melancholy fact that third-party sentiment had historically reached a promising intensity only after the major party conventions had nominated unpopular candidates—too late to organize a winning third force. Borah found the League concept too rationalist and remote. "My observations and my reading," he declared, "lead me to the opinion that no parties can be successfully organized by a few men or a few leaders, however able and sincere they may be. New parties have to come up from the grass roots.

It takes some single dominating issue, accompanied by a dramatic crisis, to swing people from their old moorings into new positions."[9]

Balked in their efforts to create a viable third party in time for the 1932 election, the League endorsed Norman Thomas for President and liberals of whatever party for lesser offices.[10] The League's own views were expressed in a detailed seven-point plan that emerged from a conference of "over one hundred economists and experts." That platform without a party emphasized relief of unemployment, public ownership of utilities, tax relief for farmers and tight federal control of banking and credit—in short, the means to attain the consumer democracy to which the League was pledged. In addition the League proposed legislation to protect freedom of expression, to grant political asylum to political refugees, to protect labor against coercive injunctions and yellow-dog contracts, and to give the Negro political equality. A final section called for broad, peaceful international cooperation. It denounced what it considered menacingly large military expenditures, while urging American entry into the League of Nations and withdrawal of American influence, whether in the form of troops or treaty, from China, Latin America, and the Philippines.[11]

In September, 1933, the League's third-party organizing began in earnest at a giant gathering in Chicago thrown open to all who professed an interest in establishing consumer democracy.[12] Dewey, Alfred Bingham, joint editor with Selden Rodman of the League's journalistic ally, *Common Sense*, and Thomas Ryan Amlie, a young Farm-Labor Congressman from Wisconsin, led the sessions of the meeting.

The Socialists were conspicuously absent. They claimed that they already fulfilled the need for a third party. As well, some of them bristled at what seemed a patronizing invitation. LIPA apparently agreed to include them as responsible leftists who would avoid the excesses of Marxism—much as though they were Pentecostals invited to a High Anglican conference on the assumption they would not speak in tongues or rend their garments. Norman Thomas expressed mounting exasperation as the decade wore on and chances for unity on the left waned. He viewed LIPA and other independent groups as niggling attempts at "rewriting the Socialist platform of 1932." If the rather academic competitors had come into the Socialist Party, "we should all have been farther along."[13] That, of course, was the issue. For the members of LIPA insisted that any group officially labeled "Socialist" carried a stigma like a cross and could never gain majority support. They hoped that the Socialists could break with their tradition—their treasured "solidarity"—to try a new coalition of forces committed to similar ends. But the Socialists stayed with their own organization and emblems, and LIPA had to look elsewhere for support. They found it in an amalgam of social critics, agrarian reformers, and the downtrodden fringe of the unemployed.

From the Farm Belt came representatives of the Farmers' Union, the United Farmers of America, the Farm Holiday Association, the Progressives of Wisconsin, and that redoubtable veteran of 1920's radicalism, the North Dakota Nonpartisan League.

The National Unemployed League, boasting more than a million members, and the Workers' Committee on Unemployment appeared, claiming to represent the scattered masses of the unemployed.

Labor, however, had only a handful of representatives from small unions present. Bingham noted their thin ranks with a sardonic observation that "labor leaders at present, at least in the A. F. of L., are riding high in the new if somewhat doubtful dignity of the NRA [National Recovery Act] and they are not ready to prejudice their positions quite yet."[14]

Amid the sort of clamor and crowding and expectant enthusiasm that chairman Dewey so much enjoyed, an eight-point platform was adopted, paralleling the stress of the League's program a year before on centralized, scientific planning. The conference closed in a hopeful mood. To sustain its spirit and carry the gospel of the new party through the states the executive committee formed a National Committee of Action with Dewey as honorary chairman and Amlie as the acting chairman. An aggressive confidence shone through such hortatory pamphlets as *Audacity! More Audacity! Always Audacity!* "If the leaders of American radical movements will exercise some of the magnificent audacity of a Danton or a Samuel Adams, of a Jefferson or a Jackson, of a Lincoln or a Lenin, they can bring into existence a new political movement which will challenge the power of capitalism."[15] The pamphlet presented a curious list, combining models of revolution and moderation into an apt illustration of the League's desire for radical change within respectable limits.

To clarify its vision the League adopted Edward Bellamy and Thorstein Veblen as patron saints. Dewey wrote of Bellamy in terms that recalled his earlier praise of Henry George as a social philosopher the like of whom in history "would require less than the fingers of the two hands to enumerate."[16] What appealed most to the pragmatic rationalists was Bellamy's description in *Looking Backward* of the coming evolution of capitalism by orderly stages, almost approaching inevitability, into a state ruled by reason and technical knowledge. In his subsequent book, *Equality* (1897), Bellamy went to the heart of pragmatic rationalism's reconciliation of individualism with a collectivist society. "Equality," Bellamy declared, "created an atmosphere which kills imitation, and is pregnant with originality, for everyone acts out himself, having nothing to gain by imitating anyone else."[17] Dewey proclaimed Bellamy "a great American prophet." The novelist's *Looking Backward* had long lain in the back of Dewey's mind as a dramatic realization of what Dewey, and Whitman before him, had steadfastly maintained: the logical kinship of democracy, science, and art. The new city of Bellamy's imagination clearly made things—machines and money —the servants of man's spiritual life. Furthermore, Dewey insisted, one could make systematic use of science without becoming tied to an ideology. He explained in his announcement of "Policies for a New Party" in 1931 that "no commitment to dogma or fixed doctrine is necessary. The program can be defined in terms of direct social needs and can develop as these change. While opportunistic in application, it will be definite and concentrated in purpose. It will not get lost in a dispersed inventory of scattered items of reform so long as it sticks to the unifying principle of the use of government to effect the subordination of economic forces to the maintenance of human justice and happiness."

Veblen's ideas had influence on both the urban intellectuals and the farm radicals within LIPA. The distinction Veblen made between the logic of industry and pecuniary greed informed the economic arguments of Dewey, Bingham, and Douglas. Quite different was the interesting, if somewhat overplayed, emphasis Thomas Amlie placed on the economist's rural background. In a review of Joseph Dorfman's monumental biography of Veblen (1935)[18] Amlie stressed the six years Veblen spent on his family's farm, after he had finished his schooling, as instrumental in developing the pungent views he was later to express. There he garnered the wisdom of the farm-labor viewpoint. "The picture of this young man with a doctorate from Yale," Amlie wrote, "following his Norwegian immigrant father about the fields for an opportunity to discuss with him difficult economic problems is one that staggers the imagination. No one will deny that it marks young Veblen as the most intelligent man who ever received a doctorate from Yale."[19] Amlie cited with approval the judgment of the philosopher and spokesman for Rochdale cooperation, Horace Kallen, who once declared, "I have a shrewd suspicion that Veblen may be to the intellectuals of the future what Marx has been to the humanitarians of the past."[20] Veblen's book *Absentee Ownership* (1923), written in the bitter style of the economist's later years, struck Amlie as the most significant of Veblen's guides to action. Veblen's greatest contribution, Amlie felt, was in giving a picture of the cooperative state to come; his great solution, drawn from the Populist tradition, was to end absentee ownership. Amlie was greatly concerned to find a place for Veblen within farm-labor politics. But ironically, by reading a rural bias into the master's economic ideas, Amlie tended to estrange himself from the economic community that derived from Veblen. Urban-oriented, they did not concur in the stress Amlie placed upon Veblen's farm back ground or his concept of absentee ownership. Clearly, the bridge the League for Independent Political Action sought to construct between farm radicalism and other more industrially geared radicalisms was not complete by 1935. And the following year the partially built span would have to undergo the earthquake of Roosevelt's great election victory.

2. The Social Engineers

The League for Independent Political Action represented a relatively conservative aspect of pragmatic rationalism, aligning itself to traditional Progressivism and hoping to work through the established medium of politics. Other pragmatic rationalists leaned more heavily on Veblen's concept of an engineered society and emphasized technological imperatives, independent of political processes. The most conspicuous, and probably the most extreme, of the social engineers were the Technocrats. The brainchild of Howard Scott, a Columbia economist who had begun researches into means for achieving technological efficiency early in the 1920's, Technocracy sought to replace the money system with a measurement of earned income based on the energy generated by the nation's productive industry. Such a scheme, Scott felt, would enable an engineering elite, whose competence earned them stewardship of the state, to direct economic enterprise and distribution with maximum efficiency. Through a baffling manipulation of figures which never seemed entirely clear even to the most devoted disciples of the mysterious Scott, Technocracy claimed the ability to provide a lordly income for all citizens. Scott's idea, really a stab at economic dictatorship, had become a national sensation by 1932, perhaps less for the plausibility of the scheme than for its sheer audacity. But almost as rapidly as it had flowered it withered under the combined attack of economists, who thought it an unlikely theory, and political idealists, who considered it a threat to democratic processes.

Strangely, out of all the inducement the Crash afforded for thinking of technological remedies, no social engineer idea has survived so long in memory as that odd failure, Technocracy. But the Technocrats in their fanatic way were persistent while others sank into doubt.

There were several reasons for uncertainty. The Crash itself showed that the lords of technology had been drastically unreliable. Just as the

Nobel Prize winner Robert Millikan won acclaim during the 1920's when he urged a greater place for science in public affairs on the grounds that science and industry are linked as parent to child, so it was natural that the economic collapse should bring some discredit to science. Also, Freudian psychology suggested that scientific reasonableness was beyond the grasp of most men. And the rise of totalitarian dictatorships warned of what could happen when the state became a machine and the citizens its cogs.

Behind those large reasons lay the residue of a debate about science that had intensified during the 1920's. Though widespread optimism accompanied the pouring forth of goods and comforts during that decade, thoughtful social critics suffered increasing anxiety. Bertrand Russell's essay in 1918, "A Freeman's Worship," measured the narrowing margin of independence toward science that people might still enjoy. We must realize, Russell insisted, that the great work of science has revealed man's insignificance as a mere "accidental collocation of atoms." Only by accepting the dominance of natural forces can one hope for any but the most abject fate. Once we abandon the false idea of mastering nature, we can concentrate on sensibly modest ambitions and faiths. Russell's message was a variation of the skepticism George Santayana had been leveling for years against the importance Americans attached to their practical affairs. After denying anyone's ability to understand truly the world, Santayana closed his famous essay on "The Genteel Tradition in American Philosophy" (1911) with the admonition: "Let us therefore be frankly human. Let us be content to live in the mind."[21] Walter Lippmann gave the American doctrine of fatalism its most popular form in the twenties. In 1929 he described the age as one when "custom is dissolved and authority is broken." He called for a "religion of the spirit" that one could carry off into stoic privacy free of science and society. While Lippmann urged "disinterestedness," others who felt the force of science could not be avoided wished to combat or contain it. C. E. Ayres in *Science, the False Messiah* (1927) warned against the passive expectation that science would resolve all human issues. If unchecked, belief in science would diminish religion and other experiences where only subjective powers could rightly serve. On the stage Elmer Rice's *Adding Machine* and Eugene O'Neill's *Dynamo* hammered home the like fear that impersonal technology would destroy human instinct. And novelists, much influenced by the mystic primitivism of Sherwood

Anderson and D. H. Lawrence, made the same point in fiction. The growing malaise about science and technology was well summarized at the close of the decade in Joseph Wood Krutch's influential study, *The Modern Temper* (1929). "Science," declared Krutch, himself an avid naturalist, "has always promised two things not necessarily related—an increase first in our powers, second in our happiness or wisdom, and we have come to realize that it is the first and less important of the two promises which it has kept most abundantly."[22]

So, the 1930's opened with an obvious opportunity for science and technology to help reconstruct a shattered society; but an uncertain spirit hindered the good work. Most pragmatic reformers shied away from the direct applications of science and technology after the Technocracy fiasco. But of those who retained a lively interest in the issue, the two leading historians of the 1930's, Charles Beard and Carl Becker, illustrated rather well the decline of hope in that period for a beneficial new Age of Power that eventually left insensitive men like Scott virtually alone as enthusiasts for a society controlled by the dictates of science and engineering.

Charles Beard, who had stressed the determining force of economics from an early point in his career, began contributing to the examination of machine-age life in the late twenties. He edited a collection of essays on the subject in 1928, entitled *Whither Mankind*, in which he defended what seemed the reasonably limited impact of science. The machine age, he contended, has not destroyed the springs of beauty, religion, and humanitarianism, only the conditions under which they take effect. "These ancient forces will become powerful in the modern age just in the proportion that men and women accept the inevitability of science and the machine, understand the nature of the civilization in which they must work, and turn their faces resolutely to the future."[23]

In 1930 Beard sponsored a second symposium, *Toward Civilization*, that would give technicians a chance to add their commentary to the critical speculations of the nonspecialists. "Are not technologists thinkers as well as doers?" Beard asked in the manner of Shylock. "Are they indifferent to the human aspects of their revolutionary activities?"[24] The contributors responded with assurance that technicians could wisely direct civilization and that America, in any case, could not return to a preindustrial state. Beard's service to the ideal of science as a positive social force reached its height, explicitly and symbolically, in the introduction he wrote for the American edition of J. B. Bury's famous work on *The Idea of Progress* (1931). Beard noted that the Century of Progress Exposition was just then honoring the works of the engineering imagination. The occasion publicized the intimate connection Beard held to exist between technology and progress—a connection Bury had significantly failed to discern. Beard insisted that "technology has a philosophy of nature and a method—an attitude toward materials and work—and hence is a subjective force of high tension." Its impact on society— pointing directly toward collectivist reform—was clear: "In societies founded on technology, the warrior, priest, and political leader sink into the background or at all events can operate only in accordance with the economic realities produced by the machine. Thus technology reinforces the social, as distinguished from the individual, aspects of historical evolution. Henceforward history must deal with masses of people, organized in associations, governed by laws of averages."[25] Beard tied his contentions to the American situation as the Depression wore on and the New Deal began to emerge from the mists. In *America Faces the Future* (1932) he extended his optimism with the declaration that "all Western civilization is founded on technology, and of inner necessity technology is rational and planful."[26] The following year he and George Smith wrote *The Future Comes: A Study of the New Deal* with the assumption that the whirlwind Hundred Days of reform legislation had begun a thorough re-engineering of society.

Beard's enthusiasm waned rapidly, however, when it began to appear the New Deal would not develop a coherently engineered program. That was a disappointment; yet perhaps a salutary one, he judged. For the nations in the world that were most fully organized and committed to engineering power had become dictatorships all too reminiscent of the harsh world of technicians Spengler had envisaged in the twenties. After mid-decade Beard decided that the great need was for firmer principles of humane control rather than greater sway to science. It was an abrupt turn. Beard moved from extolling engineers to preoccupation with history as a source of "faith" strong enough to resist the misuses of power and to erect an isolationist barrier against the totalitarian states abroad that had so evilly twisted human ingenuity. Beard closed the decade with attacks on the New Deal for involving America in the world's quarrels and pleas for his countrymen to fix their attention on the reform message in their own traditions.

Carl Becker in his essay on *Progress and Power* (1936) was both more graceful and more melancholy than Beard. Looking at the material chaos of Depression, Becker surmised that "the economic disturbance that so aggravates passions and darkens counsel appears to be the surface symptom of a more profound social dislocation occasioned by the fact that mankind has entered a new phase of human progress—a time in which the acquisition of new implements of power too swiftly outruns the necessary adjustment of habits and ideas to the novel conditions created by their use . . . never before have men made relatively greater progress in the rational control of physical force, or relatively less in the rational control of social relations."[27] Becker, the skeptic who favored order of a calm and philosophic sort, was predisposed against the steely force of mass industry. Yet he saw clearly the issue of control and was echoed afterward by scientists and others who pondered the place of science in modern society. Ironically, the sort of foreboding Becker expressed inclined science and technology toward greater irresponsibility. Awe at the difficulties of directing scientific energies stayed the hands of many persons in positions to exercise control. There even developed a rationale that scientific work should be consciously held apart from values on the grounds that, since values could not be made "objective," they were therefore not the responsibility of scientists.

The most important organized effort to apply scientific technique to human affairs—the scientific management movement—avoided excesses of ambition or of fearfulness about the relations between science and society by keeping its innovations in industry a safe distance from the outside world. Frederick Taylor, the founder of scientific management, and his followers in the Taylor Society had originally hoped to use the method of efficiency on social problems. But the complexities of those problems and the demands on businessmen's social consciousness proved too great. Industrial management expanded rapidly during the business era of the twenties. Yet that very rapidity made careful adjustment of engineering logic to society insupportably difficult. The conditions of life were changing too rapidly; and the public, beguiled by the boom, would not wait upon the patient ways of planning or tolerate the limits it set upon exploitation.

A stalwart few, including Harlow S. Person, successor to Taylor as prime spokesman for scientific management, wished to cling to the old progressive ideals of social service during the twenties; but most in the movement agreed to stress industrial efficiency and remain neutral. That decision supported the rising class consciousness of businessmen. To the social prestige they enjoyed, businessmen could add the dictates of managerial science. Strict efficiency called for unitary direction by experts beholden to the production goals of management and the higher truths of science. Short of gaining a share in setting the direction of management, the worker must inevitably decline in human worth, his independence of judgment and opportunities to contribute any wisdom to the enterprise steadily reduced by directives from above. With few exceptions, such as the garment industry, business did not share its control with the workers. The ideal of industrial democracy declined during the 1920's along with the power of labor unions, although there was a flurry of false hope early in the decade when improved working conditions were mistaken for a sign of increased industrial democracy.

The Depression disrupted that rather serene mood of efficient neutrality and gave H. S. Person and the original Taylorite insistence on industrial cooperation added importance—but not enough to overcome the aloofness of industrial management from public affairs. In the winter of 1930 Person made his plea for greater social involvement. To the Taylor Society he announced that "the operations of industrial society are not yielding substantial good to the greatest number of industrial citizens. This is because these operations are not . . . organized with that end in view . . . because of an inconsistency between the basic principle of business enterprise—*individual self-interest and intuition*—and the basic principle of the production technology which that enterprise, without full appreciation of its influence, has come to use—*co-operative integration.*"[28] But Person's colleagues were not moved, with few exceptions, to enter the cause of social reform. Their attention veered instead toward a remarkable experiment being conducted at Western Electric, an experiment that promised to realize the old Taylorite belief in the natural harmony between efficiency, happiness, and self-esteem.

The experiment at the Hawthorne plant of Western Electric began in 1927 under the auspices of Elton Mayo, a young Australian then on the staff of Harvard Business School. Mayo observed the production rate of six girls in a telephone assembly room under a variety of conditions. Having noticed the dramatic loss of efficiency through fatigue in his researches for the Fatigue Institute in England during the war, Mayo sought to make the girls' life as pleasant and relaxed as possible. Predictably, the new regimen of coffee breaks and rest periods and cheerful surroundings was accompanied by rising production. But to the amazement of all the observers, when the pleasant extra touches were withdrawn, productivity continued to climb! Mayo finally deciphered the revelation: The girls had improved their performances not because of material well-being but because they had been made to feel important. Mayo seemed to have laid bare the full implication of Taylor and Person's insistence upon the importance of "cooperative integration." Production, profits, and human fulfillment seemed to be at one. And soon the more enlightened employers rushed to effect the "human engineering" principles of Mayo. By the time of World War II employee consultation and testing had become an integral part of the business establishment.

The old desire to make industry and its technology a beneficial social force was not fulfilled, however. Though the Hawthorne experiment led to more benevolence, of a manipulative sort, it also acted to reinforce the insularity of industrial management; for the crux of industrial harmony in the Mayo formulation lay in the involvement of the worker in his surroundings, not in the reform of them. The employee was to be given a sense of being valuable, and that was not apt to come unless he felt at peace with his life situation. The logical result of Mayo's ascendancy was an effort, which reached its peak in the 1950's, to advance the conservative virtues of loyalty, earnestness, and regard for the severe limits to perfectibility. The cause of industrial democracy faded steadily during the late thirties, along with lingering hopes for a labor party, while the arguments for an elite leadership took firmer root. On the eve of World War II an industrial psychologist, Morris Viteles, expressed well a characteristic ambivalence between science, democracy, and leadership that would soon be heightened by war. He spoke of the "impartial research" that would likely produce the means for "cooperative effort by management and labor in the formulation of techniques and standards" by which "workers can be fitted to their jobs."[29] But where was cooperation to stand in such a deterministic scene? The "cooperative effort" would unfold somewhat in the style of Catherine the Great's epigram. The workers—like her subjects—would be "perfectly free—free to obey all the laws!" But that did not preclude harmony if workers agreed to the way they were fitted into place, as Viteles suggested they would. Industrial management theory had concertedly moved toward an assumption of such agreement in accord with its elitism. Ordway Tead, a key spokesman for industrial management, put it well in the midst of Depression and of burgeoning enthusiasm for the Mayo dicta: "We should never forget that people *love to be led.* . . . They can become identified with a strong force outside themselves into which with others they can pour their own increasing energy and thus feel a harmony of oneness with a power bigger than themselves." [30] Tead had always made it clear that the leadership principle he was concerned with was limited to the factory and that he did not look kindly on the intrusion of issues from the democratic swirl outside. When, for example, in 1933 he revised his textbook of 1929, *Human Nature and Management*, a standard in schools of business administration, he added a new set of illustrative problems but included no mention of the Depression that had intervened. Many years later Tead reflected that he had developed his philosophic outlook early and "wasn't to be distracted from that by a depression or by a big strike." [31]

The centers of social research that underwent vigorous growth during the 1920's and 1930's were somewhat less abstracted from the social arena and showed distinct sympathy for liberal reform. Brookings Institution and the National Bureau of Economic Research led the way in lending research talents to government on the Socratic assumption that the possession of accurate information would improve both the efficiency and the virtue of society. But relatively little reform activity issued from the earnest labors of the researchers.

Nor did the profession of economics offer activist reform programs to confront the crisis of Depression or the redoubtable power of the machine. An ominous transition period followed the collapse of the laissez-faire world of the twenties during which economists diligently searched the rubble but, except for a few Marxists, did not seek to inspire. Herbert Hoover and Franklin Roosevelt, bereft of constructive economic formulae, preached confidence, with Roosevelt emerging the winner in 1932 if only because he had not presided over the debacle. Eventually the expedient pump-priming devices of John Maynard Keynes filled the void of unitary theory and took root in the ground Roosevelt's ingenious opportunism prepared. Socialist economics, neglecting the details of how it might make itself viable in the everyday marketplace, lost out to the Keynesian "mixed economy" that was adept at providing immediate material returns. And the whole-souled kind of reform that Henry George urged and Veblen implied was left to the independent liberals.

Theorists and messiahs came forward with blueprints, only to be balked by the combination of forces that made the early thirties less a field for radical reform than they first appeared to be.[32] The crankishness of some of the schemes helped discredit all ideas for new directions. And an ugly poison entered with the revival of old anti-Semitic beliefs in a linkage between economic woes and Jewish bankers. The Social Justice movement of Gerald L. K. Smith, Dr. Townsend, and Father Coughlin strengthened American suspicions of monetary reform schemes and third parties, especially in the face of a growing Fascist menace abroad that also fed on anti-Semitism. Those suspicions broadened when the Social Credit movement, at its outset far more respectable than the Union Party, became enmeshed in Fascism. With growing alarm the movement's sponsors in America disavowed connections with its English founder, Major C. H. Douglas, who had veered to the Fascistic right; and their journal, *New Democracy*, spurned the frenetic dispatches of Ezra Pound as he lapsed in the mid-thirties into his mad Fascist obsession with Jews and money.[33]

Another unorthodox economic reform concept—barter exchange— suffered a different frustration. The idea gained wide currency through a persuasive tract by Frank Graham, *The Abolition of Unemployment* (1932). Graham urged that an exchange agency be established to bring the unemployed and the owners of empty factories into fruitful contact. Workers would send whatever they could produce in the abandoned factories for trade in a central depot. At first the idea excited support from Communists and others on the left; but they soon soured on a scheme that seemed to be breathing life into capitalist enterprise. The concept became important, however, when one idiosyncratic Socialist used it as the springboard for one of the jauntiest political adventures of the decade.

After the Crash the dauntless labor radical Upton Sinclair, who had been publicizing socialism for the entire century, decided to take political action. He noted that, though judgments varied on what the prime causes of the hard times were, the problem of unemployment appeared to most to be the central evil. Borrowing from Graham's plan, Sinclair devised a program to End Poverty in California (EPIC) and used it to secure the Democratic nomination to run for governor of California in 1934.[34] At first he seemed to have Roosevelt's support; but as large vested interests, aroused by the prospect of reforms that would threaten the availability of cheap labor, mounted a powerful, often slanderous campaign against Sinclair, the President retreated.[35] Despite the encouragement of other liberals, including the leadership of the League for Independent Political Action, it was evident at that point that Sinclair would lose. He emerged from the battle with a rueful book entitled *How I Ran for Governor of California and Got Licked* (1934). In it he professed a measure of optimism that his defeat at least gave valuable publicity to the EPIC plan of cooperation; but he seemed to sense very well that the major result was to discredit radicalism of the EPIC variety in the eyes of the general public, which saw the wild campaign as a symptom of equally wild Utopianism at the heart of Sinclair's scheme. Indeed, the cause of cooperative social planning never quite recovered from EPIC's epic fiasco.

3. Cooperative Designs

Cooperation on a private basis fared somewhat better than EPIC and other politicalized programs. Private cooperatism agreed in its general tenets with the Cooperative Commonwealth proposed by the League for Independent Political Action and at the same time incorporated the tradition of decentralized, independent neighborliness underlying the small farm cooperatives that were flourishing amid the rigors of the Depression. Such cooperatism was dependent not upon rational central planning but upon a sense of community that might proceed as well from organic tradition as from scientific reason. Thus it provided the pragmatic rationalists and the liberal traditionalists with their most commodious common ground. With its broad base of popular support and its apparent consonance with American communal ideals, private cooperatism had earned the endorsements of civic and philanthropic groups of all kinds and had even merited praise from Presidents Harding and Coolidge. If ever a chance for collectivism to seize the American imagination on a large scale existed, the troubled thirties should have provided the time and the established decentralized forms of cooperation a gauge. Indeed, during the first half of the decade the growth of cooperative movements reached a peak; but the total share of the American economy affected remained small and dwindled precipitously after 1936.

Cooperation had not been able to overcome the obstacles that had been with it from the start. It had always been injuriously divided between town and country, producers and consumers. In 1916 two contrasting movements made the differences especially concrete for the future. That year Dr. James Peter Warbasse established the Cooperative League of the United States in New York to promote the English Rochdale plan of consumer cooperation; and on the remote plains agrarian discontent gave rise to the North Dakota Nonpartisan League, pledged to secure political support for agricultural producers' cooperatives. The former urged a plan to band society together on the grounds that all men are predominantly consumers. Joint enterprises to supply their consumer-owners and return them the profits formed the crux of the Rochdale plan. But the farmers were interested in cooperative production and distribution. Their aim was not to serve consumers but to end their old unhappy dependence on the railroads and distant banks. The differing motives of the two wings of cooperation kept them apart and unable to offer a very strong alternative to competitive business. Though the Nonpartisan League faded after World War I, its concept of producer cooperation persisted in the Farm Belt, sometimes expressed militantly in farm-labor politics and at other times in commercial ventures. The Cooperative League expanded slowly but retained its zeal for the Rochdale principles, ascribing the meagerness of its progress quite plausibly to the financial, psychological, and legal grip competitive business had on the American public. Cooperative enterprises could never match the lavish advertising lobbying and marketing techniques of their competitive rivals and were always in peril of losing their best managers to higher salaried executive suites.

Cooperation was a factor in the reform effort of the thirties not as an economic power but as an example with appreciable moral and intellectual influence on community-mindedness. Marquis Childs, for example, was able to arouse considerable admiration for the Swedish achievement of social and economic equity through cooperation; but his writings did not result in a material shift toward more cooperative enterprise in America.[36] Some active sympathy came from the New Deal. The Farm Credit Administration issued loans for producers' cooperatives through a special bank; the NRA made an exception of cooperatives by allowing them to give their traditional profit rebates to consumer-owners; and the TVA provided electricity wholesale to several rural cooperatives. But that was the tenuous extent. Mounting pressure from competitive business, which singled out TVA as a particularly sinister example of "creeping socialism," checked further government aid to the cooperatives.

There was continuing speculation about the affinity between cooperation and socialism. The phrase "cooperative commonwealth" was popular among Socialists and cooperators alike; and the concepts of cooperation were among those seriously studied at the Socialist League for Industrial Democracy. But farm producer cooperation rested too heavily on the concept of private ownership to suit most Socialists; and the Rochdale group, in turn, stressed freely given cooperation whose voluntary spirit would be damaged by government direction. The Cooperative League, and Warbasse especially, grew increasingly hostile toward any form of governmental power. The New Deal appeared as a risky attempt to save capitalist enterprise. As Fascism crowded in from abroad and from the domestic fringe, many cooperators grew fearful. "What may we expect in the United States, when the collapse of profit business has gone a little farther," Warbasse asked, "when no New Deal can any longer save it, when the government is taking over the failing businesses? Capitalists then may be expected to become desperate."[37] The task for cooperation was to maintain neutrality, to serve as a haven for those who wish to escape the capitalist turmoil and as a calming example of associative living. By the end of the decade cooperation had added a distinctive moral overtone that drew from Peter Kropotkin's ideal of mutual aid and anticipated the post-World War II decentralism of the commune movement and of social critics like Paul Goodman.

4. Planning

Of all the areas of reform that pragmatic rationalists entered, planning had the most comprehensive appeal. It was rational and systematic and seemed not to be faced with the obstacles that repeatedly doomed third-party activity and repressed cooperation. Carefully wrought plans might affect politics, but could, as well, carry beyond the power of government to benefit the private community directly. The educative impact of planning appealed also to pragmatic reformers who felt that the need in the present was to implant a more systematic approach to social affairs so that public assent might come in the future for a planned society.

At the center of early efforts to make planning a large national undertaking was a jaunty, quick-minded, voluble economist named Lewis Lorwin. He was, as he reflected long afterward, "always organizing something" and always eager to absorb new experiences. Lorwin's first involvement with the study of organized power left him with a rueful appreciation of how unlikely it is that men in public life will want to accept the full implications of their attempts to explore hard problems. As a young economics instructor at the University of Montana in 1916, Lorwin was asked to write a study of the mining interests in the state because officials of the university felt sure that their struggling school was not getting the funds from local mines that the state constitution guaranteed. Lorwin plunged in and found all too many reasons why— juggled accounts, profits hidden away in Chile, and other bits of chicanery. At the last moment the president of the university asked him to suppress the report. Lorwin published it anyway, lost his job and, although he won a fight for reinstatement, left to write a column on economics for the New York *World*. Soon afterward, in 1921, he became Moscow correspondent for the Chicago *Daily News*. There ensued a fruitful time, observing the new Soviet experiment and wandering through Europe where he studied the reconstruction of several war-wracked countries and wrote an impressive book on the French labor movement.

Lorwin joined the staff of the Brookings Institution in 1925, convinced that unstable world conditions required careful thought on planning, which then scarcely existed in any systematic form. Conversations with a Polish colleague at Brookings persuaded Lorwin that the International Labor Organization was the most promising locus of planning thought because its mission to coordinate working conditions in many countries inclined it toward planful study of various economic systems and ways of integrating them.

It was with a considerable sense of the significance of the occasion, then, that Lorwin accepted an invitation to be the principal speaker at a world conference on unemployment in Amsterdam in 1931. The presence of Russian delegates for the first time at such an international conference aroused wide interest, and Lorwin's speech appeared in a sunburst of publicity extended worldwide by a public relations man who amazed Lorwin with his ingenuity. The lucid presentation Lorwin gave of plans for coordinated economic relations, prefiguring the post-World War II Point Four program, made him a leading spokesman for the enlarging field of planning.[38]

When agitation over planning as a remedy to the Depression reached Washington, the scene bore many signs of Lorwin's influence. Senator Robert La Follette, Jr., of Wisconsin, was impressed with a Lorwin article in the *New Republic* of April, 1931, that spoke "in favor of a National Economic Council." La Follette asked Lorwin to use some of the time on his ensuing European trip to write a résumé of European economic policies. Lorwin returned with a long analysis of national economic councils that the informal study group he had established at Brookings worked over to find useful applications for the American situation. At the same time a Progressive Conference attracting Congressmen and assorted reformers was busy in the capital weighing ideas to reduce the stress of Depression. In December La Follette submitted a bill to the Senate calling for a National Economic Council based on the most likely ideas he could cull from Lorwin's researches and from the deliberations of the Progressive Conference.

Hearings on the bill took place the following spring as the tempo of speculation about the nation's fate increased.[39] From the horde of witnesses who appeared before the La Follette Committee four major plans emerged, two of them conceived by businessmen. Gerard Swope of General Electric proposed that private industries form trade associations under government direction to establish standard practices and ethics. His provision for mandatory membership in the associations was a departure from older trade association ideas and disturbed many businessmen. A milder call for coordination and responsibility on the part of business came from the Chamber of Commerce. Their proposal would have a council of industrial leaders to study conditions and urge cooperative policies on the business community. The third plan was La Follette's for an economic council appointed by the President to study problems and propose action. La Follette's plan would have placed considerable initiative in the hands of government. But the strongest proposal for direct governmental control came from Stuart Chase, one of the most articulate and influential social critics of the day. Chase recommended a Peace Industries Board, patterned after the War Industries Board of World War I and endowed with decisive power over production and distribution. In Chase's view the old free-enterprise traditions and fears of centralized control had helped create chaos and should not now be allowed to hinder reconstruction, regardless of which idols had to be discarded.

When Roosevelt was inaugurated in March, 1933, he inherited the great debate on planning along with the accumulating woes of Depression. Ultimately the La Follette proposal evolved into the President's Council of Economic Advisers, an institution that has provided some useful advice and less passion than many expected. But enthusiasm for more rigorous government control over the economy, of the sort that Chase advanced, moved toward the far more turbulent drama of the National Recovery Administration. A foretaste of the troubles that would beset the NRA before it finally collapsed was provided by a debate in 1932 between Lorwin and Rexford Tugwell, for a time Roosevelt's chief adviser and one of the chief architects of NRA. At a meeting of the American Economic Association in March, 1932, Tugwell struck out with his customary vigor to speak of the large, and ennobling, demands planning would entail. Tugwell had always chosen to dramatize economics, making little secret of his belief that the science was, indeed, usually dismal. He had begun just after World War I as a leader in the "New Economics," dedicated to enlarging the questions of man's trades and livelihood to include the spirit and mind as well as the ledger book. Writing with frequent reference to philosophy, psychology, and literature, Tugwell made of economics a means for the joyful regeneration of society. As an admirer of Dewey's *Reconstruction of Philosophy*, he urged release from the Puritanical habits of an acquisitive society. Indeed, he declared in 1924, "We are just beginning to see that we shall really have to begin all over, forming our science upon relevant facts in American life." [40] Tugwell came to the economics meeting in those dark days after the Crash with his old fervor for reconstruction very much alive. He advised his audience that they must rouse themselves to the point where they could realize the totality of change which true social planning must bring. Too many had hoped against hope that a little planning would work—that we could attain "a kind of economic Geneva where all sorts of compromises may be had and where peace and prosperity may be insured." [41] The same lazy wishful thinking had afflicted the Republic for many years. "If we had been watching, describing, analyzing, industry as we should, we must have known that the greatest economic event of the nineteenth century occurred when Frederick Taylor first held a stop watch on the movements of a group of shovelers in the plant of the Midvale Steel Company. And we must have understood, when *Shop Management* was published in 1903, that, perhaps a generation later, the world could be overwhelmed with goods." [42] Warning that change would be hard, Tugwell declared that there must be comprehensive revision of the Constitution and many legal statutes to root out the old competitive bias written into them and a change in the economic structure that would amount to the abandonment of "business," which he defined as essentially a laissez-faire term. In the end the government must take control of business, for the simple logical reason that business must be coordinated and once merged into a mighty whole would have too much power for the government to allow its continuance as a free competitor.

Lorwin responded that he found little to disagree with, except for the dangerous inflexibility of Tugwell's conception. Many different kinds and degrees of planning might be advisable depending on circumstances, Lorwin commented. To think otherwise, to insist on a total blueprint or nothing, is to run athwart of the shifting, gradualist tides of society, especially in America. "That," Lorwin concluded in words that penetrated the future, "is why Mr. Tugwell comes at the end to a dilemma.

The present order does not satisfy him. Planning involves a complete revolution in institutions which cannot be achieved at once. He offers us a choice which is no choice at all."[43]

Subsequently, Tugwell joined the New Deal and helped draft the NRA, which established trade association codes somewhat along the lines of the Swope Plan and gave labor guarantees for collective bargaining, maximum hours, and minimum wages. Tugwell hoped that the bill would give public planning the dominion over business that he had predicted would naturally arise from the responsibility of broad coordinated power. Instead, the self-seeking ingenuity of businessmen found loopholes beyond plugging. General Johnson, the head of NRA planning, covered the country with *Blue Eagle* stickers and barnstormed against the uncooperative "captains of industry" turned "corporals of disaster"—all to no avail. The NRA failed to gain enough public favor or administrative precision to establish control and was finally dispatched by the Supreme Court in 1935.

Tugwell's optimism about the irresistible forward movement of planning oversold the chances at hand for planning, while it restricted its room to maneuver, as Lorwin warned. In the New Deal Tugwell found himself more and more effectively countered by conservatives and antitheorists. Senator "Cotton Ed" Smith of South Carolina resisted his appointment as Undersecretary of Agriculture because "he is not a graduate of God's Great University" meaning the rural extension of the College of Hard Knocks. From the other side, Oscar Ameringer, the agrarian Socialist, rejected the entire notion of professorial planning experts with the hard-scrabble irony typical of farm radicalism. "Why particularly this deluge of the doctorate into the Department of Agriculture?" he asked. "Before Columbia moved uptown to its present site (formerly occupied by the Bloomingdale Insane Asylum), the countryside thereabout consisted chiefly of rocks, truck gardens and far-ranging goats. It was never, so far as I understand, what might be called a natural granary. Columbia, once described as 'a mausoleum completely surrounded by factories,' was hardly a likely breeding ground for either farm products or farm experts."[44]

Tugwell, the most thoroughgoing planner of the Brain Trust, left the New Deal in an ambivalent mood that never resolved itself. Impressed by the practical accomplishments of an administration fearfully hard-pressed by events, he yet regretted the failure not to move on toward ends of a more cohesive and uplifting sort. Looking back from the sixties, Tugwell confessed, "I think now that I was too impetuous. I also think, however, that Roosevelt erred too—on the minimal side. He could have emerged from the orthodox progressive chrysalis and led us into a new world. He chose rather rickety repairs for an old one."[45]

Lorwin avoided the dilemma by staying farther afield from the New Deal and so exemplified those pragmatic reformers who felt that the political system had not yet reached the point where those within it could hope to implement far-ranging plans. The one New Deal undertaking in which he took part merely hardened his independence. In 1934 Charles Merriam of the newly created National Planning Board came to Brookings to ask Lorwin to prepare a critique of planning. But when the finished study was delivered, Merriam, perhaps thinking of the terrible wrath of the National Planning Board chairman and self-styled curmudgeon, Harold Ickes, decided to shelve it because of the criticism it contained of the NRA. Lorwin wrote off the incident as another example of the timidity one must expect from planners in the employ of a governmental system that still did not understand or trust planning. And he then set out to promote vigorous planning on a private basis. With Marion Hedges, who edited the newsletter of the progressive International Union of Electrical Workers, Lorwin conceived the National Planning Association in 1934 and a journal, *Plan Age*, to spread its ideas. The association, much in the pattern set earlier by the National Bureau of Economic Research and Brookings Institution, became a permanent and productive source of social analysis, if not the center of national reconstruction its founders hoped might be its role. But Lorwin did not remain long with his creation. In 1935 he became economic adviser to the United States delegation at the International Labor Organization and passed the directorship of the NPA on to George Soule. The choice was perfectly apt, for Soule had become by then one of the most penetrating spokesmen for national planning. His writings, bolder and more searching than the run of critical commentary, were urging liberal dissatisfactions with the New Deal onto the hard road to a rational alternative.

5. George Soule

George Soule was a quiet man with depths. He was one of those in the rising generation just before World War I whose ardor for a more compassionate and intelligent social life Randolph Bourne so keenly discerned and hoped to direct. But Soule stayed with pragmatism while Bourne and his associates moved away in reaction to war and materialism. It was Soule's steady, even stoic, dedication to the factual groundings of reform that held his strong feelings within a sober economic framework and that kept him from any rebellious escapes. In 1914, a young man in his twenties, Soule became one of the original members of the *New Republic* and gratefully absorbed an education from the persons and ideas that passed through the offices. Like other economists, Soule was struck by the way World War I simultaneously revealed the possibilities of large-scale planning and the inadequacies of the old capitalist system which had helped bring on the bloody, senseless conflict. After the war Soule expressed belief in the need to reform by joining the National Bureau of Economics and helping found the Labor Bureau, Inc., and the Technical Alliance. At the alliance he came into contact with Veblen. Intrigued by Veblen's daring analysis of the predatory inefficiency of businessmen, Soule would often go over to the New School for Social Research to hear the master murmur in scarcely audible polysyllables to a dwindling class. But Soule did not become a Veblenite in any strict sense. The doctrine, for all its usefulness in suggesting a conflict between profit and production, seemed too dogmatic to Soule, too insistent on the idea of "instincts" governing economic activity and on the superior character of technicians. He turned instead to practical politics and labor-union organizing.

In 1919 Soule joined the study group sent to Gary, Indiana, by the National Council of Churches to investigate the battle of strikers at the steel mills to escape the seven-day week and the twelve-hour day. There he met William Z. Foster, the steel union leader whose bitter experiences at Gary and elsewhere eventually drove him into the Communist Party. Soule followed up the earnest talks he had with Foster in those bleak surroundings with an independent study of Marxism that confirmed Soule's distrust of ideological dogma. Resistance to such absolutism was, he avowed, "part of his very nature." Yet he was touched by Foster. When he returned to New York, he sought a union cause to which he could commit his energies. In the recently formed International Ladies Garment Workers Union, headed by Sidney Hillman, Soule found his ideal. Neither doctrinaire like the Marxian unions nor merely after tactical material gains like the AFL, the Amalgamated displayed three cardinal virtues. First, it was active in independent political action, lending support to the farm-labor candidates of 1920 and 1924, while pressing for a distinct labor party. Second, it disavowed sabotage as a tactic, thus distinguishing itself from the self-destructive wildness of the IWW. And, finally, it stressed the cultural benefits a union ought to bestow on its members. Soule looked admiringly on the staunch efforts of the Jewish unionists to found schools that would examine tactics and ethics and also provide enrichment for workers' leisure. Felix Adler's social philosophy of ethical culture stemmed from that concern for the quality of workingmen's lives. So, too, did the Rand School of Social Science, begun in 1905, and the numerous labor colleges, like the famous Brookwood Labor College which the remarkable pacifist radical A. J. Muste made the most famous of its kind.

Soule was one of the many post-World War I social critics who felt an acute need to study the complex ramifications of industrial society. His experience with the Amalgamated convinced him that "workers everywhere are awakening to the necessity of having sources of information upon which they can depend."[46] In issuing a call for intellectuals, Soule was acutely aware of class differences and self-conscious about the sorts of privileges he enjoyed. He invoked the example of Powers Hapgood who went directly from Harvard to digging coal in Pennsylvania in order to learn enough of miners' work to qualify for a position of union organizer. Hapgood's humility as well as his respect for experience appealed to Soule. Above all, Soule held that the intellectual's task within the unions was to serve the needs of workers, not to seek leadership. The intellectual must be willing to do tedious clerical jobs and stay within the bounds of hard facts. "Unless the inner spirit of a man is robust enough to bear such a matter-of-fact analysis, his courage and enthusiasm certainly will not endure through an experience of the reality. I am confident that a deep fire of conviction can and must be capable of a straight look at the facts and will be willing to prove itself in the unromantic drudgery necessary to accomplishment. There is no discouragement for those who have such a spirit in what I have tried to say."[47]

Some of the experienced union professionals found Soule rather too earnest and Puritanical, perhaps because he was trying too hard to atone for the arrogant treatment given labor by the white-collar class out of which he had come. Morris Hillquit, speaking in favor of partnership rather than a concept of the intellectual as servant of the workers, answered that "it is the recognition that the class struggle of the workers inevitably leads to a higher social order that furnishes common ground for the intellectual idealists and practical trade unionists in the political and economic struggles of organized labor." And, added Muste, an ordained minister, one should remember that honest labor is a source of great moral example, a source in need of a new "statement of ethics" by those whose intellectual talents fitted them to the task.[48]

Soule took the advice to heart and went on to hold a higher opinion of what the intellectual could contribute to practical causes. Yet he always remained deliberate and self-effacing. He was a splendid archetype of the intellectual pilgrim as reformer: optimistic, yet skeptical of panaceas; at home in the pandemonium of labor meetings and radical demonstrations, yet gentle and scholarly in bearing; mentally receptive to any change that reason should dictate, but not eager to overturn conventional mores or to alter the austere middle-class New England character of his life. His major aim, lucidly expressed in numerous articles and books, was to extend experimental reason into the dark continent of prevailing economic thought. Soule guessed that the result of rooting out conservative orthodoxies would be an increased socialization of control over resources, moving toward a cooperative rather than a competitive society. But that conjecture remained of secondary importance for him. The task at hand was to experiment scientifically with each facet of economics to see exactly what method of operation, authoritarian or cooperative, best suited the public interest in a rationally ordered society.

During the 1920's Soule supported Progressive movements and in the election of 1920 was even on the slate of Presidential electors for the Farm-Labor Party in New York. But the Progressive Party did not greatly influence his views on reform strategy. Third parties, he decided, did not suit American conditions. Moreover, the industrial age had rushed on past Herbert Croly and the moralistic spear-bearers of his era, the Teddy Roosevelts and the Robert La Follettes, to a stage of complexity that required extensive new study before any logical political structure could be devised. Liberals, he recalled later, became increasingly discouraged as the twenties wore on because "our civilization appeared to be unmanageable."[49]

Soule confronted the Depression with the optimism of many pragmatic rationalists who believed that the great crisis must certainly lead to a new public willingness for fundamental change. He rejoiced to observe that Roosevelt's mind, at least in terms of economics, seemed a blank slate. Reformers with persuasive logic and evidence, long barred from the centers of influence by a cordon of economic dogma, could now hope to be heard.[50] With his surmise that the force of necessity could turn established institutions onto a reasonable course and the diffidence he had acquired toward insurgent political action, Soule chose not to join Dewey and the rest in third-party activity.

At the same time Soule kept aloof from the New Deal. He was offered several posts in Roosevelt's Brain Trust, but despite his admiration and liking for Rexford Tugwell, who offered the lures, he chose to remain a fully independent commentator. From his post on the *New Republic* Soule fired suggestions for action at the New Deal that became critical enough on occasion to ruffle the feathers of the financial "angels" of the *New Republic*, who were friends and partisans of the President.[51]

Soule's views in the *New Republic* and elsewhere were gathered into an analysis and positive program for change published under the title *A Planned Society* (1934). The way ahead lies open, Soule declared, now that the most destructive phase of the twentieth century had ended. Perhaps those years, from 1914 to the present Depression, for all their rigors, had been a salutary experience. At the time of the Great War, Soule reflected, "as the doctrinal foundations of religion became undermined by modern skepticism, and as the limitations of patriotism in the traditional sense began to be revealed, these systems of values lost, for a majority of the more sensitive and intelligent, the touch of reality."[52] Science, it was then hoped, would perfect civilization, and in that spirit

H. G. Wells, the Webbs, and G. B. Shaw filled the popular mind with millennialist visions. But the dismal results at Versailles blasted that faith in reason and left social critics without firm values or policies. A gloom settled in, obscuring the opportunities for learning from the recent hardships and for appreciating a new freedom from old, outmoded customs. In Soule's mind three key factors disputed the pessimism of the twenties: first ,the displacement of belief in absolute natural law by pragmatism; second, the tremendous growth of empirical data describing economic and social conditions; and, finally, the provocative example of Soviet Russia.

Soule added to the optimistic promise of those three factors by indulging in a mild determinism of his own. "There is something in mankind," he asserted, "that forbids permanent surrender to disorder, ignorance, regression, no matter how hopeless the struggle may at times appear. The values inherent in the effort to build, to organize, are of primary and lasting importance; they are in harmony with man's own organic being."[53] Soule's support of a collectivist "organizing faculty" reflected Veblen's idea of the instinct of workmanship. Veblen did not predict an outcome in the struggle between that instinct and the secondary pecuniary instinct. But in Soule's view "the same sort of habit which has been observed in the past ordering smaller areas and endeavors, planning, changing and improving them, can be counted upon to attempt to bring order out of the chaos of the new world community. That impulse is irrepressible; whatever obstacles or groups stand in its way are bound in the end to suffer for their obduracy."[54]

Soule agreed with other pragmatic rationalists in believing that the leadership for the coming planned state must come from a responsible minority. Thrusting at the opposing Marxist view of historically determined mass action, Soule declared that "there is nothing more destructive than an undisciplined and undifferentiated crowd, acting on the highest common denominator of their several impulses—which is bound to be an exceedingly low denominator indeed."[55] The Russian example and the native example of the War Industries Board during the First World War demonstrated to Soule the wisdom of installing a rigid pyramid of command extending from regional councils, established to coordinate local resources to geography and inhabitants, on up to a National Economic Board directing all the planning agencies. Soule discussed the functions of that monolith without alarm at its power. We

need not fear that the planning structure will become despotic, Soule
stated reassuringly. "Public opinion in the world has been so conditioned by industrialism and the liberal democratic slogans which accompanied its birth, that the main objective of policy in any country would
almost necessarily be the same as the Russian objective—enhancement
of the general popular well-being."[56]

As the New Deal moved through its first term in power, Soule sharpened the outline of his blueprints for a planned society. In a 1934
address to a gathering in honor of the efficiency expert Frederick Taylor,
Soule prophesied that the climax of the struggle Veblen predicted between engineers and profit-takers was near. Consumers must rise up
and demand an economy of abundance run for their benefit. He amplified that theme later in the year in *The Coming American Revolution*.
With his increasing intensity came disillusion over the slow pace of the
New Deal. "Since [Roosevelt] was not prepared in his own mind or by
the organization of social and political forces behind him to press the
issue against [the capitalists]," Soule concluded despairingly, "he had
to surrender to them."[57] In tones of a *Nunc Dimittis* Soule declared
that "the virtue of the New Deal will probably be seen, in the light of
history, not as successful social planning, but as a step in the educational
process which is necessary if the workers, the farmers and the professional and white collar classes are ever to become sufficiently mobilized
and conscious enough of a program so that they can engage in successful social planning."[58] Soule then turned to the third-party eventuality
he had scorned in the early days of Roosevelt's administration. A
measure of his optimism remained. He saw the elements for a successful
party of rational social planning coming together as the alternatives
faded. The New Deal, he reasoned, had slipped the hangman's hood
over its eyes by aligning itself with the old capitalist order. Communism,
given its mistaken emphasis on spontaneous lower-class revolutions, was
hopeless. The third alternative, Fascism, Soule dispatched along with
the New Deal. The policy of linking business interests with government
in the NRA appeared to Soule to obviate Fascism. "We are," he stated,
"by way of trying out the economics of Fascism without having suffered
all its social or political ravages. If it succeeds, as is most improbable,
we shall not have to undergo the unpleasantness of the political dictatorship. If it does not succeed, and the reasons for its non-success are sufficiently well understood, any American Fascist movement would have

to think up a new economic philosophy. It is possible that the New Deal is a relatively painless inoculation against Fascism."[59]

Soule's unruffled appraisal of Fascism as a possible contender for power in America gave an interesting insight into the coolness of his mind and temperament. As he had done in *A Planned Society*, Soule had slain the enemy with logic and left the way open for a new order. But the question of who was to clear the field and initiate social planning remained unanswered. True to his insistence that significant change and organization proceed from an intelligent minority, Soule called for the liberal intellectuals to provide tutors for such a minority. Admitting that the majority of intellectuals and professors were still apologists for the Old Order or the New Deal, he saw two hopeful signs. First, "the forefront of the white-collar workers, the productive professions, are just beginning to assume some of the political prerogatives which their actual place in a highly organized industrial society warrants, and to which their superior competence in matters of social theory entitles them."[60] Secondly, "the more sensitive of the writers and teachers have, with surprising unanimity, ceased celebrating the virtues of the Old Order and embroidering its traditions, but rather have been busy exposing its failures and corruptions and ridiculing many of its leading figures."[61] Faith in the irresistible advance of the "organizing faculty," as industrial society becomes more complex, and in the lesson afforded to the nation by various idols—capitalism, Communism, Fascism, and the New Deal —crumbling under the weight of their own unreason, must sustain the liberals through the hard times. If that long period of trial and error happens to proceed painlessly, "it will be the first time in history that a social revolution has been completed with neatness and dispatch. What is more likely is that there will be a prolonged period of turmoil and uncertainty, that the moderates will ingloriously fail, that there will be fighting, swings to the left and reaction. . . . Eventually the outcome will be the final disappearance of government by private profit-makers over the means of production, a chance for social management to learn its task by experience." "This will not be Utopia," Soule hastened to add.[62] It was, however, far more idealistic than any vision he had entertained since the defeat of La Follette's gallant campaign in 1924. Within three years he would declare emphatically that such hopes for a collectivist revolution were Utopian indeed.

6. Stuart Chase

Stuart Chase stood out during the thirties as the most conspicuous and perhaps the shrewdest spokesman of the pragmatic rationalist viewpoint. An economist by profession, Chase became an effective gadfly among social critics after a youthful period of unrest and soul-searching.

Chase's resolution of character was a specimen of the awakening many young Americans underwent during the years just before World War I, prompted by growing awareness of social iniquities and the sense that a sea change must soon set in against the iniquitous. Chase's conventional middle-class upbringing gave him something immediate to react against, but his optimistic temperament made him the least gloomy of rebels. Bright, gregarious and athletic, Chase trained as a certified public accountant at Harvard so that he could smoothly enter his father's Boston accounting firm. His first tinge of social awareness came shortly after graduation in 1910, when he shocked his earnest uncle Arthur by confessing to no particular social philosophy. He was duly set to work on the writings of Henry George and found much in *Progress and Poverty* to impress him. Always energetic (he once counted all the billboards between New York and New London from a train window in order to document the excesses of advertising), Chase began studying the statistics of income distribution in his spare time on the assumption those figures would give a reliable idea of what sort of social justice and happiness obtained in America. He was struck by the discovery that the Census Bureau listed $600 as the average family income in 1914 and tried to envision what that meant in flesh and blood terms. Finally, to the mingled dismay and amusement of their families, Chase and his new bride decided to investigate by spending their honeymoon looking for jobs in Rochester, New York, without any help whatever from home. The results were shattering. In a remarkable, melodramatic little book called *A Honeymoon Experiment* (1916) the Chases recounted their adventures. They began with a typical Chase survey—by trolley car—and found to their surprise that Rochester had no slums! Then their story took a surprisingly contradictory turn that indicated the Chases' lack of preparation for getting along in the American jungle and an earnest desire to find a need for reform. From the time they began trying to support themselves in "the city with no slums," the tale was one of misery on every hand: dingy boardinghouses whose inmates were helpless against cockroaches and decay; an army of the unemployed crowding the park benches or clamoring to get the few miserable jobs available; sweatshops; dingy five and dimes; and all manner of tawdry fates befalling the people the Chases came to know. All of Stuart's energy and ingenuity failed to turn up any acceptable work—only a few grinding part-time jobs and a beckon to his wife from the white slave trade. In the end the couple became literally suicidal about American life as they found it. "If we had been genuinely faced with the necessity of living through an indefinite future in the same manner that we had lived for the past six or seven weeks," Stuart intoned, "we should undoubtedly have chosen not to live at all!"[63] The Chases left Rochester shaken and with a resolve, which never left Stuart, though it became less tragic, to explain what they had discovered and work to improve it. On departure, as Stuart recalled it, his wife asked:

> "Do you think we can make them understand—all this?"
> "We'll try," I said.
> And we have.[64]

Chase's subsequent efforts to understand and explain were broad and vigorous. During the war that followed closely, he worked with the Federal Trade Commission as a consultant and gained permanent enthusiasm for the possibilities of governmental planning. After returning to New York, he came briefly within the expanding bubble of Howard Scott's strange career. Ripe for the idea of social engineering, though not in the authoritarian form that Scott was later to propose, Chase agreed to join in the formation of the Technical Alliance for the purpose of studying technology and industry. There Chase discovered Thorstein Veblen, who became his unchallenged mentor until John Maynard Keynes came to his attention in the mid-thirties. It was Veblen who interested Chase in the study of waste which preoccupied Chase all during the indubitably wasteful business spree of the twenties.

As for Scott, his flamboyant posturings never made much difference to Chase. As Chase rather laconically put it, "The question is not whether Scott has lived in Greenwich Village or in Lung Tung Pen, but what his figures show."[65] In saying that, Chase was not declaring himself the dull slave of the ledger; but, rather, captive of the *idea* that technical study might be able to make sense out of the American experience and induce vital reforms. It was a prophet's approach. Chase launched himself upon his new career as technical critic and reformer with a buoyancy that produced a swift flow of witty and urgent writings and a cheerful nature which the losing of many battles to chaotic free enterprise could not seriously depress.

Chase's liaison with the Technical Alliance was only a part of his determined search for answers. He also joined the League for Industrial Democracy and became for a time an enthusiastic Socialist, even, in his more fervent moments, a "near Communist." For a time he was on the editorial board of *Forward*, an organ for the modified socialism of Sidney Hillman's Amalgamated Clothing Workers' Union, and was a consultant for the Labor Bureau, Inc., a nonpartisan agency for the study of ways to improve bad working conditions. Yet, with an aroused social conscience and thrown together with many Socialists in the heartland of Socialist activity and thought, Chase did not find any ideology to which he could commit himself. His mind sifted through the doctrines of Henry George, Marxism, guild socialism, Fabian socialism, and consumer cooperation and finally emerged grateful to all but converted to none. He was committed only to a thorough examination of American institutions, in the anthropological and economic mode Veblen had prescribed. His strategy was nonpolitical—Chase described himself as an "ignoramus" in that respect—and so not given to the same frustrations that beset political reformers during the twenties. Still, much of the fire in his commentaries was generated by a strong aversion to the laissez-faire policies of Calvin Coolidge's New Era, which, in its mindless drift in the shoals of special privilege, seemed to Chase a direct repudiation of the capacity of human nature to create a just society.

Chase's fluctuating experiences and views during the twenties moderated his attitude toward the economic crisis of the 1930's. He prided himself on the hardheaded rationalism of his approach. He commissioned himself to assay economic conditions without wandering off into speculation about social or political questions that were more properly in the realm of different experts—and of secondary import, at that, in the midst of unprecedented economic collapse. Yet he was not able wholly to escape the impressions of a trip to Mexico in 1927, which produced a book praising the preindustrial aesthetics of that country, or his reading of Ruskin, Wells, and Kropotkin while he was searching among various Utopian ideals for a star to follow. In criticizing capitalism he felt it apt to say that "the system called capitalism, for all its sprinkling with holy water in the nineteenth century, is at heart irreligious, without internal unity or public spirit. . . . Great religious movements have usually been grounded in collectivism, in the brotherhood of man, leaving laissez-faire, in the last analysis, a cold and ferocious anti-Christ."[66] In the cooler mood of detachment that he favored for himself he promoted his belief in an engineered society by asserting that "the technological imperative is impersonal, amoral, and non-ethical. Like the Nile, it sets the boundaries within which a given culture must operate."[67]

Chase reflected the ideas of many pragmatic rationalists who had experienced World War I by suggesting the War Industries Board as an appropriate model for a central planning agency. He made a plea for such a board as early as 1925. As the thirties began, Chase added the Republic of Mexico Planning Commission and Soviet Russia as exemplars of social planning. "Russia is no dream," he advised in 1931. "Day by day her shadow falls sharper, bolder, upon the face of the world. . . ."[68] "Why," he later added wistfully, "should Russians have all the fun of remaking a world?"[69]

But Chase's enthusiasm for Russia's Brave New Experiment was limited to its economic feats. He was impressed that the backward, war-wracked Soviet Union was able to build a powerful industrial base in the twenties when it was a pariah among the wealthy Western nations, and then able to augment it after 1929 when the capitalistic world was floundering in depression. Chase's visit to Russia in 1927 reinforced his view of the irrationality of capitalism's money economy. Wealth, he reasoned, resides in the fruitful use of manpower and natural resources, not in bank vaults. How else could one explain Russia's phenomenal advances when she was utterly broke? How wonderful it would be if Russia's Western neighbors would ponder that "miracle" and begin rethinking some of their own free-enterprise pieties.[70]

Chase did not wish to emulate other features of the Russian state, however, recognizing the harsh repressions to which it was given and the ideological fixity of its social and political views. Chase agreed with other pragmatic rationalists in deploring ideologies of all sorts; similarly, he was immune to the temptation of romanticizing Russia's Glorious Revolution, as so many Americans did in the twenties and thirties after leafing through the praiseful books of Maurice Hindus, Anna Louise Strong, Walter Duranty, and others on the new Russia.

Chase found the example of Mexico far more persuasive on the issue of how to nurture the human spirit. In 1930, exhausted by his "studies of life in the machine age" and intrigued by the advice of his artist friend George Biddle that he ought to go to a land with little sense of time and admire the murals of Diego Rivera, Chase arranged a two-month stay in the village of Tepoztlán. He did not abandon his planning sense altogether, however. Tepoztlán attracted him because that was where Robert Redfield had done his pioneer study of Mexican Indian life. With Redfield's book in his luggage, Chase carried a travel guide par excellence. He also packed a copy of the recently completed study of Muncie, Indiana—*Middletown* (1925)—by Robert and Helen Lynd so that he could ponder the facts of another "village." With a delighted sense of the valuable equation that could be made between the two books and his own observations, Chase satisfied his need to be useful and was freely able to release the rest of his spirit into the new surroundings. There in the languid, picturesque mountains, touched by the dignity of the Indians and their facile craftsmanship, Chase's romantic sensibilities rose to the surface. His comparison of Middletown and Tepoztlán was emphatically weighted on the side of Tepoztlán. Middletown merged into Gopher Prairie as Chase unloosed some of his most antagonistic comments toward his countrymen, whose faults he usually described more genially as foolish aberrations. The spectacle of Americans viewed directly against the background of Mexican life provoked his full wrath. Chase used the Buick touring car as a symbol of American machinery and metamorphosed it into a predatory monster. Perhaps, he concluded wistfully when he contemplated the crude and greedy Americans invading his beloved mountains, "the Buicks may fall off the unguarded hairpin turns which distinguished Mexican mountain roads."[71]

But however harshly Chase's true resentments were brought out by his sojourn, he did not abandon his enthusiasm for social planning. He gave high praise to the Programme Department of the Mexican government for its ability to carry out sweeping social plans without bureaucratic delay. "Outside the Russian Gosplan," he declared, bringing his various observations into focus, "I know of no such far-reaching and powerful agency since the collapse of our own War Industries Board in 1919."[72] To Chase's mind the Indian handicrafts economy did not conflict with the strategy of central planning. Both were designed to advance security and abundance. And both, if one looked closely enough and was not balked by conventional beliefs, fulfilled the ideal of efficiency. "Mass production cannot compete in charm, and probably not in quality, with the Mexican handicrafts," Chase declared in accord with what everyone already knew. But there was an unrecognized economic backbone supporting the Mexican handicraft system, making it a viable part of the modern world and not merely a quaint relic. "I am convinced," Chase concluded, "in the teeth of all the doctors of economics, *that [mass production] cannot always compete in price.*"[73] For the village craftsman had few costs to worry about, in contrast to the rising expenses of distribution and advertising that afflicted United States manufacturers.

The lessons of his varied experiences and observations left Chase convinced, well before the Great Crash occurred, that American prosperity was hollow. He advocated a Supreme Economic Council, residing in Washington, to convert the apparent wealth of nimble speculators into actual wealth in the hands of pinched small businessmen, farmers, and factory workers. With hucksters in command, he lamented, "the technician is the modern Prometheus in chains."[74] At another time he remarked that "Plato once called for philosopher kings. Today the greatest need in all the bewildered world is for philosopher engineers."[75]

In 1931, as the blackness of the Depression was deepening, Chase called for a bloodless revolution by engineers and their allies in the professions and the ranks of white-collar workers against the organized Babbittry of the business civilization Hoover continued to support. "We shall seek to sharpen the line which Thorstein Veblen once drew between industry and business, between applied science as an economic agent and profitable speculation, between the economies of planned abundance and the economies of manipulated scarcity."[76] Chase was enough caught up in the crusading zeal of the time to plump for a radical infusion of leftist righteousness into politics and for a reinvigoration of America's intel- ‑

lectual tradition by the enlightened few. "It is time," he announced, "that the intelligent minority should realize that it cannot serve God and Mammon." [77]

Chase presented his program for a rational administration of the nation amid doubts that a smooth transition to that desired state was likely. "Free competition is a dying institution," he intoned. But "the big problem before us is what is going to take its place. Four champions are already in the field—more perhaps will come." [78] Those immediate contenders Chase saw to be:

1. Dictatorship by great corporations and mergers
2. State Socialism
3. Cooperative Commonwealth—control of industry by volunteer groups of consumers or producers
4. Continuation of the present "hodge-podge"

"The first," Chase concluded, "is probably the next phase for America. The second is the going system in Russia. The third is the going system in Denmark. The last is the going system everywhere else in the Western world." [79] Chase's presentiment of a form of Fascism coming to America, occurring to him even before the Nazi revolution, is an interesting example of a common pragmatic rationalist tendency to fear rightist dictatorship in America. Undoubtedly that fear reflected distaste for the "associational" policy of the Republican administrations during the twenties. Ruling coalitions of businessmen and politicians had come to seem far more consonant with American conditions than ruling coalitions of workers.

Chase's book *A New Deal for America* (1932) provided a clear statement on the hopes for collectivist reform that he held at the outset of the thirties. It also catapulted its author into prominent public notice by providing Roosevelt with part of the text for his Inaugural Address in March, 1933, and perhaps with the title of his famous program. To Chase a viable New Deal meant following a third road, somewhat to the left of those in the Democratic Party who considered themselves liberals, but well to the right of Marxist territory. The Communists, he felt, for all their outcry, could never sell class solidarity to American workers. Rather sardonically he dismissed earlier fears of a Fascist ruling clique as an illusion based on the false notion that business and financial tycoons could ever temper their selfishness long enough to form an effective combine.

The third road, Chase suggested, would be lit by a "torch . . . borne by another class, one hitherto unknown to history: the men and women who have grasped the hand of science." [80] The way would be illumined far beyond the horizons of such tinkerers as John Maynard Keynes and Arthur Salter, who, Chase felt, had failed in their critiques of the *workings* of capitalism to make a searching enough examination of the deficiencies of capitalism as a way of life. The minimum requirements for the reconstruction that Chase advocated were: (1) a managed currency, (2) drastic redistribution of the national income through income and inheritance taxes, and (3) a huge program of public works geared to the elimination of all unemployment, which was the cardinal waste of the nation's resources as well as an unwonted cruelty to many who were trapped in an economic system they could neither understand nor control. Such a program, Chase felt sure, could only take effect through an all-powerful Central Planning Board. The divisive political system currently in effect should give way to a more rational, stabilized arrangement. In that plea Chase reiterated the common view of intellectuals who had weathered the twenties that politics were apt to be venally subordinate to forces maneuvering privately for power and economic advantage. Referring to social pressures as a partner to political process in forming two "governments" Chase reflected that "the voter's power, as in Russia, is, broadly speaking, negligible. It acts ineffectively on the weaker of the two governments under which the American lives." [81] The best hope, then, for the needed radical reform would be (1) education and agitation, and (2) a new political party against which the Democratic and Republican parties would coalesce into a frankly conservative opposition. "If the party, supported by the mass of the electorate, were voted into power they could inaugurate the planning authority forthwith, which in four or eight years' time might dig itself so deeply into the economic mechanism that it would not be dislodged in subsequent elections unless it failed dismally to solve the problem of distribution." [82]

The accession of the Nazis to power in Germany strengthened Chase's conviction that only a fully rationalized planning system with full power to propose and dispose would stand a reasonable chance of achieving the necessary reforms in the United States. The Weimar Republic illustrated the disastrous error of trying moderate, patchwork control over industry. Instead of coordinating all industrial operations under a central planning authority, the German government set up separate regulatory agencies for the various enterprises. Both government and business were precariously uncertain of what the sum of separate controls would equal at any given time. The Nazis were able to play on that fear and forge alliances with certain economic interest groups that sought a measure of security should Hitler come to wield a significant measure of power. In the end, of course, Hitler gained far more than a "significant measure" of power. Chase concluded that Hitler built his absolute domination on the concessions granted to him in a vain effort to make him their subservient ally. [83]

Thus by 1934 Chase was in the resolute frame of mind required for his most militant planning manual, *The Economy of Abundance*. Recounting his earlier formulas of government control, Chase declared himself in favor of "an industrial general staff with dictatorial powers covering the smooth technical operation of all the major sources of raw material and supply. Political democracy can remain if it confines itself to all but economic matters; democracy in consumption will make enormous strides as standards of living are levelled upward; industrial individualism—anarchy is a better term—in the sense of each business man for himself, each corporation for itself, must be disallowed." [84] Concerning the loss of individual freedom that such rigid collectivizing would entail, Chase remarked laconically, "I think I could adapt myself to it without developing Freudian complexes. It would be irksome for a time, in that it was different, but a retreat to Stratford would be even more irksome." [85]

With that statement of acquiescence, Chase's challenge to the political and economic order was complete: He was prepared to support a third party to set the country on a collectivist course, giving the federal government and the engineering principles that would animate it control over the economy and, by implication, over much of the social and political life of the citizenry. To speed the transition to the new consumer state Chase was eager to call a Constitutional Convention to hack away the network of checks and balances that tended to stay the hand of the state from taking firm control over otherwise chaotic economic activity. [86]

But what of Roosevelt and the administration bearing Chase's own slogan? "Considering the character of the emergency and the speed which was demanded," Chase observed guardedly the same year that *The Economy of Abundance* appeared, "I have very little criticism to direct against the administration for its first year's performance. . . ." [87]

"But," he went on, "a continuation of the patch-work means a gradual disintegration. Nobody is satisfied, now that the fear of imminent disaster is passed."[88] Chase was echoing the growing pragmatic rationalist clamor at the middle of the decade for outright collectivism to displace policies of gradualism that seemed to be falling behind the rush of events. Clearly the New Deal had not resolved the crisis; who could expect the nation's many disaffected sufferers to refrain patiently forever from disruptive, even violent, attempts to better their lot? And did the rapid rise of collectivism abroad not indicate that the large planned state was the inevitable answer to the complexities of life in the Western industrial nations?

But the confidence of those rhetorical questions appeared before the demonstrated failure of any collectivist program to take hold in America, before the electorate expressed rousing approval of the New Deal in 1936, and before the collectivist states in Europe plunged into war in Spain, filling the last half of the decade with menace.

7. Against the Revolution

Of the several pragmatic rationalist characteristics perhaps the most distinctive was its consciously middle-class nature. Repeatedly, its spokesmen declared the necessity of an informed middle class to generate the intelligence required for effective, rational reforms.[89] Dewey's emphasis on education, which so filled his reform writings, found a fundamental place in pragmatic rationalist thought. In turn, the educative temper of pragmatic rationalism made it congenial to reform agencies that stressed persuasion and reason, organizations such as the League for Industrial Democracy, the American Civil Liberties Union, the People's Lobby, and numerous cooperatist alliances.

The bourgeois nature of pragmatic rationalism provoked conflict with the Marxists, who looked for a proletarian revolution. The more vehement, doctrinaire Marxists simply dismissed middle-class reformism as an enemy of history. Their cooler-headed colleagues, recognizing the absence in America of a significant proletariat, in the classic sense of a downtrodden horde of class-conscious workers, set about to convince the bulk of wage earners and white-collar workers, who considered themselves middle class, that they had a common cause with the lower classes against capitalist exploitation. Pragmatic rationalists they lumped in with the New Deal as aiders and abettors of current abuses. The English visitor John Strachey put the case for the Marxists succinctly. "The truth is," he announced, "that nominally 'left' or progressive parties have before now, and perhaps unconsciously, carried out programmes which had undeniable affinities with Fascism. . . . It may be that the final verdict of history is that the present Democratic administration in America represents not American Fascism but American 'Social Fascism.' "[90] The shrewd Marxist critics Benjamin Stolberg and Warren Jay Vinton saw the New Deal as a captive of scientific social work on the Hull House model. By trying to assuage the pain of the

Depression for workers in the lower middle class and draw that class into accord with "housebroken" capitalism, the New Deal, they claimed, had actually undercut itself as an effective reform force. For "the tragedy of the New Deal is that the [conservative] middle class which it politically represents immobilizes it psychologically; and thus demobilizes it as an effective force in combating Big Ownership."[91]

In rebuttal, the pragmatic rationalists discounted talk of revolution and charged that the Marxist dogmatists were guilty of confusing American conditions with those that prevailed in czarist Russia in 1917. In America, pragmatic rationalists insisted, belief in the likelihood of revolutionary upheaval by the masses was the near exclusive property of literary radicals and Park Avenue conservatives. In truth, revolutions, violent or orderly, are managed by well- informed organizers who must, necessarily, come from the middle classes. In America the very practical question of material loss would stay the hands of leaders and followers of any incipient revolution. In Russia the tide of revolution swept over a backward nation. Revolution in America would involve a terrific struggle that would not be worth the candle; pitting revolutionists against powerful entrenched forces would result in a monstrous loss of life and the demolition of an intricate industrial complex that would take a prohibitive amount of time, money, and effort to replace. Stuart Chase summed up the case for the pragmatic rationalists:

> One thing such a revolution can do; it can teach mankind once and for all the degree of interdependence and technological tenuousness in its environment. If dwellers in glass houses cannot throw stones, those in a highly mechanized society cannot hit valves with sledgehammers. The lesson is one we must learn. . . .
>
> That brings me to the second main difficulty with this particular road. How far is America prepared psychologically for violent revolution? Technologically the thing is unthinkable, but it does not follow that it will not happen if enough citizens are determined to try the experiment. Who is for the experiment? I call for a show of hands. Farmers? No. Emphatically no. Yet they would be the least ravaged class. Skilled laborers? No. Their unions are weak, their discipline poor; with few exceptions they have never absorbed the ideology of the class struggle, which means they have no tradition, no unifying ideas to build revolution upon. Unskilled laborers? No. They have fewer unions and on the whole less tradition than the skilled workers.

That American labor may become violent, no one who knows its stormy history will dispute. It will be violence, however, of spasmodic, almost tropismic, outbreaks, not the planned and desperate will of nationwide revolution. White collar workers? No. Their spinal columns have been broken by decades of yessing the boss. The learned professions? No. They will line up with their bread and butter—what is left of it. . . . The engineers? No. Here more rank-breakers may be found, but the mass is not ready. It is doubtful if this generation of engineers will ever be ready—such has been its early conditioning.[92]

8. A Literary Impasse

The cool reasonableness of the pragmatic rationalists did not arouse much enthusiasm in the literary realm. Creative writers, swinging sharply from a sense of alienation during the 1920's to an intense social concern in the face of the Depression, were too burdened with emotion to feel moved by the plans of social engineers. Arthur Schlesinger, Jr., has popularized the charge that the pragmatic rationalists were either-or extremists: either radical reconstruction of America into their own version of a cooperatist utopia or else the dark.[93] To be sure, the pragmatic rationalists did reject the New Deal's prescription for gradual change as milk-water liberalism, a rejection that withheld them from the dominant trend of the time. But the choice pragmatic rationalists felt the country faced does not look so foolishly either-or when compared with the far more polar choice posed by a very large number of novelists, poets, and social critics during the thirties, who insisted on either-Communism-or-Fascism. The ideas of pragmatic rationalists occupying more moderate ground in between were pointedly avoided by writers entering into either-or radicalism.

The pragmatic rationalist view that ideology has a corrosive effect on the mind was vindicated in the case of the leftist attempts to politicalize literature. Tales of strikes and lower-class suffering appeared, received strong literary praise on the basis of their relevance to the radical cause, and then quickly died from lack of any real artistic merit. Elmer Davis, the hardheaded Hoosier realist, remarked perceptively in 1931, when proletarian literature began to appear, that radical writers were in effect writing for each other. The supposed proletarian readership was a shadow audience, by no means a reality to be inferred from praise of certain books by well-educated critics. The Hearst Press, Davis concluded, contained writing that was far more proletarian, judging from those newspapers' enormous circulation.[94] Louis Adamic helped to document Davis's charge by traveling around the country to talk to workers about their reading tastes. Everywhere he discovered that those few workers who had sampled proletarian literature were indifferent, baffled, or repelled by the Marxist message.[95] The evidence suggested to Adamic that another of his acquaintances, the somewhat seedy paper-back-book tycoon E. Haldeman-Julius, had more success in drawing a wide reading audience by giving voluptuous new titles to the classics than the Marxists did by weaving revolutionary doctrine into stories about the downtrodden masses.[96] If the proletariat wanted an easement of their lot, their reception to literature indicated that they were more apt to seek it through temporary escape than by clashing with their circumstances head on in revolution or fiction.

Pragmatic rationalists, devoted to a technical reconstruction of society, did not feel drawn to using creative literature as a medium of expression or persuasion. Upton Sinclair wrote a novel called *Co-Op* to publicize his EPIC doctrines, but it met much the same critical fate as its predecessor, Edward Bellamy's *Looking Backward*, which the English utopian William Morris greeted as "a vulgar cockney dream."[97] In general, literary critics tended to discount pragmatic rationalist programs for their lack of any inspirational fire. Archibald MacLeish set the tone in his attack on the Technocrats for being "as inept and outmoded as the Communists and less than half as persuasive. For the Communists have the great advantage of recognizing that the mechanization of industry means eventually a human world of human values: a world in which a man may not only live and work but believe."[98] Where criticism was not so harsh, especially in reference to pragmatic rationalist programs that were not as susceptible to the charge of robotry as those of the Technocrats, concern still arose over the remoteness of the rationalists from the public passions. With regret Walter Peck, reviewing Dewey's *A Common Faith* in 1934, concluded that "we know the warmth of heart and expansive social faith of John Dewey; if such a book as this has limitations it is because he must still be *Professor* Dewey. The man of generous impulses . . . will be heard only by intellectuals, not by the masses whom with his whole soul he would like to reach, and whom it is a tragedy not to reach."[99]

9. The Fascist Specter

The feeling of pragmatic rationalists during the first half of the thirties that the tide of collectivism was setting in made them increasingly disappointed with the vacillating New Deal, at the same time that it made them increasingly fearful of the menace of Fascism. Those who became active in the League for Independent Political Action were from the outset always skeptical of the New Deal, committed as they were to the view that both the Democratic and Republican parties were incorrigibly linked to reactionary groups. But a significant number of pragmatic rationalists withheld support from dissident political movements on the chance that the President might prove willing to experiment with a new collectivist order. Their hopes tended to dwindle. In July, 1933, George Soule reviewed the work of the whirlwind Hundred Days with cautious approval but also doubts "whether the 'thin red line' of experts who have at heart the welfare of labor and consumer, who want to build a collective economy, can survive the attacks of the reactionary profiteers who are already out for their scalps. If recovery comes and the Devil begins to convalesce, will he still wish to be good? Shall we relapse to the old anarchy? Or shall we enter a capitalist dictatorship?"[100] By October he noted with dismay that no central planning agency had been established by the administration. "Little is heard any more about the 'Brain Trust'—always a picturesque fiction. What there ever was of trustification in brains has now succumbed to the free competition of ideas."[101] Soule decided that at heart "people distrust any mobilization of knowledge and of analysis. They distrust the power which might grow from it."[102]

Soule's disappointment was a commentary on a rift within the liberal community as well as a reaction to the New Deal. As Roosevelt took command, a flush of hope for New Deal collectivization spread briefly over a large front. Individuals as conservative as William McAdoo and

Nicholas Murray Butler expressed support for central planning.[103] But once mild signs of recovery began to appear, they, along with the moderates, began to relax. The New Deal seemed to have averted the need for collectivism. The pragmatic rationalists, however, took the opposite tack and viewed the measures taken by Roosevelt as cause for alarm. They seemed mere palliatives that weakened the reform zeal of liberals without correcting the underlying faults of the old capitalistic system. Moreover the linkage of Big Business with the government in the NRA suggested the possible development of the New Deal into a front for undemocratic elements.

These fears constricted the range within which the pragmatic rationalists felt free to develop their own plans for society. Though they wished to promote cooperation, they were doubtful about the capacity of businessmen to shed arrogant ways and join in fruitful cooperation with the government or with private interests. At the same time, as we have seen, they shunned any resort to force and emotional dogma. Their hopes resided in an educational drive designed to enlist public support for scientific planning.

With only a narrow educational passage open to them, it is not surprising that pragmatic rationalists became highly sensitive to evidence of unreason in the world. They measured the significance of growing totalitarian strength carefully and, although the air was filled with talk of the Soviet experiment and the growing strength of Marxism, concluded that Fascism was the more imminent danger for the United States. Their diagnosis depended in part on Lenin's dictum that Fascism was the last agonized stage of capitalism. Certainly, American capitalism was suffering agonies; and did the drive by Big Business to achieve monopoly through the NRA not indicate Fascist tendencies? More important in pragmatic rationalist thinking was the view that Fascism squared more logically with American customs than did Marxism. It was middle class, whereas Marxism aimed toward a class-conscious proletariat, which did not exist in America. The oppressive feature of Southern life, recently dramatized by the Gastonia strike and the fate of the Scottsboro boys, the tendency of Americans to worship businessmen, and a recurrent streak of violence in the American character all suggested possible avenues by which Fascism could enter the country. "The American middle-classes are in fact ripe for Fascism," Alfred Bingham concluded in 1935. He listed all the incipient dangers: "An anti-labor policy, outlawing the strike, forcing the collaboration of capital and labor in a corporative system (while the dominant controls still remain largely in the hands of Capital, however much codified), quelling the subversive elements that would destroy the institution of private property, extolling the national virtues, suppressing alien influences—this is all quite possible. Much of it is already apparent in America. What seems to be wanting is a year or two more of depression, and the emergence of the Strong Man to lead the crowd."[104]

Bingham's analysis of the American middle-class bias toward Fascism gained support from Robert and Helen Lynds' notable study of Muncie, Indiana. Returning to "Middletown" in 1935, ten years after their original study, the Lynds observed that "Middletown seems recently to have been building its fences higher. The city is more antagonistic to outside groups; individuals in the city are seemingly more wary of each other; need of protection and security is more emphasized."[105] As anxiety mounts, "those elements in the culture with more information, more perspective on the issues, and more power of money and propaganda may chafe under the dragging unawareness and 'uncooperativeness' of their brethren in the Middletowns, and may spend their money to invoke symbols useful in persuading Middletown to jump through the appropriate hoops. And herein one glimpses once more the possible seeds of an eventual coercive control which in Europe today goes under the name of Fascism."[106]

The association many Americans made of Fascism with war helped spread the pragmatic rationalist fear of totalitarianism. As early as 1933 Matthew Josephson published a pamphlet urging Western nations to draw a *cordon sanitaire* around the Nazis in order to break their warlike spirit at the outset.[107] The *Modern Monthly*, edited by the able Marxist critic V. F. Calverton, published an interesting symposium on the subject of what to do "When America Goes to War." A wide array of social critics, including Dewey, Beard, Chase, Archibald MacLeish, and Walter Lippmann, were asked to consider various alternative approaches Americans might take toward entry into another war. In answering the questions, all of them made the assumption, as did the questionnaire, that any future war would be instigated by Nazi Germany.[108]

Sinclair Lewis, by inclination an apolitical writer, provided the most widely discussed speculation on how Fascism might come to America in his novel *It Can't Happen Here* (1935). Lewis' stature as a novelist, although on the decline, earned all his writings wide notice; yet it is a remarkable testament to national concern about the Fascist menace that his unrealistic picture of American political conditions, embodied in a narrative that often lapses into implausible melodrama, should have received so much attention as a prophetic glimpse at political possibilities. Perhaps part of his success came from the fact that, in the midst of such improbabilities as Frances Perkins shouldering Roosevelt aside and contesting for the Democratic nomination in 1936 against Senator Joseph Robinson of Arkansas, Lewis drew his political hero in the image of farm-labor collectivism so strongly favored by the League for Independent Political Action. In one scene Lewis depicts a meeting between that hero, Senator Walt Trowbridge, and a wealthy oil baron angling for influence. Senator Trowbridge, the Republican Presidential candidate defeated by the Fascists in the election of 1936, is directing resistance from a remote base in Canada. Regarding his tempter with the shrewd, squinted gaze of the plainsman he had once been, Trowbridge drawls a refusal: "Nope, sorry, Will. But we can't use you. Whatever happens . . . you and your kind of clever pirates are finished. Whatever happens, whatever detail of a new system of government may be decided on, whether we call it a 'Cooperative Commonwealth' or 'State Socialism' or 'Communism' or 'Revived traditional Democracy,' there's got to be a new feeling—that government is not a game for a few smart, resolute athletes like you, Will, but a universal partnership in which the State must own all resources so large that they affect all members of the State, and in which the one worst crime won't be murder or kidnapping but taking advantage of the State. . . . Eh? What's going to happen to magnates like you, Will? God knows! What happened to the dinosaurs?"[109]

The hopes and fears of the pragmatic rationalists pointed toward the election of 1936 that Lewis described so grimly. Surely its outcome would be a crucial measure of what expectations collectivist reformers might fairly hold. A strong showing by the Union Party of Long, Coughlin, and Townsend would confirm the fears of Bingham and others that Fascism was rising to fill the gulf between the lower classes and the capitalist New Deal.[110] Should Landon run well, even though falling short of a majority, the New Deal experiment would be revealed as a failure in its attempt to lead the country toward modified capitalism. Socialism and Communism did not seem to be serious contenders, but they might draw sufficient lower class support to force a consideration of their views by the nation's rulers.[111] Only a smashing Roosevelt victory would leave the pragmatic rationalists with a need to reconsider seriously their hopes for a cooperative reconstruction of America. Expecting a narrow Democratic victory that would settle none of the political uncertainties,[112] *Common Sense*, on the eve of the election, urged that "since the presidential election is not of prime importance, let [us] concentrate on state and Congressional campaigns—*and on the future!*"[113]

II. John Dewey: Philosopher of Action

1. Dewey's Philosophy of Democracy

The 1930's have impressed many observers as an "age of ideology." Surely the intense concentration upon Fascism and Communism and a host of formulae designed to ease the crises of the period indicate a certain logic in that viewpoint. But, as the pragmatic rationalist movement suggests, much of the fervor for social reconstruction was stanchly anti-ideological. Malcolm Cowley, whose own erratic pilgrimage through the thirties showed the effects of social crises upon sensitive critics of that time, perhaps captured the Depression era more exactly by calling it an "age of faith."[1] The faith he remembered was faith in a social Second Coming, based not on firm principles of dogma but on the negative view that the old social order had fallen apart too completely to allow repair. Many could only believe that some new order of a vaguely defined Utopian shape would surely appear to build on the wreckage of the old.

Pragmatic rationalists, who looked to social engineering and reason as the means to usher in the new society, operated in the shadow of John Dewey. His philosophy framed their hopes, even as he worked with them to bring specific reforms into being. The philosopher Charles Frankel has perceptively noted Dewey's share in the visionary temper of reformers: "Oddly enough the philosopher who wrote so badly, whose thinking seems so homely and prosaic, and who is remembered for his glorification of science, had essentially a poet's vision of the possibilities of human life."[2] A trust in man's ability to change his surroundings, and even his own inner nature, by rational inquiry was Dewey's "vision, . . . the source of the excitement and the sense of importance that his work communicated, and still communicates, to others."[3] Dewey did not forecast Utopia, but he denied that there were any impassable barriers blocking the way. And he so firmly equated the scientific method of inquiry with human virtue and power that he felt

99

justified in labeling faith in science "religious." "There is such a thing," he asserted, "as faith in intelligence becoming religious in quality. . . ." It becomes so as "the scientific methods that define intelligence in operation are pushed further into the mysteries of the world, being themselves promoted and improved in the operation." The expansion of man's understanding of such "mysteries" is "one reason," Dewey concluded, "why personally I think it fitting to use the word 'God' to denote the uniting of the ideal and actual which has been spoken of. . . ."[4]

Dewey's enthusiasm for science and his deep concern about social problems encouraged him to construct an elaborate philosophic bridge between scientific method and social control. His efforts provided the logical core for the pragmatic rationalist faith in scientific planning.

Because the bulk of Dewey's philosophic logic appeared before the formation of pragmatic rationalist thought in the 1930's, there is a temptation to proclaim him the official father of the movement. Pragmatic rationalists were, however, singularly wary of acknowledging philosophic debts. Their reticence matched their commitment to a presentist attack on social problems, free of dogma and tradition. The most loyal of Dewey's defenders, Sidney Hook, has aptly explained the logic behind the lack of any closely knit Deweyan school. "Since every man's philosophy, when he thinks it through, is his own," Hook explained, "Dewey expects that the philosophies of those who are in general agreement with him will to an appreciable degree be different. . . . That is why so many who agree with Dewey do not agree with each other."[5]

But if Dewey does not stand as the acknowledged leader of pragmatic rationalism, he was surely its guiding spirit. His defense of a planned democracy, congruent with the views of Stuart Chase, George Soule, and Alfred Bingham and others of like mind, helped spread his philosophy, tentlike, over twentieth-century liberal rationalism.

Dewey's involvement in pragmatic rationalism's share of the Faith had prime importance. In the first place, it provided pragmatic rationalism with philosophic underpinnings from the thought of the greatest American philosopher of the twentieth century. And it posed a great test for Dewey himself.

The saying has it that philosophies are seldom refuted, only forgotten. They may approach the world of affairs, but they seldom touch it, remaining at best mere descriptions of what ought to be. But the 1930's, with their chaotic search for a faith, offered a rare chance for a philosophic conception to take hold and shape society anew. The philosophy Dewey urged was notably suited for such a role. It proposed to link philosophic speculation with science and, ultimately, with social affairs, thus justifying the term "instrumentalism" that Dewey applied to it.

Dewey was alert to the promise of the thirties. He recognized that the League for Independent Political Action and similar reform movements embodied a chance for applying that instrumentalism. So, optimistically, he cut numerous ties of compromise with the prevailing ways and became more fully engaged in social affairs than ever before.

Dewey placed his ideas at the service of radical reform efforts far more fully than other notable philosophers before him had done. Emerson lectured his contemporaries on the need for radical change while remaining aloof from concrete reform movements. Thoreau criticized society and walked away from it. Other American thinkers acted similarly, either making accommodations with the prevailing order or else standing apart from it, sometimes in an aggrieved mood. But Dewey, true to the logic of instrumentalism, placed his views on the line and sought to use them directly as agents of change. His activism was a significant gauge of what opportunity existed for drastic concepts of change in the thirties and an important measure, too, of just how practical America's great philosophy of practicality really was.

Throughout his career Dewey insisted on an inherent link between philosophic logic, the scientific method and social realities. He so strongly opposed the notion of philosophy as a means to enjoy separation from practical life that he very quickly rejected most of the philosophers of earlier eras as hopeless wool-gatherers and dream-spinners. To an extent Dewey's rejection of his predecessors reflected his skepticism about lessons to be learned from the past, a skepticism he shared with other pragmatic rationalists and, rather inconsistently, which he derived partly from his admiration for Jefferson and Emerson. More fundamentally, he rejected the earlier philosophers for foolishly seeking "ideal truth," as though there were really such a Holy Grail resting in an enchanted spot outside the real world.

A prime point of departure from many pragmatic rationalists was Dewey's attachment to humanist values, which led him to make a sharp distinction between science and technology. In that regard he was farthest from those who, having been trained as technicians in economics or engineering, tended to conceive of scientific benefits in terms of mechanical function. Dewey claimed that "the needs of modern industry have been tremendous stimuli to scientific investigation." But the form of scientific investigation that had resulted seemed restricted in an important fashion. Because the industrial impulse had aimed squarely at mechanical function rather than at the great ethical and esthetic issues, it never reached out beyond the means in life to touch ends. Any effect upon true human aims had been accidental. Change had been "technical rather than human and moral, . . . economic rather than adequately social."[6]

Dewey felt great progress in drawing the human concerns of life into the scientific orbit would be made by breaking away from a lingering Aristotelian belief in the superiority of pure contemplation and by recognizing that all meaningful science must be applied science. Then the technicians would not imagine a rift to exist between their practice and scientific theory that deals with matters of human thought and feeling and does not express itself in purely mechanical applications. "'Pure' science," Dewey advised, "is of necessity relational and abstract: it fulfills its meaning and gains full truth when included within a course of concrete events." "If we could free ourselves from a somewhat abject emotion," Dewey went on to say, meaning Aristotelian medieval scholasticism, "it would be clear enough that what makes any proposition scientific is its power to yield understanding, insight, intellectual at-homeness, in connection with any existential state of affairs, by filling events with coherent and tested meanings."[7]

One of the momentous contributions Dewey foresaw from thus extending scientific method into all areas of human existence was a correction of the common tendency to subordinate practical scientific accountings of nature to fixed dogma. Dewey paid tribute to the eloquent dissent of Francis Bacon against that mysticism and to the ensuing success of the Newtonian revolution in approaching nature with a scientific spirit of inquiry. Yet despite great gains, for the mass of the people recourse to supernatural dogma had kept science a dark and mysterious art. Unhappily, Dewey concluded, the great technological strides of the late nineteenth and twentieth centuries had only deepened the mystery by making science increasingly complex and abstruse in its details.[8] Stating the case in language appropriate to the occult thinking that he observed, Dewey declared that "for most men, save the scientific workers, science is a mystery in the hands of initiates, who have become adepts in virtue of following ritualistic ceremonies from which the profane herd is excluded. . . . For most persons, the reality of the apparatus is found only in its embodiments in practical affairs, in mechanical devices and in techniques which touch life as it is lived."[9]

Dewey saw in that stunted view of science profound dangers that extended far beyond the initial issue of man's ability to understand his natural surroundings. Ominously, the divorce of science from humanity had left society fragmented into a welter of uncontrolled, often conflicting passions. John Stuart Mill, supporting laissez-faire liberalism, mistakenly attempted to justify such a rudderless condition. "Men in a state of society are still men: their actions and passions are obedient to the laws of *individual* human nature."[10] But what Mill failed to observe, Dewey contended, was the inextricable connection between men and their social surroundings. Indeed, the connection seemed to a large extent a dependent one. To Dewey the "activities and passions" of individuals that Mill spoke of were "in the concrete what they are, their beliefs and purposes included, because of the social medium in which they live. . . . They are influenced throughout by contemporary and transmitted culture, whether in conformity or protest."[11]

Mill's apparent oversight provided Dewey with the cue for his crucial definition of the public. Dewey used the term "public" in a special way, intending it mainly to describe a role played by the individuals in any society when gathered together by common concerns. The public was not an aggregate of separate persons, as the laissez-faire theorists would have it. Nor was it a social force destined to carry out a mission described or imposed by an ideology. To Dewey the public was a force akin to the town meetings he knew during his youth in Vermont. The concern of citizens to solve problems cooperatively created the public and determined its characteristics.

Dewey's pragmatic concept of a voluntary public created from individual concern over common problems resembled the views held by his old friend Jane Addams and his colleague at the University of Michigan, Charles Horton Cooley. But Dewey was not as satisfied with the strictly empirical as they were. He wished to enlist systematic scientific methods in settling human affairs and saw a telling similarity between the proper functions of the public and science. Both ideally call for cooperative effort to analyze and control events. Both, also, stress experimental reason.

Yet despite their marriage in the heaven of logic, science and social life had somehow failed to come together. To Dewey technology seemed the villain. He noted unhappily that his era was undergoing a technological chaos that had "formed such immense and consolidated unions in action, on an impersonal basis, that the resultant public cannot identify and distinguish itself."[12] As a consequence, a severe imbalance had occurred: "The knowledge which regulates activity is . . . the monopoly of the few, and is used by them in behalf of private and class interests and not for general and shared use."[13] Dewey interpreted that imbalance in terms strongly reminiscent of Thorstein Veblen, with whom he was then in close contact at the New School for Social Research. In *The Public and Its Problems* Dewey observed that "the pecuniarily economic phase of society is something radically different from industrialization, and from the inherent consequences of technology in current life." Rather than advancing human welfare, "knowledge, divided against itself, . . . has played its part in generating enslavement of men, women and children in factories in which they are animated machines to tend inanimate machines."[14]

For all its dark overtones, Dewey's analysis of society retained an essential optimism. The break from superstitions that had long shrouded human history and impeded science seemed to him irreversibly complete. "Change," Dewey wrote in 1920, "rather than fixity is now a measure of 'reality' or energy of being; change is omnipresent. The laws in which the modern man of sience is interested are laws of motion, of generation and consequence. He speaks of law where the ancients spoke of kind and essence. . . ."[15] To use the law of change in a fruitful way men must recognize that the universe, as a coordinated complex of objects and functions, requires a collectivist approach to scientific inquiry and, concurrently, a collectivist approach to the organization of society. "Variability of elements in mathematical science is specious," Dewey asserted; "elements vary independently of one another, but not independently of a *relation* to others, the relation or law being the constancy among variations."[16]

Here, in one of his subtlest and most controversial logical turns, Dewey avoided drawing the inference suggested by his matrix view that individual units of being are bound and unfree. Instead, he cited approvingly that "the present tendency among scientific men is to think of laws as statistical in nature—that is, as statements of an 'average' found in the behavior of an enormous number of things, no two of which are exactly alike. If this line of thought be followed out, it implies that the existence of laws or uniformities and regularities among natural phenomena, human acts included, does not in the least exclude the item of choice as a distinctive fact having its own distinctive consequences. No law does away with individuality of existence, having its own particular way of operating. . . ."[17]

Dewey's rather mechanical delineation of something so fraught with subjectivity as "individualism" provoked sharp opposition. Critics with a slighter attachment to the methods of science than Dewey have accused him of unfairly dismissing idealism in the heat of his polemical war on traditional philosophy and of failing to appreciate recent studies of the subconscious, especially those stemming from the work of Freud.[18] Dewey's arch philosophic foe, George Santayana, aimed the most elegant shafts. "It would be hard to find a philosopher in whom naturalism . . . was more inveterate than in Dewey," Santayana charged. "He is very severe against the imagination, and even the intellect, of mankind for having created figments which usurp the place and authority of the mundane sphere in which the daily action goes on."[19] Santayana went on to present the argument that most persistently plagued Dewey's long career. Dewey is driven to pragmatism, Santayana concluded, because "he is the devoted spokesman of the spirit of enterprise, of experiment, of modern industry. To him, rather than to William James, might be applied the saying of the French pragmatist, Georges Sorel, that his philosophy is calculated to justify all the assumptions of American society. . . ." The results of such a mundane philosophy seemed depressingly predictable. Santayana found in Dewey "a pervasive quasi-Hegelian tendency to dissolve the individual into his social functions, as well as everything substantial or actual into something relative or transitional."[20]

Horace Kallen, a philosopher whose idealism was far less world-weary than Santayana's, posited a vital choice between James and Dewey on the latter's failure to recognize the actuality of mystical experience. Numb to that vital element of life, Dewey offered a sharp and restrictive alternative to James, one that removed much of the human claim for individuality. Kallen felt that human beings without a mystical sense would be subdued members of a social herd who take their characteristics from the group. Indeed, that is how he thought Dewey described them. "As for me," he declared in rebuttal, "I stand here with James." For James recognized the crucial role of the intuitive and the mystical in generating distinct individuals and, from them, distinct social groups. Drawing strength from his eloquent guide, Kallen declared himself to be with those "who think the world's determinism a consequence of the succession of its ongoing piecemeal determinations, with perhaps every single item of it—certainly every human being—holding fast to its integrity, and every so often crying out to the residual universe Hands off!"[21]

Dewey never acknowledged the radical disagreement with James that Kallen suggested, although he did not show the same filial devotion to James that he did to Emerson. Dewey found the Concord sage's efforts to free the common man in democracy from the toils of conformist thinking highly ennobling. On a lower plane he considered James' radical empiricism valuable as a weapon to slash through the distinction dualist philosophy posed between mind and reality. To overcome the contention of Hume that man's awareness is limited to his own sensations Dewey had at first adopted a Hegelian view that simmered all phenomena together in a cosmic fusion of mind and the material world. James' naturalistic solution, which began to impress Dewey when he read *The Principles of Psychology* in 1890, made *consequences* the test for significance. Judgments on Ultimate Reality James would leave to the scholastics—fine work for the fastidious intellect burdened by pangs of anxiety about final causes.[22]

Endorsing that connection between the individual and the natural world, Dewey added that the interests of the individual and his environment were coextensive—measured by the *consequences* the actions of each had upon the other. Since scientific study is a collectivist enterprise, it follows that the study and organization of society should be similarly collectivist.[23] Through its efforts to gain a full knowledge of the nature and needs of individuals, the collectivist scientific method promises to propel the individual upward to his highest possible state. "Science has made its way by releasing, not by suppressing, the elements of variation, of invention and innovation, of novel creation in individuals."[24] The urge toward freedom, which Dewey felt to be "grounded in our very beings,"[25] manifests itself in "that secure release and fulfillment of personal potentialities which take place only in rich and manifold association with others. . . ."[26]

Dewey fitted the great issues of morals and ethics into the same cooperatist frame. He acknowledged that morals are "personal because they spring from personal insight." Yet men are associated in their moral awareness. Dewey insisted that "judgment and choice . . . are wholly consistent with the fact that *what* men think and believe is affected by common factors, and that the thought and choice of one individual spread to others. . . . At the present time, almost all important ethical problems arise out of the conditions of associated life."[27]

From his views on the scientific method and the associational quality of human life, Dewey concluded the wisdom of granting all individuals equality of rights and opportunity. Scientific inquiry, Dewey reasoned, produces accurate results only when its subjects are viewed without prejudgment and move without artificial restrictions on their activity. At the same time one must recognize that "human beings combine in behavior as directly and unconsciously as do atoms, stellar masses and cells. . . ."[28] Thus, to secure the highest degree of human development society must maintain a creative tension between close communal interdependence and individual freedom.

Long before the turmoil of the thirties Dewey pointed to the polar threats dictatorship and laissez-faire posed to the required social balance. Dictatorial states, he observed, have characteristically regarded that requirement as a hindrance, a Gordian knot to be cut through by means of simple tyranny. At the other extreme laissez-faire has resisted balance by encouraging irresponsible, uncooperative individualism. But both of those "final solutions," by ignoring the character of man and the natural world, have created pain and insecurity where they attempted to establish order and a confident sense of purpose. They have left their human victims hanging because they inconsistently claimed to have the answers to human needs while dogmatically refusing to consider many of those needs. To Dewey, the just "demand for consistency, for 'universality,' is a demand to survey consequences broadly, to link effect to effect in a chain of continuity. Whatever force works to this end *is* reason."[29]

The premium Dewey placed upon the unfettered development of

individuals led to his insistence upon free choice and, consequently, upon consent as the basis of society. "The power, the ability to command issues and consequences, that forms freedom must," Dewey insisted, "have some connection with that something in personality that is expressed in choice." [30] Of course, the factors of luck and chance remain. But with his will firmly set on acting by free choice "a person forms the habit of choosing and acting with conscious regard to the grain of circumstances, the run of affairs." [31]

A successful community requires an acute individualistic social consciousness on the part of its members. "No amount of aggregated collective action of itself constitutes a community. For beings who observe and think and whose ideas are absorbed by impulses and become sentiments and interests, 'we' is as inevitable as 'I.' But 'we' and 'our' exist only when the consequences of combined action are perceived and become an object of desire and effort. . . ." [32] Ultimately, a successful society must stem from the separate intelligence of each of its members. For consciousness is a wholly individual matter. And it is "the clear consciousness of a communal life, in all its implications, [that] constitutes the ideal of democracy." [33]

Dewey's prime role as shaker and mover in American education stemmed directly from his social philosophy. For scientific intelligence to operate, he maintained, individuals must possess a large fund of knowledge about their world. And for free choice to act beneficially, worthy values must be present for guidance. Clearly, then, the central social issue was one of "effecting a more general equitable distribution of the elements of understanding and knowledge in connection with work done, activities undertaken, and a consequent freer and more generously shared participation in their results." [34] A further implication followed. Because of the need to develop positive values, Dewey maintained that education was closely involved with morality. Simply and directly he stated that "all education which develops power to share effectively in social life is moral. It forms a character which not only does the particular deed socially necessary but one which is interested in that continuous readjustment which is essential to growth. Interest in learning from all the contacts of life is the essential moral interest." [35]

As Dewey's instrumentalist philosophy developed early in the century, it held fast to the ideal of the philosopher operating busily in the stream of events. He would act not as a king but as a common citizen, a citizen-scientist. Dewey's record of active support for social and political causes was the practice that matched his preachments. Appropriately, he worked to establish a cooperative community, one that would gain power and wisdom through constant experimentation.

One of Dewey's friends remembered several years after the philosopher's death that "Dewey liked a non-academic atmosphere much better than any other philosopher that I know."[36] Indeed, more than any other American philosopher Dewy put his philosophic ideas at the service of concrete democratic reforms. He built a platform along pragmatic rationalist lines for truly native American reform to stand upon. Then he ventured out, himself, to face the crowd.

2. Reform Before the Crash

The thread of concern for public affairs ran unbroken through all of Dewey's career, though it frayed at various critical times. As a young philosophy instructor at Michigan from 1884 to 1894, he gave support to humanitarian reforms. When he became part of Rockefeller's new University of Chicago in 1894, Dewey involved himself in Jane Addams' Hull House, a project that provided some of the inspiration for the famous experimental school he started with several of his colleagues at the university. With his move to New York in 1904 and the gathering momentum of the Progressive movement, Dewey became enmeshed in broader efforts to reform society. His association with Herbert Croly's *New Republic*, beginning in 1914, brought him to a peak of involvement.

Just then the outbreak of World War I prompted Dewey to expand his reformist view to international size. Reacting against German authoritarianism, displayed with shocking effect in that nation's march through Belgium, Dewey incorporated the critical assaults he had made for many years on German idealistic philosophy into a general attack on the German Imperial State, *German Philosophy and Politics* (1915). His efforts earned him both praise and scorn as a skillful propagandist.[37] When the United States at last became involved in the struggle, Dewey wrote a series of articles for the *New Republic* proffering his instrumentalist view of intelligence as a proper weapon for Wilson to use in the crusade to "make the world safe for democracy."

When the frightful carnage of the Great War finally ended and the world was presented with the Treaty of Versailles as its fruit, liberals felt sadly betrayed. Dewey, as an optimistic supporter of the war, stood within range of crtical blasts emanating from the *Dial* and similarly pacifist journals. Of all the attacks upon him, the most wounding for Dewey was Randolph Bourne's "Twilight of the Idols," which dismissed instrumentalism as a tarnished form of opportunism. Bourne commanded great respect as a social critic. When he died shortly after the article on Dewey appeared, he achieved martyrdom in the eyes of many admirers. Frail and humpbacked, Bourne seemed a symbolic casualty, killed without gunfire in his dismaying fight against war itself.

Under the circumstances Dewey's entry into the 1920's was a clouded one. His biographer, Sidney Hook, credits Dewey's growing acuteness on social questions during the twenties to a measure of cynicism that grew out of his disappointed hopes and the tawdry business civilization that displaced them.[38] While cynicism may be too strong a term to describe his cast of mind, Dewey was becoming sharper and more skeptical. His wariness was not an unmixed blessing. It tended to inhibit him in carrying out his own philosophic plea for full social participation. While continuing to encourage liberal reforms, Dewey's energies throughout most of the twenties were largely directed to projects at least one step removed from the public arena.

During that period Dewey made several noteworthy trips abroad. He visited China in 1919 and discussed his concepts of democracy and education with the attentive rulers of the new Chinese republic. In 1924 he answered the call of Turkey's revolutionary government to organize the new nation's school system. Two years later he visited Japan and Mexico and was impressed, contrastingly, by the burgeoning industrial power of the former and the latter's tradition of esthetic craftsmanship. Dewey's most dramatic journey of the decade took him to Russia in 1928. In his book evaluating his travels, *Impressions of Soviet Russia and the Revolutionary World, Mexico—China—Turkey* (1929), Dewey displayed cautious approval of the new Soviet state, predicated in large measure on the hope that its repressiveness was merely a holdover from centuries of czarist rule and would dissolve as Socialism impressed cooperative ways on the Russian mind.

The twenties, as we have seen, were also years of culmination for Dewey's philosophy. Beginning in 1920 with *Reconstruction in Philosophy* and extending through *The Quest for Certainty* in 1929, Dewey distilled his thoughts into a series of books that attempted to present the Common Man, whom Dewey always considered his proper audience, with the philosophic rationale for a democratic faith.[39]

Dewey released some time from his traveling, writing, and teaching to participate in several active social ventures. He joined Wesley Mitchell, Thorstein Veblen, James Harvey Robinson, and others in founding the

New School for Social Research in 1919, which set its course by Dewey's instrumentalist compass in an attempt to foster an experimentally scientific approach to the study of social conditions.[40]

Dewey sought to implement another key feature of his democratic philosophy by continuing to support organized labor and its allies. Believing that a progressive society depends upon equality, Dewey decried the increasingly inequitable distribution of wealth and opportunity.[41] Dewey's association with the League for Industrial Democracy was especially fruitful as an entry into labor-union activities, the Socialist Party, and related reform organizations.[42] In 1920 Dewey supported the forlorn Farm-Labor Party, and in 1924, with prospects for the farm-labor concept making an impact upon the electorate appearing significantly brighter, he spoke out in favor of Robert La Follette's Progessive movement.[43]

Dewey's most concerted reform efforts were given to the American Committee for the Outlawry of War, led by the indefatigable peace-monger Salmon O. Levinson.[44] He welcomed the opportunity to rebut the notion that nations could justifiably advance their aims through war—even the sort of war in behalf of democratic principles that he had urged America to wage in 1917. From 1921 until 1927, when the empty promises of the Kellogg-Briand Pact fatally undercut the American Committee's attempts to establish multilateral nonaggression agreements enforced by a World Court, Dewey spoke and wrote frequently in support of the committee's aims. In unhappy recollection of his support for World War I, Dewey remained a vigorous spokesman for pacifism long after the American Committee dissolved.[45]

The year 1927, with its several disappointments, was a critical juncture for Dewey. The failure of the Outlawry movement struck the harshest blow at Dewey's attempts to influence society directly; but the emotional impact upon him of the Sacco-Vanzetti case was deeper. Indeed, the fate of the two anarchists seemed to seal the fate, as well, of many liberals' faith in the efficacy of gradual social reform.[46] Dewey responded to the episode with an article angrily denouncing the commission headed by Harvard's retired President, A. Lawrence Lowell, for vindicating Judge Thayer's efforts to "get those anarchist bastards."[47] Sidney Hook remembered Dewey's outrage and that "he never again placed faith in the willingness of those who were in high place to reverse themselves when they were in error."[48]

3. On the Political Front

By 1929, at the end of his battered passage through the twenties, Dewey was ready to accept the invitation of Paul Douglas to join the League for Independent Political Action. There, in the midst of an organization designed to confront the faltering political powers with a radical new collectivist alternative, Dewey began to speak forebodingly of "irrepressible conflict." When the stock market dove toward the depths shortly after the League began, Dewey declared firmly that the time had come to answer "the basic question of whether, under the guise of rugged individualism at the top and ragged individualism at the bottom, agglomerations of great wealth are to make our democracy a farce and stench." [49] Dewey looked for the League for Independent Political Action to be an adventurous experiment in social activism that would meet his ideal of instrumental change. He discounted the shrill, hostile cries that would surely arise from partisans of the *status quo*. Given the needs of the country, their sound and fury would signify nothing; and as for the logic of their complaints: "Well, they say we aren't practical; I have a number of editorials telling me how impractical I am. I am not, thank God, what is called a practical politician. But I am practical enough in my mind to see that there is an irrepressible conflict coming as real and as deep as that to which Lincoln called attention. In the face of such a conflict I think the practical thing is not to shut one's eyes, or to shilly-shally and postpone, hoping some run of the tide will make it safe to come out on the side of the people and against the big business interests." [50]

Because the new political movement was to be novel and experimental, operating in a rapidly changing milieu, Dewey felt it to be the better part of wisdom not to present a detailed program to which the League would be committed. Instead, in a series of articles appearing in the *New Republic* shortly after the Crash in 1929, Dewey contented him-

self with describing general attributes of the new party the League would
one day bring into effect. A flexible view on policy matters would help
at first because "liberals are notoriously hard to organize. They must
depend upon ideas rather than upon established habits of belief; and
when persons begin to think upon social matters they begin to vary."
Conservatives, by contrast, have "a natural bond of cohesion. . . . They
hold together not so much by ideas as by habit, tradition, fear of the
unknown and a desire to hang on to what they already have."[51] Before
trying to launch an action program or a full-fledged new political party,
the League must carefully fashion a unified set of goals that will fasten a
secure hold on the aspirations of liberals. "For thirty years, at least, the
story of liberal political movements in this country is one of temporary
enthusiasms and then steady decline. If liberals are 'tired,' it is chiefly
because they have not had the support and invigoration that comes from
working shoulder to shoulder in a unified common movement."[52]

Not only must the reform view of organized liberals be brought into
harmony, but the general public, long the dupes of Big Business and the
mirage of "rugged individualism," must come to realize their true stake
in reform. The League's executive committee, of which Dewey was
chairman, expressed a strong conviction that "any political movement
will be premature and futile, which is not based upon a recognition on
the part of the underprivileged groups of the necessity of militant
political action, and upon the realization of citizens of all groups of the
necessity of the social control of economic power."[53] The required
education would aim partly at mitigating Americans' suspicion of
collectivism. In all probability Socialism bore too heavy an onus ever
to achieve wide acceptance in America.[54] But new programs supporting
central planning might succeed if they skirted the Socialist stigma and
did not harden their proposals for economic reform into political
ideology. Dewey felt that a cautious approach of that nature would
prevent the League from inadvertently helping the present floundering
political forces or any new authoritarian movement that might rise out
of the chaos. "After the depression has lasted a year or two more,"
Dewey predicted, "and the inefficacy of the palliative measures now
being taken is evident, I expect to see representatives of this system
themselves put forward definite stabilization plans for congressional
action. But that is, quite literally, their funeral. I do not see why radicals
should help them." Dewey ended his blast with a rather prescient warn-

ing that Fascism might soon become, or seem to many to have become, a danger in America because of its appeal as a possible way out of the Depression. He cautioned radicals urging planning to save the fading economy that they must include encouragement for individual freedom within those plans or else "they will find it difficult to enlighten the public mind when they are forced to begin opposing Fascist schemes for stabilizing the speculative-profit systems." [55]

Despite his gradualist view, Dewey held no hope that either of the two dominant parties could be enlightened to the point where it might serve as a useful vehicle of reform. Both of them Dewey wrote off as hopeless captives of the illusion of automatic progress that had been inspired by the rapid industrial growth of the nineteenth century. They could not cope with an economy that was contracting and individuals who were suffering from basic wants that they could not possibly satisfy themselves. "Here . . . we have the reason why the present unrest is so unlike any in the previous history of our country. The needs, experienced where men live, concern themselves in a political situation where no provision is made for this necessity, where interest is centered almost wholly upon stimulating production and distribution without any reference to the way they impinge upon consumption." [56]

The sense of uniqueness and urgency that Dewey felt about the crisis moved him to acknowledge a radical new awareness. "At last," he confessed, "I am disillusioned; I am humiliated at the recollection of the length of time it has taken me to pass to something like political maturity. For, I submit, it is an infantile cherishing of illusions, a withdrawal from the realities of economic and political facts, to pin one's hopes and put one's trust on the possibilities of organic change in either of the old major parties." [57] There, at another crossroad of his long life, Dewey momentarily abandoned the mood of objective, pluralist reason so characteristic of him. He now saw, he announced, that "everything points to a simple conclusion. The only way to achieve any lasting reform is to find the one great issue on which all others converge. . . ." In his emotional mood Dewey was quick to grasp at the view of Veblen and most of the more excitable heroes of America's radical past to declare that Money was the great issue. "Those who control the giving and withholding of credit govern the country, whoever controls government in name." [58]

Thus the new party that Dewey and others in the League sought to midwife should, in his opinion, tie all its varied reform hopes to a rational program of economic reconstruction. Like others of the pragmatic rationalists, Dewey concluded that a planned economy under cooperatist management would fulfill the major requirements of equitable distribution and democratic procedures.[59]

Dewey's political activism reached its peak in 1932 and then subsided after the overwhelming defeat of Norman Thomas, whom Dewey and the League for Independent Political Action supported in the Presidential election. Dewey faced the setback in the optimistic stance of one who believed that the real test and opportunity were going to come after the election. "We believed and still believe that the greater Governor Roosevelt's vote, the bigger would be the mass of voters doomed to sure disappointment. It is part of our job to catch these citizens on their rebound and make them see that a New Deal means a New Deal and can be carried out only through a new party."[60] But the situation called for a reappraisal of the time needed to educate the public into readiness for significant political reform. The small Socialist vote registered in industrial centers was the most discouraging part of the situation. Dewey deplored the comparatively slight support given to the only candidates and only measures supporting workingmen's interests as "a sad commentary on the leadership of organized labor."[61] But, as one who shared the general pragmatic rationalist view that an intelligent middle-class minority must lead the educative crusade to secure political reconstruction, Dewey expressed his greatest concern over the fact that the 90 per cent of the intelligent people who are in favor of radical change are basically unorganized. In that spirit he rebutted the counsel against fear in Roosevelt's First Inaugural Address with the somber warning in March, 1933: "I fear the consequences if radicals do not combine to work out and work for a definite political program."[62]

In the face of the public's inadequate support of radical reform, Dewey emphasized the role of educator that had been central to his career for most of its duration. He wrote no more political pieces for the League after 1933 and confined his remarks on politics outside that forum to general analyses of the changes in heart and mind that must precede meaningful reform. Dewey's withdrawal from the public front lines was accompanied, and perhaps in part quickened, by his increased concentration on producing several large works synthesizing his views on philosophy and society. In 1933 his 1910 book, *How We Think*, appeared in revised and enlarged form. The same year he resumed his publication of books on education with the volume *The Educational Frontier*. Dewey reached the creative peak of his work in 1934. In *Art as Experience* and *A Common Faith* he projected his thought into the complex regions of esthetics and religion with a thoroughness and depth beyond his earlier treatments of those subjects.

4. The Character of Dewey's Social Concern

Dewey's social commentary during the first half of the thirties generally exemplified the pragmatic rationalist position but differed significantly from the more militant believers in social engineering in its suggestion of individual freedom as the logical outcome of a collectivist organization of society. *Individualism, Old and New* (1929), the salvo with which Dewey opened his reform efforts during the thirties, made his position clear. He spoke of the inevitability of a Socialist reformation in terms suggesting that vestiges of Hegelian idealism still clung to him. The influence of Veblen was, however, far more pervasive. "We are in for some kind of Socialism," Dewey prophesied, "call it by whatever name we please, and no matter what it will be called when it is realized. Economic determinism is now a fact, not a theory. But there is a difference and a choice between a blind, chaotic and unplanned determinism, issuing from business conducted for pecuniary profit, and the determination of a socially planned and ordered development. It is the difference and the choice between a socialism that is public and one that is capitalistic."[63] Clearly, a cooperatively realized ideal was necessary to replace shattered loyalties. The Great Crash had borne Jeffersonian individualism down with it, even as it had disgraced the irresponsible self-seeking that businessmen had followed in Jefferson's name. Only a vacuum remained. "It would be difficult," Dewey contended, "to find in history an epoch as lacking in solid and assured objects of belief and approved ends of action as is the present."[64]

Dewey felt that such a vacuum, as in nature, would tend to be filled. But his expectation that collectivist ideas would rush to the center was not an endorsement of organized socialism. His hopes for that movement were dim. Too many charges of "alien subversion" had tarred them. Furthermore, the vestiges of Marxism that remained in American socialism seemed to Dewey an affront to science. In the modern world, he contended, "the rise of scientific method and of technology based upon it is the genuinely active force in producing the vast complex of changes the world is now undergoing, not the class struggle whose spirit and method are opposed to science." [65] Dewey adopted the coolness of other pragmatic rationalists toward established protest groups, as well as toward established institutions. Only a radical new start seemed warranted.

The disillusionments of the 1920's left Dewey with a measure of skepticism that helped him reach accord with pragmatic rationalists and the generally hard-boiled temper of the 1930's. He went far enough in the direction of those steely social engineers who measured success purely in terms of results to remark that "in view of the influence of collective illusion in the past, some case might be made out for the contention that even if it be an illusion, exaltation of intelligence and experimental method is worth a trial. Illusion for illusion, this particular one may be better than those upon which humanity has usually depended." [66] The crux of the issue was "the success of the method . . . ," suggesting that "the case for trying it in social matters is not altogether desperate nor yet illusory." [67]

In almost the next breath Dewey revealed the tension within pragmatic rationalists between their skepticism and their urge to action. They could not credit notions of absolute knowledge, but neither could they tolerate hesitant inaction. The Aristotelian ideal of gaining the wisdom to guide action through passive contemplation has proven mistaken, Dewey asserted. "Hence the first effect of acceptance of the idea that the operation of control of social forces has something to learn from the experimental method of the physical sciences is a radical alteration in the prevailing conception of social knowledge. The current assumption is that knowledge comes first and then action may—or may not—proceed from it." [68] Enlarging on the applicability of the scientific method to social affairs, Dewey declared that the advisability of policies is "all a question of what kind of procedures the intelligent study of changing conditions discloses." [69]

Speaking of logical practice in that broad vein, Dewey joined many pragmatic rationalists in drawing an analogy between the affairs of society and the affairs of science. But the analogy remained unstable. Dewey chose not to grapple with the question of differences between the laboratory and society, crucial though that issue was to his concept of democracy. After granting the wisdom of suspending scientific judgments until the results of careful experimentation are understood, could one then apply that reticence to the business of politics? How much could one expect of cautious promises that experimental inquiry would someday make it possible to devise a reform program? Could they compete in gaining the loyalty of the crowd with crusaders who held firm convictions and vowed to find the Promised Land?

Occasionally Dewey seemed to acknowledge the wisdom of separating scientific method and social action. He did at one time, as we have seen, advocate flag-waving and declare that emotion is the bulwark of all major social movements. But in his deepest considerations he drew back from supporting any sort of dramatically doctrinaire program. Intelligent campaigns educating the public to realize its long-term interests seemed to Dewey the only tolerable weapon to use against those who would exploit mass delusions.[70]

Dewey was in step with pragmatic rationalism in proposing that the middle class should exercise the leadership needed for social reform. Leadership from that quarter would be natural because America is, by dint of its political and social ideals, a middle-class country.[71] In addition, persons in the professional and white-collar classes alone have the education and skills needed to establish a scientific collectivism.[72] Dewey felt there was no cause to fear oppression from such a minority. Minorities have always spearheaded new movements. Of necessity they stand fending off the blows of the entrenched enemy until the masses come to understand enough of the workings of the new order to take reliable control over its workings themselves.[73]

Dewey plainly distinguished between the necessity of having specialists manage the operation of complex social machinery and the error of giving social engineers massive control over the final ends of society. The issue of elitism, inherent in pragmatic rationalism, worried him mightily. In his strongest call for radical reform, *Liberalism and Social Action* (1935), Dewey issued clear warnings. There at mid-decade the memory was fresh of Technocracy and its dictatorial leader, Howard Scott, striding like a colossus among the faithful. That year also saw the publication of Stuart Chase's plea for a general staff of planners to run the nation's economic business in crisp fashion, as remote as possible from interference by the electorate.[74] Shortly before, George Soule in *A Planned Society* (1934) spoke of the imminent time when America would follow the

Russian example and institute a social planning system that would extend from small local councils to a central authority in Washington.

The danger signals outside the pragmatic rationalist movement alarmed Dewey far more than the strong statements of his allies. In 1934 the title of a popular book echoed the apprehensions of many Americans by asking, *Do We Want Fascism?*[75] The next year Alfred Bingham reviewed a book predicting revolution and asked the companion question: "How Red is America?"[76] Fears of elitists of both those stripes, brown and red, affected Dewey greatly. He insisted that any moves toward elite control carried with them dictatorial dangers and declared that only a democratic society could rightfully determine final ends. He decried the logic of those who held that "the average citizen is not endowed with the degree of intelligence that the use of [scientific inquiry] as a method demands." That seemed to him "the last stand of oligarchical and anti-social seclusion." If there are only a few who have the native capacity to make significant scientific advances, yet there remain the many who are needed to put those advances to work. The telephone dialer is the essential complement to Thomas Edison; and the locomotive engineer gives meaning to Watts' teakettle experiments. The key factor, Dewey insisted, returning once more to his theory of balance between science and society, is partnership. On one side a few great minds stand out. And, happily, "there are none so mean that they cannot intelligently utilize these embodiments of intelligence once they are a part of the organized means of associated living."[77]

Dewey's vision of a cooperative commonwealth based on an economy of abundance partook heavily of Veblen's indictment of the capitalist system. Dewey was, however, far more optimistic than his old colleague at the New School and more insistent on giving the individual the central role in society. Consistent with Veblen and pragmatic rationalism, he was skeptical of dogma, dismissing Marxism and capitalism even-handedly. Adherents of both of those viewpoints have led society into drift, he insisted, the former by positing laws of historical inevitability, which paralyze the mind's will to think for itself, the latter by laissez-faire sanctions against purposeful community action.[78] Both dogmas, Dewey charged, have relied on force and terror and are allies in spirit of the forces threatening the world with dictatorship. "Communism, with its doctrine of the necessity of the forcible overthrow of the state by armed insurrection, ... with its threats to exclude all other classes from civil rights, ... is itself an unwitting, but nonetheless, powerful factor in bringing about Fascism."[79] Capitalism, Dewey judged, had generated fear of an opposite sort, "a vague but influential dread lest a monkey-wrench be thrown into the economic and financial machine. The dread is as general among the workers as among small traders and storekeepers. It is basically the asset that keeps the dominant part in office." Thus, "our presidential elections are upon the whole determined by fear."[80]

The economy of abundance Dewey proposed was directly in line with the general pragmatic rationalist position. "Regiment *things* and free human beings," Dewey urged in summary. "Regiment machines and money and other inanimate things, and give liberty to human beings."[81] That way lay escape from the baleful effects of corporate life and a return "to the spiritual factor of our traditions, equal opportunity and free association and inter-communication. . . ."[82]

Dewey felt that the key to solving the corporate predicament lay in making a closer distinction between *economic means* and their proper *esthetic ends*. On that issue Dewey walked a tightrope stretched between the Marxists and the prevailing capitalist culture. Marxism recognized a clear distinction between means and ends but sinned by permitting any means for reaching worthy ends. Capitalism, on the other hand, failed grievously to distinguish between means and ends. The true "rugged individualist," Dewey contended, found competition its own justification, leading merely to more competition. "When we take means for ends," Dewey cautioned, "we indeed fall into moral materialism."[83]

Dewey's view of the relation between ends and means rested on his philosophic belief that they are logically interdependent. Actions— *means*—change the situations in which they operate and, thus, change the forms of the *ends* they call into being. The ends-in-view become the ends-in-fact, links in a continuous chain of new ends-in-fact.[84] As for the ideal end of human life, Dewey cast his vote for art, the highest form of individual self-expression—and thus the most intelligent. Characteristically, Dewey brought in science to explain his choice. "It is explicable," he declared, "only when it is realized that scientific and artistic systems embody the same fundamental principles of the relationship of life to its surroundings, and that both satisfy the same fundamental needs."[85] But art contained the higher value: "Art—the mode of activity that is charged with meanings capable of immediately enjoyed possession—is the complete culmination of nature, and ... science is properly a handmaiden that conducts natural events to this happy issue."[86]

Discussing art's proper setting and function, Dewey turned to his underlying belief that the highest degree of individualism, in this case taking the form of esthetic creativity, derives from collective unity. Dewey insisted:

> The moral office and human function of art can be intelligently discussed only in the context of culture. A particular work of art may have a definite effect upon a particular person or upon a number of persons. ... But a less conscious and more massed constant adjustment of experience proceeds from the total environment that is created by the collective art of a time. ... Even technological arts, in their sum total, do something more than provide a number of separate conveniences and facilities. They shape collective occupations and thus determine direction of interest and attention, and hence affect desire and purpose.[87]

In the end, then, Dewey's purpose, however it might be obscured by the epithet "naturalism," was a spiritual one. He believed that an esthetic sense lay in common within the depths of all men, and he sought a community that would work to discover that sense and develop it. In his quest Dewey moved in the shadow of the transcendentalists and their spiritual brethren of the mid-nineteenth century who established Utopian communities as monuments to beauty and true reason. Dewey did not attain the reputation of a latter-day Utopian largely because he departed from Utopian practice by seeking to work in close association with the materialist centers of American life rather than in flight from them. Consequently, to many observers he seemed himself to be a materialist, or else an apostle of passive adjustment. But he was, in fact, a radical believer in change, endowed with the strengths and weaknesses of other American visionaries who have promoted the ideals of individual creativity, equal opportunity, and humane cooperation in a nation whose traditional values support them but whose practices often belie them.

Dewey's support of the esthetic soul of America's radical tradition strengthened the spiritual side of pragmatic rationalism. But not adequately. As we have seen, pragmatic rationalism did not attract the more imaginative minds of the decade. Some in its ranks, Stuart Chase and George Soule among them, showed concern over the aloofness of creative artists. Their absence meant the loss of valuable mental resources; and it lent worrisome support to those critics who found the movement materialistic and dull. Disturbingly, the best pragmatic rationalist efforts to light a general reform fire were only able to produce smoldering in some quarters.

In that spirit Dewey indicted capitalism for repressing the free development and exchange of ideas. A free press under the capitalist system, he declared, citing Veblen, is a manifest impossibility.[88] No one could expect the moneyed owners of the communication media to permit the publication of views contrary to their vested interests. That condition, Dewey maintained optimistically, would simply dissolve when a collectivist democracy replaced capitalism. "Does anyone imagine," he asked, "that under a cooperative economic system, controlled in the interest of all, it would be necessary to have official censorship of, say, the Hearst press? Would not such a press under such a system be inherently impossible?"[89]

Civil liberties, Dewey felt, are susceptible to similar repair. Under laissez-faire, individuals have lived in fear of government on the ground that it was the natural enemy of their liberties.[90] The result has been a critical lack of awareness that the term *civil* is directly connected with the idea of citizenship.[91] Failure to see that simple truth, Dewey noted, has misled many persons into thinking that civil liberties derive from the natural order rather than from citizenship in a civil state. Since secure liberty is tightly bound up with a sound civil state, Dewey concluded, individuals must realize that "social control, especially of economic forces, is necessary in order to render secure the liberties of the individual, including civil liberties."[92]

True to his belief in democratic persuasion, Dewey exerted considerable energy in behalf of making the teaching profession a vital moving force for democratic reform. He gave notable help in founding the Association of American University Professors and the American Federation of Teachers, imbuing both of them with a measure of the viewpoint Veblen had broadcast in his famous diatribe against American colleges, *The Higher Learning in America* (1918). Dewey accepted the contention that the nation's schools had fallen into the hands of militant defenders of the *status quo*, including American Legionnaires, the DAR, the Ku Klux Klan, and religious fundamentalists.[93] He noted the widespread fear of violence from radical leftist groups and decried it as a distraction from the real center of coercive power in America. "The reactionaries are in possession of force, in not only the army and police, but in the press and schools. The only reason they do not advocate the use of force is the fact that they are already in possession of it, so their policy is to cover up its existence with idealistic phrases—of which their present use of individual initiative and liberty is a striking example."[94]

In addition to his work for teacher organizations Dewey became a member of the board of a new periodical militantly devoted to making teachers socially conscious and active. The magazine, *Social Frontier*, began in 1934 under the guidance of William Heard Kilpatrick, a professor of education at Columbia and a devoted disciple of Dewey's activist philosophy of education. Another of Dewey's followers, Sidney Hook, and his colleague at the New School, Alvin Johnson, joined him on the board, along with social critics, such as George Counts and Harry Overstreet, who had no direct connection with education.

The journal began publication with a pronouncement that "for the American people the age of individualism in economy is closing and an age of collectivism is opening. Here is the central and dominating reality in the present epoch."[95] Unfortunately, the editors concluded, the teachers' representatives in the National Education Association seemed unaware of the momentous changes in process and at the recent convention in Washington showed a deplorable tendency to continue toadying to reactionaries who had fastened their mossy grip on education. Teachers should instead use their position as disseminators of ideas to influence social development toward collectivism. Dewey promised that "if the teacher's choice is to throw himself in with the forces and conditions that are making for change in the direction of social control of capitalism—economic and political—there will hardly be a moment of the day when he will not have the opportunity to make his choice good in action."[96]

Dewey contended that the unity of social purpose needed for teachers to break out of bondage and help in the collectivist reeducation of the country called for a national system of education. Carefully distinguishing between "national" and "nationalistic" education, Dewey spoke for an arrangement that would give individual teachers classroom autonomy within a nationally coordinated organization that promoted individual freedom. In that way the nation's schools would have the power to escape the grasp of selfish private-interest groups while avoiding the danger of following the Soviet Union and the Fascist nations into the error of turning classrooms into propaganda forums. Then "the freedom and impetus that result will enable the schools, without a centralized system, to develop a system of truly national education—by which I mean one animated by policies and methods that will help create that common purpose without which the nation cannot achieve unified movement."[97]

In 1935 Dewey gathered his collectivist concepts together into his most comprehensive reform manual, *Liberalism and Social Action.* Coming at midpassage in the decade, the book served as a marker, summarizing pragmatic rationalist concepts and setting off the first half of the decade and its full swell of collectivist hopes from ensuing doubts about the individual's ability to gain full freedom in the midst of a planned society.

Dewey argued forcefully that "liberalism must now become radical, meaning by 'radical' perception of the necessity of thorough-going changes in the set-up of institutions and corresponding activity to bring the changes to pass."[98] Because of their supine past, liberals fail to command the enthusiasm of the public. The liberal camp must commit itself boldly to the reality of constant change and to the use of scientific method in governing society's response to that change. The notion of many liberals that mere open debate will somehow produce solutions to problems struck Dewey as a faulty kind of "watered down version of the Hegelian dialectic, with its synthesis arrived at by a union of antithetical conceptions."[99] Science and technology had too admirably rationalized the modern world, Dewey felt, for any simple appeals to the Agora to be tolerable substitutes for reason and careful scientific planning.

Thus Dewey faced the middle of the decade with firm confidence in the ability of men to discover the single true mode of democratic life. Such sturdy faith left him face to face with two troubling dilemmas that perplexed other pragmatic rationalists in varying degrees. How, in a community predicated upon free choice, could one enforce scientifically determined precepts for managing social affairs? And how could one believe in a constantly evolving world and at the same time advocate an intricately planned society? Could the massive machinery required possibly be flexible enough to keep pace with continuous changes in the conditions it was engineered to meet? Dewey's hopes that these critical difficulties could be resolved rested on his belief that enlightened free choice would naturally turn to favoring the very actions that science warranted, and on the kindred belief that a reformed educational system would provide the needed enlightenment. The final years of the thirties were to confront Dewey's large and fragile conceptions with severe tests. The increasingly violent tenor of collectivism in Europe disputed Dewey's equation of collectivism with liberated individualism. And at home, as the election of 1936 demonstrated, the enormous success of the New Deal in capturing public favor had extended Roosevelt's power beyond the reach of any challenger on the left. It was clearly time for pragmatic rationalism to reexamine its vision—and that time was to last only the short interval until the Second World War cast an untimely pall over the liberal debate.

III. The Liberal Traditionalist Response

The Liberal Traditionalist Response

The election of 1936 marked the start of a steep road downward for pragmatic rationalist programs seeking collectivist social reform through politics. Although the League for Independent Political Action lingered officially for another year, it survived the election without much hope or impetus. Technocracy had lost its intellectual following some time before and was beginning its later career as a fanatical fringe movement. Upton Sinclair's EPIC program had been mortally wounded in the California election of 1934. And the Farm-Laborites who had aligned themselves with the Leage for Independent Political Action either returned to the fold of Democratic and Republican Progressivism or else joined the efforts in Minnesota and Wisconsin to begin a third party along Populist lines.

Events abroad gave further cause for discouragement. Collectivism as a principle suffered in the light of oppressive and often violent tactics by Fascists and Communists. The special villainy of the former, quickly recognized and easily rejected by the American public, fitted snugly into the mind's chamber of horrors. But Russian Communism, which seemed under Stalin to be abandoning the character of a Brave New Experiment and returning to the tyranny of the czars, caused the additional pain of disillusionment.

Particularly damaging events occurred in quick succession at mid-decade. The invasion of Ethiopia by Italy in 1935, and the involvement of Italy with other collectivist states, Germany and Russia, in the Spanish Civil War, which began the following year, suggested to many Americans a linkage between collectivism and war. Hard on the heels of these disasters came the Moscow treason trials, climaxed by the virulent denunciation of Leon Trotsky by his former, less illustrious colleagues.

A spate of antiwar books in the mid-1930's indicated America's concern over the rising level of hostility in the world. Similarly, a strong anti-Fascist feeling showed itself in the growing volume of writings on Nazi Germany and the war in Spain.[1]

Within that general atmosphere appeals to tradition, as a counter to rational collectivist planning apparently gone berserk, gained an increasingly attentive hearing. Those appeals centered on the reformist mode of thought described earlier as liberal traditionalism. Their original aim was to offer defensive arguments in behalf of particular geographic areas and social groups. The great regionalist cause of the 1920's, for example, was that of the Southern agrarians, who condemned the industrial North as they praised the special virtues of rural Southern ways. Cultural pluralism, as originally devised by Horace Kallen, was not as defensive. But Kallen was first moved to invent that doctrine as a way of protecting minorities from the sort of nativist abuse that he, as a Jew, had suffered.

During the thirties the restrictive bounds of regionalism and cultural pluralism were gradually enlarged in an attempt to include the entire nation. The spokesmen for both groups sought to draw generalizations from their special sets of values and apply them broadly. Partly, that trend reflected both the collectivist planning emphasis of the early years of the 1930's and the increasingly interdependent nature of American industrial society. Apartness for special groups no longer seemed feasible. An effective integration of small groups into the larger America had to be made; and the great concern now had to be to find the means of doing so while protecting the soul of the nation's several minorities.

To some extent the nationalist trend also indicated a growing concern over the Fascist menace. A gathering of national purpose for humane democratic ends seemed the surest way to avoid a Fascist alternative. Otherwise a danger existed that Fascism might take hold in neglected, suffering pockets of American life, festering there like a deadly bacillus.[2]

1. Reshaping Regionalism

The first major indication that regionalism was stirring from the position it had been left in by the Southern agrarians was the appearance of Distributism in 1934. Herbert Agar, a journalist and historian with a rather aristocratic Southern heritage, promoted the concept and soon gained the valuable assistance of the prominent poet Allen Tate, who had been one of the leaders of the Southern agrarian school. Distributism borrowed its name and the major elements of its program from the conservative English land reform program led by the Catholic writers Hilaire Belloc and G. K. Chesterton. The impetus for English Distributism came from the hardships visited upon displaced yeomen by the Enclosure Acts of the late eighteenth and early nineteenth centuries and from Pope Leo XIII's encyclical, "Rerum Novarum" (1891), aimed at alleviating the ills of industrialism without resorting to socialism. At the heart of the program was the idea that human productive enterprise could be carried on at least as well in small units as in large. Industry, then, should decentralize, and in recognition of the virtues of agrarian self-sufficiency, many persons should return to agriculture on land powerful landowners made available through conscience or coercion. Henry George's writings, steeped in passionate Christian moralism, appeared at a crucial time, and the American writer achieved a greater fame for his method of restoring ill-used land to its full potential in England, where land was scarce, than in America. The Americans, then, who adopted Distributism in the thirties were welcoming Henry George home while they were reinvigorating the agrarian side of Jefferson's principle of self-sufficiency.

The logic of their position led Distributists to oppose the New Deal. In his first appeal for Distributism in 1934 Agar criticized the administration as a patchwork quilt devoid of unifying principles and wrongly devoted to reviving the old discredited finance-capital system.[3] The following year Agar linked his Distributist views with the concept

Charles Beard advocated in *The Open Door* (1935) of a self-contained Western Hemisphere economy that would secure American isolation from the mounting troubles of Europe and Asia. Agar added to his argument for insulated self-sufficiency the conviction that "self-government is only possible in a state where real property is widely distributed."[4]

A Jeffersonian ideal of self-government and self-reliance made Agar critical both of Marxism and of the laissez-faire economics advocated by Friedrich Hayek and others.[5] Those systems erred, in Agar's judgment, by promoting an inequitable distribution of wealth and power and by emphasizing competition and class warfare rather than co-operation. America, Agar concluded, was founded to provide a third way between tyrannical state control and self-interest: the way of the independent property holder and the small producer.

Agar's ideal of decentralization led him to minimize the role of economics in society. He stressed that "only by ruthlessly subordinating economics to political and moral aims, can a nation hope to gain inner peace and self-esteem, and to give its citizens a way of life in which the plain man can know happiness and dignity."[6] The strong emphasis on economic determination, both among the growing legion of Marxists and the apologists for capitalism, seemed to him a stultifying trend. Creative writing suffered accordingly. "At the moment," Agar observed in 1935, "our literature offers surprisingly few examples of pure economics. One reason for this, I think, is that our aimless society is making a false demand upon the economists, which the economists are trying to meet. We are asking our economists to provide us with a substitute for a moral purpose."[7]

Agar joined Allen Tate, whose agrarian views had lost some of their conservative sectional character during the Depression, in editing a set of regionalist essays in 1936 under the questioning title, *Who Owns America?* The book marked the culmination of Distributist theorizing, offering samples of the thought of the leading figures in the movement. Southern views asserted themselves strongly in essays by Lyle Lanier, John Crowe Ransom, Frank Owsley, Donald Davidson, Robert Penn Warren, and John Donald Wade—all veteran writers in behalf of Southern institutions. But their arguments were balanced by Northerners —David Cushman Coyle, William Fisher, and Cleanth Brooks—and two Englishmen, Hilaire Belloc and Douglas Jerrold.

From the Southern writers came familiar pleas for protection of agriculture from predatory Big Business. Lyle Lanier warned "that the peculiar dissociation of ownership from control of property which characterizes the corporation, and the reduction of a progressively increasing number of real property owners to the status of wage-earners, create conditions not contemplated by the founders of the American Republic." That situation represented in Lanier's mind far more than a personal tragedy for the individuals directly involved. "These conditions are so complex that democracy throughout the world is giving way to one or the other of those two poles of political absolutism, communism or fascism. If we are to avoid some such outcome in America, it is imperative that some formula be discovered whereby the benefits of technology and organization can be utilized to promote, rather than destroy, the fundamental aims of democracy."[8]

The Distributists worked hard to establish an incriminating, though unwitting, link between Marxism and capitalism. In his introduction to *Who Owns America?* Agar spoke anxiously about the traditional American dream of a stable, egalitarian, familial life. "Today that dream is derided by two groups: first, by the communists, who say that any attempt to realize it must be vain, since the attempt would contradict the laws of Marx; second, by the friends of Big Business, who dishonor the dream by saying that it has been realized, that it lies all about us today."[9] Allen Tate drew the linkage more tightly, more positively, suggesting that a subtle bond of common interest brought Marxism and finance capitalism together. Both worked to establish control by large organizations over productive resources, thus eliminating the sense of individual liberty that comes from personal control over property. Both the Communists and the Liberty League vouch for the "ownership" of the means of production by the people under their social systems, the former by placing economic control in the hands of the peoples' representative, the state, and the latter by arguing that the stockholders who "own" the American corporations are a diverse group, spanning all levels of society. But Tate felt that both had made hollow arguments. The citizen shareholder of the Soviet state and the obscure small shareholder in a large American corporation lacked the benefits of *true* ownership because they lacked *control* over the use of their "property."[10]

Furthermore, Tate contended, Marxists have been very quick to agree with Big Business that finance capitalism represented the highest logical outcome of capitalism. The time thus had come, Marxists argued, to move on to the next stage of dialectical evolutionary development. Through resolute class warfare the "final stages of capitalism" would give way to the classless society.

Tate called on traditional individualism to confound Communist claims that they alone could represent the masses in the crusade against the two thousand or so super-capitalists who exercise oppressive control over society. He expressed confidence that "if the people were convinced that the collectivists wished to eliminate the two thousand men only to disposses the rest of us more thoroughly, they might decide to eliminate the two thousand themselves—to get control of their property again."[11]

Others among the Distributists felt a similar antipathy toward Marxism but tended to consider Fascism the more immediate threat. "Unless the people are aroused," Agar warned, "monopoly will go its way, not because it is fun for the monopolists. If monopoly goes its way, it will drift into fascism—the political tyranny that must implement an economic tyranny."[12] Only after Fascist trials would Communism emerge. Indeed, "if we once get fascism, we shall probably get communism in the end, for the reason that fascism is too bad to be endured."[13]

For all its criticism of Fascism, Distributism yet showed an inclination in some quarters toward Fascist aims. The periodical *American Review*, begun in 1933 by Agar, among others, to promote the fortunes of traditionalism—both the Jeffersonian individualism urged by the regionalists and the authoritarian veneration for classical models that the New Humanists wished to impose—became in the late thirties little more than an organ for Fascist propaganda. Agar left the journal before it had reached that pass. Nonetheless, the emphasis of Distributism on anticapitalist self-sufficiency resting on an agrarian base was reminiscent of European Fascism's praise for similar agrarian values and provides a clue as to how the American Fascists who took over the journal were attracted to it.

None of the American contributors to *Who Owns America?* expressed anything but distaste for Fascism. It was left for one of the Englishmen, Douglas Jerrold, to give the only direct praise. That was not altogether surprising, for England in the mid-thirties harbored a number of organizations and individuals that expressed at least guarded sympathy for Fascist desires to create a Homeland for her scattered peoples. A policy that would combine strict imperialist direction over "inferior" peoples with domestic social reform had had a long list of advocates in England since the late nineteenth century, with the Fabians perhaps the most influential among them. George Bernard Shaw, the celebrated veteran of Fabianism, was at the time of the writing of *Who Owns America?* traveling from country to country, including the United States, delivering controversial lectures in praise of Fascist nationalist policies.

Jerrold's argument stressed the importance of national self-sufficiency in the midst of world crisis. He used his Distributist forum to praise such self-sufficiency as an analog to regional self-sufficiency within a single nation. Nations that were not critically dependent on outside resources could avoid the basic uncertainties of international economics at the same time that they could help in imposing economic sanctions against those nations that threatened peace by thrusting outward for power and possessions.

At that point Jerrold's argument turned in upon itself. Sophistically he claimed that, since self-sufficiency is such a great international virtue, the democracies must not be too unbending in their opposition to the territorial ambitions of Germany, Italy, and Japan. Crippled economically by the Great War and the settlement that followed, their peoples scattered about under a multitude of different sovereignties, those nations were faced in the thirties with difficult obstacles in their efforts to gain stability. Acquiring additional power and territories would enable them to gain self-sufficiency and tranquillity. In his sympathy for the alleged needs of Fascist nations, Jerrold was blandly inclined to take the Fascists at their word. He spoke optimistically of the rising fortune of the agrarian self-sufficiency movement and declared that "England is reviving her wheat and livestock production, has already re-established her pig product and will soon turn to develop her markedly rich potential resources in dairy produce. . . . Germany is being forced by international Jewry along the same path and Italy by internationalist politicians." [14]

No truly unified Distributist program ever existed. We have noted the basic desire of the movement to return to Jeffersonian individualism and to revive the humane tradition that flourished within the bounds of that concept prior to the Civil War. The ramifications of the desire, however, were many and never subject to any central discipline.

Most Distributists felt little need to tinker with the Constitution: Legislation putting business corporations under strict control would be sufficient. But some felt a need for drastic regional reconstruction. They wanted to call a national convention and amend the Constitution.

A book by William Yandell Elliott, *The Need for Constitutional Reform* (1935), which appeared just before *Who Owns America?*, stirred many of the more militant Distributists. Elliott, a Harvard professor of political science, suggested reorganizing America into a cluster of large regional commonwealths. He proposed a national convention for the writing of a new Constitution that would base national policy upon protection of unique regional characteristics and a federation of them in a manner that would make the most efficient possible use of the total national resources.[15]

Sweden's socialized state provided the Distributists with their most attractive model. Marquis Childs' very influential writings on that nation's cooperative experiments seemed almost blueprints for survival to many Distributists. Sweden, they felt, had struck an intricately successful balance between collectivism and laissez-faire individualism. The private Swedish cooperatives, begun against the concerted opposition of large private enterprise, won out in the manner most heartening to the Jeffersonian mind: They simply outcompeted their corporation rivals by producing goods of higher quality at lower cost. Swedish Big Business, when put at such a bad disadvantage, proved as cringing and helpless as American business had during the collapse after 1929. To Agar that demonstrated the emptiness of commonly voiced fears that Big Business, if hard-pressed, would fight with the fierceness of a cornered animal, even to the point of adopting Fascism. It was growing success and power, Agar felt, that would tempt Big Business to foist Fascism upon the country.[16] What remained, then, was the task of persuading the public of the relative ease with which a shift of national energies toward their true interests could be accomplished. That optimistic vision of cooperative reform helped carry the Distributists on their own way against the tides of Marxism and the New Deal.

The Distributist manifesto, *Who Owns America?*, was followed closely by a major publication that carried regionalist thinking a step further toward cooperative nationalism. In *Southern Regions of the United States* (1936) Howard Odum collated the fruits of many years of work by the Southern Regional Committee of the Social Science Research Council and concluded from his labors that America needed drastic overhaul along regionalist lines. Odum's writing—cautious, massively factual, and folksy in a rather staid, professorial way—did not electrify public opinion. But Odum did make two valuable contributions to the cause of regionalism. He provided it with a great battery of statistical, sociological ammunition. And, by carrying on an extended attack against the sectional viewpoint of the Southern agrarians, Odum fostered the impression that the romantic Fugitive position was at odds with any careful assessment of the facts. His shower of scholarly cold water settled much of the dust that had been stirred up by strong sectional emotion and so gave the nation at large a far clearer view of the essentials of the regionalist position.

Southern Regions of the United States followed a decade of writing in which Odum discussed particular aspects of the South and toyed with questions about the nature and uses of quantitative sociological analysis.[17] A professor at the University of North Carolina, he generated an intellectual flowering in the social sciences at that university that was in striking contrast to the work of those students and teachers at Vanderbilt who rallied around John Crowe Ransom and the agrarian cause. Odum disapproved of the Fugitives for what he considered to be excessive emotionalism and narrowness. In judging the needs of the South, he inclined more to the approach of Henry Grady and Walter Hines Page, who wished to find a way for the South to participate in the modern industrial world. The answer for the South's predicament of poverty and alienation from the rest of America was assimilation, Odum believed, not an aggrieved effort to stay apart. Indeed, the gloomy tendency of Southerners to turn inward during the 1920's had meant that "before Hitler's Nazi Germany, part of the South were revivifying an emotional culture through attack upon universities and intellectual life; through religious coloring of politics and statescraft; through appeal to sectional patriotism; through intolerance of criticism and opposition; and through continuing emphasis upon racial issues, Nordic superiority, and one hundred per cent Americanism." Fortunately, a saving glimmer of loyalty to national ideals and cooperation remained. "There was lacking . . . sufficient sectional isolation and strong leadership to furnish good soil for open outbreaks. Dictatorships of demagogues were ample, but localized."[18] But in the midst of depression what remained of that negative policy of reaction took on added menace. Indeed, "the task of regional reconstruction and readjustment is all the more urgent because the South, now facing its own peculiar crises in the midst of and in relation to national recovery, appears almost equally capable of making the best or the worst of all possible contributions to the national culture of the next generations."[19]

The precarious nature of the national, as well as Southern, existence left all the regions of the nation more interdependently partners than ever—sharers in a great but dangerous opportunity. "Nowhere is this merely an academic problem," Odum declared. "It is stark reality. The Southern States, like the nation, are in the remaking; they have their big chance. How long will the option last? The South has reflected a peculiar fortune and social heritage often likened unto Germany in the sense that facing a crisis it has a tendency to take the wrong road.'[20]

Though he advocated national reform, Odum was not a partisan of the New Deal. He had other plans, calling for far more detailed and massive national planning than Roosevelt seemed willing to institute. Nonetheless, he felt gratitude toward the administration for helping to nudge the regionalist cause along. "The New Deal with its projection of planning hypotheses and of administrative problems had," Odum judged, "greatly augmented the need for regional analysis, and more regional analysis."[21]

Odum differed with conservative Southern agrarians by drawing a sharp distinction between *sectionalism* and *regionalism*. True regionalism, he asserted, should logically put the nation first, the region second. Sectionalism does the reverse. Moreover, sectionalism emphasizes the barriers erected by political boundaries, and this encourages separatism, whereas regionalism stresses the coordinated interests of the various parts of the country. Consequently, sectionalism encourages inbred, jealous individualism, while regionalism fosters a fruitful cooperative spirit. The sum of sectionalism's many flaws was a somber menace. "Not only does sectionalism sooner or later . . . constitute 'potential bases for forceful resistance,' and thus necessitate federal coercion, but it gives excuse for the theory and practice of dictatorship which ignores regional, cultural, and geographical differentials, and almost inevitably goes too far in coercion and regimentation."[22]

Odum's program for regional reconstruction resembled W. Y. Elliott's plan of regional commonwealths. Odum felt that America divided naturally into six regions of markedly different natural and cultural endowments: Southeast, Southwest, Far West, Northeast, Middle States, and Northwest. Like Elliott, he advocated a reorganization of the nation's political structure, but he cautiously stopped short of advocating a new Constitution. Instead, Odum hoped that the current enthusiasm for planning social affairs would result in a national planning commission and a careful program of regional development.[23]

Odum believed that despite increasing enlightenment, too many Americans were wary of social planning and expertise. Hence, any regionalist planning movement would be wise to move cautiously, avoiding ideological dogma, talk of social revolution, or a broad, fixed intent to change basic institutions. That caution, along with his penchant for massive fact-gathering, prevented Odum's work from becoming any sort of clarion call for reform. Yet it was significant in the way its tolerant attention to the content of American life, down to the humblest detail, encouraged the national tendency in the late 1930's to examine and sympathize with the long neglected underside of America. Nowhere was that tendency more vividly illustrated than in the attempt of the Roosevelt administration after 1936 to align itself with minority groups and the cause of civil liberties.[24] In literature a similar spirit showed itself when much of the rather impersonal ideological fervor that frequented creative writing during the first half of the thirties gave way to a close study of particular human beings caught in the toils of the Depression.[25] The same period witnessed the rapid development of documentaries— from the films of Robert Flaherty to the impressions of American life recorded in prose and photographs by Erskine Caldwell and Margaret Bourke White.[26]

The cause of regionalism flared brightly in literature. A vigorous outcropping of little magazines in the hinterlands had begun just before World War I with the appearance of *Midland* in Iowa City—"The Athens of the West." With the addition of Southern counterparts in the twenties—most notably the New Orleans *Double Dealer*, which discovered Faulkner and Hemingway, and John Crowe Ransom's *Fugitive* in Nashville—regional literature was ready for a great insurgence. The experimental literature enthusiasms of the twenties encouraged would-be writers to develop their talents; and the troubles of the thirties added a social dimension: the sense of need to search through regional cultures to find lost virtues and the elements of a new beginning. By 1936

Robert Penn Warren, one of the original Fugitives and a brilliant, increasingly liberal writer of poetry and fiction, concluded that the great literary struggle of the time was that between regionalist and proletarian literature. His comparison of the two rivals was shrewd and provocative. "The regionalist movement," he declared, "may be defined, in brief and in part, as the attempt of a writer to reason himself into the appropriate relation to the past; the proletarian movement, as the attempt to reason himself into the appropriate relation to the future."[27] Thus the regionalists are blessed with many patron saints, the proletarians none; and to Warren's traditionalist mind, to be devoid of such moral guidance, as the leftists were, was to be without sufficient resources to attain the stature of a Hawthorne, Melville, or Whitman. Warren's distinction between the two forms of literature had persuasive bite. Yet he drew the contrast too sharply by overlooking a basic shared sympathy. Both the proletarian writers and the regionalists ardently praised the common life: the workman's arts and crafts on the one hand and, on the other, the richly inventive use of leisure by country folk and slum-dwellers alike.

The growing interest shown by writers and critics during the thirties would seem to have borne out Warren's insistence on regionalism's importance. In 1936 the *Saturday Review of Literature* decided to publish a debate on regionalism, after noting the swelling emotions of that movement's friends and enemies.[28] The contenders, Joseph Baker supporting the regionalist argument and Paul Robert Beath attacking it, disputed most sharply on the issue of whether America was drastically divided along regionalist lines. Baker contended that the regionalists have shown that the melting pot has not obliterated major differences. Quite to the contrary. "Has the Negro or the Jew been losing his separateness in recent literature? The tendency is all in the opposite direction."[29] America is a welter of distinct groups. The newly grown cities possess no genuine cultural identity of their own but are merely depots for people torn from their roots. In seeking inspiration from the long-settled countryside, the regionalists, Baker felt, were reaching closer to the cultural source of art than were the proletarian writers who rummaged among the displaced persons of the cities for themes.

Beath countered with the charge that regional literature, by confining itself to backwater areas, was displaying feelings of inferiority. Baffled by America's city culture, regionalists had retreated into the myth that only the primitive held virtue. What good reason was there for the regionalists to select the simple and the mediocre to write about? Could they not be equally *regional* by occasionally dealing with intelligent, educated, even wealthy individuals who helped populate America? To Beath such primitivist tactics seemed a wrongheaded denial of the Great Tradition in the best Matthew Arnold sense of a refined, matured culture.

The interest of the *Saturday Review of Literature* in regionalism, expressed in various editorials and reviews of books with a regionalist flavor, reflected the liberal traditionalist viewpoint of both its editors-in-chief during the decade, Henry Seidel Canby and Bernard De Voto. Both men combined small-town backgrounds with education at centers of genteel learning. Canby was raised in New Haven, attended Yale just after the turn of the century, and later taught there.[30] De Voto had a more diverse background. Raised in Ogden, Utah, he blended the rough, still-pioneer values of that area with the teachings of Emerson and Thoreau that he absorbed at Harvard.[31] Both men ended with a great respect for the traditions of America's early years, a fondness for the intellectual milieu of the universities where these traditions were preserved, and a corresponding dislike of the materialist chromo-civilization they observed around them.

In 1934, as the fever of collectivism was reaching its peak, Canby urged literature to come to the aid of individualism. Canby expressed the widespread view of the time that the trend toward collectivism was irreversible. "Our modern societies require social control; they can subsist only by mass production, can be educated only by mass methods, can become civilized only by a beneficent standardization of the instruments of culture. Literature and religion, the first for the many, the second for the few who can take their religion that way, will thus become the safeguards of such individualism as is essential if we are to socialize without depersonalizing the world."[32]

Canby's repeated expressions of that humanist theme were accompanied in lesser volume, but greater heat, by De Voto's championship of the American individualist tradition. Marxist writers and the expatriates lacked enough courage, De Voto charged, to support American values. They were given to retreating under fire—either to a foreign land or into the comforting arms of some rigid ideology. Against Marxism De Voto pitted the theories of the great but erratic Italian sociologist Vilfredo Pareto. Pareto's concept of "residues"—crucial nonrational memory patterns that determine individual reactions—fitted De Voto's emotional attachment to American tradition and his distrust of large concentrations of power.[33] To a degree De Voto's use of Pareto's theories provided an answer to regionalist attacks on the rootlessness of cities. De Voto saw the mind itself in "regional" terms, a landscape of inherited memory sets that could, with properly vigorous nurture, prove strong enough to give a person the strength to retain and transmit his cultural values in the face of geographic uprooting and pressure from various social and economic forces.

The regionalist penchant for rural life was abetted by the homestead movement, led by an ex-advertising man, Ralph Borsodi. Borsodi, like the Distributists, made a connection between Henry George's single-tax emphasis upon land and the superior virtues of self-sufficient farming. In 1918 Borsodi began his active reform career by working for the Single Tax Party in the New York elections; and in 1920 he moved easily to advocacy of projects for removing discontented urbanites to the soil. His shrewd book, *The Distribution Age* (1927), made a case for decentralization by stressing a neglected economic issue. As Borsodi pointed out, the advantages of centralization were outweighed at a certain stage of growth by the difficulties of transporting and marketing goods from their central place of manufacture. Yet, centralization increased ever more swiftly, spurred on by advertisers and distributers who profited from the inefficient marketing conditions.

Beyond the economic issue Borsodi saw a problem of human scale. Men were lost in the new urban world, inconsequential units in their vast communities and in the giant businesses where they were usually consigned to dreary, repetitive tasks. Borsodi's antipathy to machine culture on these grounds was radical and quite romantic. In the end, he insisted, "the world—to be a tolerable place for a really civilized people—would consist of only two classes: artists and patrons of artists."[34]

After his brief association with Single Tax reform, Borsodi devoted himself to subsistence farming as a way to escape a mass society that seemed virtually impervious to reform. That was his message in *This Ugly Civilization* (1929). The less dependent people become upon machines and the market, Borsodi counseled, the better chance they will have of joining the two favored classes—the artists and the patrons of artists. Partly, that would mean becoming more rational; for the self-sufficient man understands the bases of his life, how things work and how nature can be made to support him, as well as what nature demands in return.

Borsodi spent the 1930's on his farm in Suffern, New York, which he managed with unusual skill. His example and his writings made him well known and often consulted. He joined Herbert Agar in 1937 to begin the Distributist journal, *Free America*, and later took part with O. F. Baker, and M. L. Wilson of the Department of Agriculture in a widely noted discussion, *Agriculture in Modern Life* (1939). Throughout the decade he was the leading figure in a return to the soil movement that was interrupted on the rise by World War II.

But Borsodi did not seek to inspire broad social reform. His desire was to help provide a means of escape for the few who could show the character and intelligence to make a go of subsistence farming. In that he was frankly elitist. With repeated references to Nietzsche he attacked the mass institutions that had been drugged by ignorance and churchly superstitions. Looking around him at industrial desolateness, he concluded that "in every age and in every region of the globe men have always consisted of three types of individuals: an immense majority of herd-minded men who have the characteristics which predatory, acquisitive, power-seeking, ruthless men have in common, and a still smaller minority of quality-minded men."[35] Inevitably, democracy has been a bust. The herd is incapable of exercising power and cannot avoid being preyed upon by a cunning few. What was needed was an aristocracy of talent of the sort envisioned by Jefferson. But modern mass society had excluded that possibility and instead rewarded the ruthless self-seekers. So, a soured Jeffersonian with little faith in the Republic, Borsodi took to the country and urged others with the necessary ability to do likewise.

2. Cultural Pluralism Reemerges

The views of the regionalists, the homesteaders and the singers of American values such as Canby and De Voto gained strength in the latter years of the 1930's as the appeal of collectivism declined and the rigors of the Depression eased. At the same time another appeal to tradition, cultural pluralism, began to gain momentum. Cultural pluralism, unlike the other forms of traditionalism we have examined, was concerned with aspects of American life of relatively recent origin. Not the innate qualities of geographic areas or the core of American tradition that sprang from New England beginnings but the place of non-Anglo-Saxon minorities, most of whom were descendants of immigrants who first arrived in America in the late nineteenth or early twentieth centuries, captured the attention of cultural pluralists.

The term "cultural pluralism" was originated by Horace Kallen, a philosopher and, as the son of Jewish immigrants, an active participant in the Zionist movement. Kallen was the favorite student of William James at Harvard and later was a close associate of John Dewey at the New School for Social Research. He combined their pragmatic views of the plural, changing character of the universe with his own special involvement in an oppressed minority to produce the view that America, if it is to retain its democratic integrity, must provide opportunity for all its citizens to preserve their own ethnic traditions while enjoying equal rights and privileges of citizenship.[36]

An article in 1915 by the noted economist E. A. Ross advising restrictions against non-Anglo-Saxon immigrants provided the occasion for Kallen's first major discussion of his cultural pluralist concept.[37] Ross, Kallen charged, was masking his intent. The economist proposed a blockade against eastern and southern Europeans on the unscientific claim that those people were inferior to Anglo-Saxons and would thus plague America with the woes that come of having vast disparities of talent in the population. But Ross was really echoing the long-standing Anglo-Saxon concern about differences of nationality, not offering evidence of differences in innate capacity. By considering deviations from the dominant Yankee standard to be signs of inferiority, Ross and his ilk were placing impossible burdens upon non-Anglo-Saxons. They could not assimilate to an Anglo-Saxon model because their inheritance and the cultural groups which nurtured them forbade it. Employing a rigid view of heredity, Kallen asserted that "men may change their clothes, their politics, their wives, their religions, their philosophies, to a greater or lesser extent; they cannot change their grandfathers. . . . The selfhood which is inalienable in them, and for the realization of which they require 'inalienable' liberty, is ancestrally determined, and the happiness which they pursue has its form implied in ancestral endowment." [38] The destiny of democracy, then, if it is to be a noble one, must be wrenched from the hands of the restrictionists. Sowers of confusion and disunity, they have kept the American spirit "inarticulate, not a voice, but a chorus of many voices each singing a rather different tune." [39] The only way to bring the American democracy into harmony, Kallen felt, was to cast it culturally as a "federal republic, its substance a democracy of nationalities cooperating voluntarily and autonomously in the enterprise of self-realization through the perfection of men according to their kind. The common language of the commonwealth, the language of its great political tradition, is English, but each nationality expresses its emotional and voluntary life in its own language, in its own . . . aesthetic and intellectual forms." [40]

During the 1920's Kallen fought a stubborn rearguard action against the prevailing mood of nativism. [41] But nativistic emotions subsided late in the decade after strong immigration restrictions had gone into effect. Kallen then turned to consumer cooperation, a doctrine of sharing that fitted logically with cultural pluralism. His economic preoccupation increased during the Depression and gave him implicit linkage with regionalists and other liberal traditionalists who stressed their own versions of cooperation. Like them, Kallen felt that the Scandinavian cooperative experiments offered Americans promising guidelines for reconstructing their own economy. [42]

With Kallen's detachment from the cultural pluralist cause and the whir of economic debate that filled the air, cultural pluralism faded from general notice during the first years of the 1930's. Yet as the decade wore on, increasing interest in the underdog and antipathy toward the example of Fascism's brutal treatment of minorities provided the base for a revived cultural pluralist movement, should a persuasive spokesman appear.

Louis Adamic answered the need for such a spokesman. An immigrant who had become a successful free-lance writer, he was, as his friend and fellow social critic Carey McWilliams observed, a man who "believed in the absolute necessity of excitement in human life." [43] He came to America in 1914 as a boy of fourteen to find the sort of adventure he had heard about from the Amerikanci who had returned home to his village in Yugoslavia. Eighteen years later he was able to say: "Nearly all the promises that my boyish imagination had exacted from America when I was still in the Old Country have been fulfilled. America has given me thrills and experiences I had not even expected. . . ." [44]

Adamic's commitment to cultural pluralism came late in his career. His humane sympathies corresponded essentially with those of Kallen; but Kallen had the special provocation of anti-Semitism to make him seek an explicit place for minorities within the American Idea. Moreover, he was a philosopher who was attracted to system-making and who saw the uses of William James and John Dewey for a pluralist interpretation of America. Finally, Kallen spent most of his life teaching in one place, removed essentially from the fluctuating passions of the crowd. Adamic, by contrast, was a drifter, chronically restless for new places and new confrontations with flesh and blood specimens of humanity. McWilliams remembered him as a tireless collector of eccentrics. "In fact, I have never known anyone with such a talent for the discovery of characters as Adamic." [45] But it was in ways a limiting talent. Adamic's absorption in his panoramic study of individuals never seemed to leave him time to organize his views on cultural pluralism in any systematic way. He was always vague when he spoke of his vision of a "New America, America overhauled inside and out. . . ." [46]

In 1934 Adamic published his first plea for a national policy of cultural pluralism. He suggested a national organization:

> The organization I have in mind, which, let us designate here as XYZ, would have, during the next fifteen or twenty years, a vast and complicated task to perform—namely, to give these millions of New

Americans a knowledge of, and pride in, their own heritage, which, to some extent, would operate to counteract their feelings of inferiority about themselves in relation to the rest of the country; and simultaneously, to create a sympathetic understanding toward them on the part of older Americans. . . .[47]

Adamic supplemented his call for a national organization with attacks on the bigotry of ultrapatriotic societies and on the milder nativist tendencies shown by the American labor movement, Congress, and the Federal Immigration Service. In offering an environmentalist explanation of the problem, he set himself apart from Kallen, who considered cultural inheritance the most potent social force. "The current xenophobia," Adamic declared, "is a product of the socioeconomic crisis of this decade, and of the fear among the dominant economic and cultural groups of mass unrest or even of revolution." [48]

In 1940 Adamic embarked on the greatest cooperative effort of his life by helping to found the periodical *Common Ground*. For nine years *Common Ground* offered a limited readership information on the state of affairs among the nation's minority groups and graphic pleas for tolerance. Its editorial board and contributors formed a galaxy of prominent liberals. Adamic himself had become a widely known figure, and even domesticated enough to be a heavy contributor to the *Saturday Evening Post*.[49]

Adamic capped his efforts for cultural pluralism with an ambitious series of books, *From Plymouth Rock to Ellis Island*, which were designed to chronicle the historic contributions to the American tradition made by non-Anglo-Saxon minorities. According to Adamic, there are two ways of looking at American history:

> One is this: that the United States is an Anglo-Saxon country with a White-Protestant-Anglo-Saxon civilization struggling to preserve itself against infiltration and adulteration by other civilizations brought here by Negroes and hordes of "foreigners."
>
> The second is this: that the pattern of the United States is not essentially Anglo-Saxon although her language is English. . . . The United States is a new civilization . . . owing much . . . to the plenitude of resources and the skills which we all of us have brought here or developed here in the past three centuries.[50]

Adamic's brand of cultural pluralism—really a great, fond bearhug for all peoples in America—represented a shift in direction for cultural pluralism toward a broad, national inclusiveness in much the same way that regionalism was moving at that time from Distributism to the tolerant nationalism advocated by Howard Odum. Kallen had focused on the rights of minorities to remain separate, suspended colloidally in the midst of American life. But Adamic concentrated upon the contributions minorities had made to a common American civilization.

In his enthusiasm and forcefulness Adamic was highly effective in stirring a public response. William Allen White, the Sage of Emporia, paid Adamic the highest compliment that might come from one so long and vitally in touch with American life by saying that Adamic's book *My America* (1938) had discovered the "essential America."[51] Adamic, in turn, was delighted to find an increasing number of books at the end of the decade that were written with sympathetic understanding of minority groups, and often by members of those groups themselves.[52]

Adamic's approach had its ambiguity, however. He was often prey to overexcitement, and his analysis of American conditions and ethnic customs was rather defensive. Rather than striking out boldly for the merits of distinct differences between ethnic groups, Adamic tended to stress similarities in an effort to combat prejudices against minorities. He expressed cultural pluralist opposition to the idea of America as a melting pot producing a single alloyed type. But at the same time, he theorized that a definite American character did exist. He proposed a national organization to assist immigrants to perceive that national character and come to terms with it. The organization would perform "a great educational-cultural work . . . to try to harmonize and integrate, so far as possible, the various radical and cultural strains in our population. . . ."[53] By so focusing on the common experience of all Americans, Adamic skirted close to the assimilationist point of view that cultural pluralism denied. Eric Goldman recognized the dangers of that approach in his review of *A Nation of Nations*. He warned that "Adamic's concern to give everybody ancestors as edifying as William Bradford bends his major thesis toward an extreme which the facts simply will not permit. For good or for bad, the United States cannot be described as a country which is no more 'essentially' Anglo-Saxon than anything else."[54]

By 1941, when he was presented with the Anisfield Award for his contributions to racial and ethnic harmony, Adamic had clearly taken the lead in the cultural pluralist movement. His broad, reformist outlook helped link cultural pluralism with a growing concern for civil rights and social welfare. As regionalism had become more national in scope toward the end of the thirties, so Adamic helped significantly to impart a nationalist flavor to cultural pluralism. His interest in finding the individual of minority status a secure place within a unified pattern of American life made strong inroads against the earlier cultural pluralist emphasis upon holding minorities together as islands in the midst of an Anglo-Saxon sea.

The liberal traditional programs of regional and cultural pluralism challenged the pragmatic tenor of the early thirties. In those first years of the decade the experiments of the New Deal and the complaints of Marxists and social planners had infused reform thought with presentist attitudes, skeptical of the old ways and of anything that smacked of mysticism. Regionalism, in opposition, encouraged a sense of continuity with the past by stressing the wisdom of having areas retain their innate characters. Cultural pluralists placed the regionalist argument within an ethnic framework. They would preserve not the quality of a region but the inner qualities of groups with common racial and national heritages.

3. *Unity Through a Great Tradition*

A third group of liberal traditionalists striving to conserve supra-rational values were believers in what many of them called the Great Tradition. The growing force of the appeal to a Great Tradition as the 1930's drew to a close was a logical outcome of trends we have observed. The broadening of regionalism and cultural pluralism embodied a growth in tolerance and traditionalist feelings, encouraging Americans to find a common standard to which all could rally.

Those seeking the Great Tradition divided into two paths following the same roadway. One group sought a distinctly American tradition, the other a larger heritage which would place the American experience in relation to the rest of Western civilization. The first group, the Americanists, were less inclined toward collectivist designs than other reformers on the right and left. Rather, they were drawn to the central American premise of individualism and, so fixed by history, could not unreservedly join in any campaign for a planned society. Nor could they find in the American past guiding examples of social movements based on religion, racial doctrines, or mystic nationalism that had achieved grand success.

Liberal traditionalists who included the European past within their conception of a Great Tradition found collectivism more congenial. They honored the classical belief in correct models of beauty and social behavior and the Renaissance ideal of the fulfilled man who lives in an understanding relationship with the whole of his surroundings. Their attention, then, could be focused on the task of applying a tradition of social unity to the chaos of self-seeking American individualism in order to create what Mumford described as "basic communism" and Waldo Frank, with more mystic religiosity, called the "Whole." To pull together the fragmented consciousness and feelings of machine-led men and integrate them with the American setting was their mission—a high-flown mission, but one that seemed urgent and very much concerned with hard facts.

Both strands of traditionalist thinking benefited from the widespread shift away from enthusiasm for materialist collectivism after 1936. Many events reflected the changing mood. The growing force of concern for tradition and of protection of the individual against bigness helped to determine such fateful matters as the enlargement of protection in the courts for civil liberties, the rise and fall of the Communistic Popular Front, the sympathetic response toward victims of Fascism, and a heightened compassion in creative literature for the fate of individuals.

Liberals entered the 1930's in despair over the prospects facing civil liberties within the courts. The liberal ideas of Holmes and Brandeis remained active only as gallant dissension against the loyalty of the majority to laissez-faire. As judicial obstruction to reform efforts mounted during the early thirties, liberal commentators pressed for restrictions to be placed on the powers of the "nine old men." Some, like Robert Carr, Edwin Corwin, and Max Lerner, wanted to curb severely the practice of judicial review.[55] Other liberals lined up in support of Roosevelt's ill-fated attempt in 1937 to pack the court with justices more amenable to reform and thus clear the tracks for the New Deal without radically altering the prerogatives of the judiciary.[56]

In the end the simple expedient of old age provided the remedy. The "Four Horsemen of Reaction," Van Devanter, McReynolds, Sutherland, and Butler, rode out of the court into retirement and were replaced by the more liberal Black, Reed, Frankfurter, and Douglas. C. Herman Pritchett and Alan Westin in *The Third Branch of Government* aptly summarize the nature of the great legal divide of 1937. Before that time, the authors state, the Supreme Court emphasized property rights; after 1937 it stressed human rights, which in the American context meant lending support to the concept of Jeffersonian individualism.

Liberal traditionalism received another more inadvertent boost from the Communist Party. In 1935 the militant revolutionary policy prescribed for the various national branches of the International Communist Party since the late twenties gave way to the Popular Front. Fearful of the growing menace of Fascism and disappointed over the failure of hard-nosed revolutionary tactics to bring on the decisive class struggle, Moscow turned to the subtler tactic of a Popular Front that would align Communists with other groups to the left of center. In the United States talk of Marxist third-party upheaval ended abruptly after the election of 1936, and Communists hurried over to support the New Deal. Earl Browder, replacing the more militant old warhorse William Z. Foster as party secretary, was lauded by his comrades as the reincarnation of another famous Kansan, John Brown of Osawotamie. In response Browder wrapped himself in the flag and proclaimed fervently that "Communism is twentieth-century Americanism."[57]

Along with their efforts at interpreting American history in their own image, the Communists sought alliance with minority peoples. They eased their extreme demands for a Soviet black republic in the Deep South and were thus able to enlist the sympathies of a limited number of prominent Negroes, including W. E. B. DuBois, Paul Robeson, and the young novelist Richard Wright. By abandoning the anti-Zionism Stalin had earlier invoked, the Communists increased their appeal among Jews.

The effect of the new Popular Front policy on the relations of intellectuals with Communism was remarkable. In fact, the shift to the Popular Front may have saved the Communist Party from almost entirely losing its grip on the intellectual community. In the early years of the thirties, when the Communist Party was running its harsh revolutionary course, intellectuals entered its ranks in a mood of self-abasement. They felt a measure of guilt over the Depression hardships foisted upon the proletariat by the privileged middle class, from which most of them had come. Meekly they submitted to the party's design to use them as propagandists, grinding out authorized social and literary criticism and party line poems and stories dramatizing the workers' cause. By the middle of the decade, however, the hair shirt was wearing thin. Irving Howe and Lewis Coser in their study of Communism in America described the situation aptly:

> The pitch of fanaticism and self-destruction to which the fellow-traveling intellectuals drove themselves could not long be sustained in America. Where, as in some European countries, the party was a mass organization vitally participating in the social life of the nation, the process of rationalization—or the act of faith—by which the intellectuals sealed their loyalty to the party could find a certain grounding in reality. But in America, where the party had never been anything but sickly and the cultural arena was one of the few in which it could claim any significant influence, the process of illusion tended to take the form

of a galloping fever that quickly reached a hysterical climax and broke. As a result, the turnover of intellectuals within the party was rapid, and the turnover among the fellow travelers still more so.[58]

By 1937, following the meliorative Popular Front line, and with the Loyalist cause in Spain to serve as a focal point of broad agreement, the Communists had managed to enlist many non-Marxian liberal allies. The American Writers' Congress, which the Communists sponsored, included as members such non-Communist luminaries as Ernest Hemingway, Thomas Mann, Kenneth Burke—and even the apolitical humorists S. J. Perelman and James Thurber.[59]

But the mood of brotherhood reigned only briefly. The Nazi-Soviet Pact in 1939 blasted the props out from under the Popular Front. A mass exodus of intellectuals from the American Writers' Congress began, and the hard-core Communists were left to try to accommodate themselves to Molotov's bland description of Fascism as merely "a matter of taste." Two years later, when Hitler invaded Russia and the Communists veered dizzily back to their old belligerent anti-Fascism, the intellectual appeal of Communism to any but a handful of inveterate disciples utterly vanished.

While the golden glow of the Popular Front lasted, however, it helped to light the way for a growing interest in traditionalism. Generally, accounts of the Popular Front have tended to look at the matter the other way around, to suggest that the blending of Communists with non-Marxist liberals represented a great success for the former. The poor liberal fish had been, lamentably, lured into the net.[60] In fact, the reverse seems closer to the truth. It was the Communists who had to change their ideological clothing to comport with the Popular Front, not the liberals. And it was the Communists who were left floundering most helplessly in contradiction when the Popular Front dissolved in 1939. In the end liberals benefited significantly from the increased national fervor for American traditions and the opposition to Fascism that the Popular Front promoted.

Creative literature reflected the sense both of liberation and disillusion that came from waning collectivist enthusiasm. Looking back on the decade just as it was ending in December, 1939, James Farrell noted that "many . . . writers and intellectuals feel that bitter reaction, fascism, is imminent. In the early 1930's there was some hope and confidence. At the end, there is anxiety, apprehension, even signs of panic."[61] But, though he regretted the fervent radicalism that had closed so many writers' eyes and minds during the period, Farrell observed acutely that at least one worthwhile advance had been made. In American fiction, he remarked, "we notice increasingly a difference in the types of environment described by the younger writers, and an attempt to introduce types of character that have not hitherto been treated seriously in American fiction. The 1930's in fiction attempted, briefly, to tell the story of the actuality of the American Melting Pot. Most of the younger writers of the period come from social backgrounds new to American fiction, though not to American life."[62]

Farrell's observation that fiction had begun to treat the theme of minorities in American life was partial recognition of a larger trend. Interest in the melting pot was one indication of the aid and comfort given to traditional American individualism and tolerance by cultural pluralism, regionalism, and the New Deal—and even, blunderingly, by the Communists. Literature, generally, reflected the developing mood. Before 1935 proletarian literature, dictated by the Communist International Union of Revolutionary Writers, made widely heralded headway. But it was feeble art. Shortly after the midpoint of the decade it died almost entirely. In its place appeared fiction that displayed an increasingly compassionate view toward men and carried that approach into formerly ignored quarters of minority life and poverty. John Fante, Pietro DiDonato, James Farrell, Meyer Levin, Nelson Algren, and Richard Wright explored the slums of the large cities. Others— Carson McCullers, Erskine Caldwell, Thomas Wolfe, and William Faulkner among the most notable—surveyed the physical and psychological landscape of the South and in a similar vein Wallace Stegner, H. L. Davis, Paul Engle, Vardis Fisher, and a growing complement of regional writers described life in the outland West.

The new mood of humane compassion in literature reached the dramatic height of its impact on the pub'ic in John Steinbeck's novel of suffering migrants, *The Grapes of Wrath* (1939). Wretched caricatures of the westward-moving pioneers, the Okies in Steinbeck's story portrayed an America that was adrift and in need of a reaffirmation of ties of love and tradition to end its anguish.

Observers who sought to draw the threads of a special American tradition together into a program of understanding and reform found an eloquent spokesman in the poet Archibald MacLeish.

MacLeish's career prior to the 1930's sheds considerable light on a certain development of character that many intellectuals who came of age just at the time of World War I also underwent. The vivid portrait Malcolm Cowley gives in *Exile's Return* (1934) of the young expatriates who fled America just after the war and then returned home in the late 1920's with a chastened sense of appreciation for their native land approximated MacLeish's own experience during those years.

Born into respectable middle-class circumstances in Glencoe, Illinois, in 1892, MacLeish went to an Eastern preparatory school, where he showed enough rebelliousness to hate its rigid upper-class tone. Nonetheless, he entered Yale in 1911 committed to the rather stolid idea of becoming a lawyer and then practicing with one of the established law firms in the East.

When the United States entered the First World War, MacLeish interrupted his straight-line course to join a hospital unit in France. After the fighting had ended, he returned to America, finished Law School at Harvard, and began the expected career with the venerable Charles F. Choate law firm in Boston.

But, like so many of his generation, the memories of war and of France and of an interlude in 1917 when he published a volume of poems, *Tower of Ivory*, would not leave him content with his original prudently chosen goals. In 1923 he abandoned the law and set out with his wife and small children for the southern coast of France to begin as a writer.

With less turbulence than most of the other expatriates, MacLeish achieved a sense of liberation from his origins and from Yankee notions of duty and social utility. In one of his most celebrated poems he struck the keynote for his sojourn in France:

A poem should be motionless in time
As the moon climbs,

Leaving, as the moon releases
Twig by twig the night-entangled trees,

Leaving, as the moon behind the winter leaves,
Memory by memory the mind—

A poem should be motionless in time
As the moon climbs.

A poem should be equal to:
Not true.

For all the history of grief
An empty doorway and a maple leaf.

For love
The leaning grasses and two lights above the sea—

A poem should not mean
But be.[63]

By 1930, as the world was entering a time of renewed trouble, MacLeish, like Cowley and most of the other exiles, had returned home. The reunion revived old feelings of kinship with America, making them deeper and more conscious. In "American Letter" (1930) MacLeish expressed the new mood:

> This, this is our land, this is our people
> This that is neither a land nor a race. We must reap
> The wind here in the grass for our soul's harvest:
> Here we must eat our salt or our bones starve.
> Here we must live or live only as shadows.
> This is our race, we that have none, that have had
> Neither the old walls nor the voices around us,
> This is our land, this is our ancient ground—
> The raw earth, the mixed bloods and the strangers,
> The different eyes, the wind, and the heart's change.
> These we will not leave though the old call us.
> This our country-earth, our blood, our kind.
> Here we will live our years till the earth blind us—[64]

Curiously enough, MacLeish credited a large measure of the social consciousness he developed during the thirties to a job he landed in 1930 on the editorial staff of the new business magazine *Fortune*. That outcome was largely accidental. *Fortune* had been planned as a prestigious, finely turned-out journal for rising executives. But its inauspicious beginning, as the Great Crash was reverberating loudly, left it with little chance to glorify business. Instead, its early issues were filled with reports of disaster and read almost like a reform journal.

An assignment in 1932 to write a summary history of the Fourteenth

Amendment strengthened MacLeish's disapproval of the power organized conservatism had long wielded in the courts and in government.[65] Four years later the field work he did for a story on the Dust Bowl shocked MacLeish into an awareness of the suffering which many Americans had undergone during the Depression.[66]

MacLeish's poetry reflected the rising intensity of his antagonism toward the world of Big Business and his concern for social reform. *Frescoes for Mr. Rockefeller's City* (1932) described the massive new Rockefeller Center in New York as a symbol of the ruthless conquest of America by greed. It seemed to MacLeish an ironic, cold-concrete monument to the Indians, the hopeful immigrants, farmers, and other common folk who had been trampled down in the rush for wealth and power. *Panic* (1935), a verse play, gave a vivid account of the disintegration of a great industrial manipulator as his financial empire collapses. And *Public Speech* (1936) presented MacLeish's critique of the times in the form of a collection of short poems.

MacLeish warned against the spiritual numbness of the age. Those who would reform, as well as those who were simply downcast, had lost through discouragement a vital sense of beauty and, hence, of true optimism. In "The Social Cant," an article appearing in the *New Republic* in 1932, MacLeish emphasized the need for "poetry" in the reformed society that is sure to succeed the present sick state of affairs. Too many prophets of the coming order, he warned, were ignoring the esthetic qualities of life in their fervor for social planning and for war against the inequities of the Old Order. In this crumbling industrial world, MacLeish contended:

> The answer will depend upon the view to be taken of the nature of Industrialism. For the social critic, whether he so realizes or not, rests his whole case upon certain industrial hypotheses. . . . But the justification of his belief he has never established. And for one good and sufficient reason. Which is that no one, engineer, scientist, philosopher or literary critic, has as yet succeeded in discovering what exactly the thing called modern industrialism is. . . . These are the prophets of planned economies and Marxian-socialism-cum-twentieth-century-machines. The geography of industrialism is irrelevant to them because they will shortly change it. But all the available evidence suggests that industrialism is itself organic, a product of life which has long since passed beyond human control; that plans for the limitation of pro-

duction in the interest of economic balance must fail in the future as all similar attempts to truncate an evolutionary process have failed in the past; and that the greatest danger to our civilization proceeds from our inability to chart the slopes and courses of the land in which we must continue to live.[67]

Those final lines, lambasting pragmatic hopes for planning society, touched the heart of MacLeish's social outlook. He was highly skeptical about the ability of any scheme or ideology to revolutionize a society built upon firm values of long duration, and in that spirit he sharply attacked Technocracy and other mechanistic panaceas.[68] Yet he remained optimistic. The same tradition that inhibited revolutionary change also encouraged, through its espousal of democratic freedom and progress, a continuous advance in the civilized virtues. Holding that faith in his own inheritance, MacLeish was impatient with the supine willingness of many in his generation to submit to foreign, determinist concepts of society. American radicals, particularly, had taken on a sour, negative air. While they rightly attacked war, they were often guilty of unjustly sneering at those who died in wars, especially the First World War, as mere "victims."[69] In the same way, radicals had lost their perspective on capitalism and Republicans. To be sure, MacLeish was glad to grant, "it is a pleasure—almost a duty— to hate them." But too often radicals failed to take themselves beyond the morbid joy of shaking their fists at the enemy.[70]

The American democratic tradition calls for Utopian thinking, MacLeish felt. He urged his countrymen to believe that they could build castles in the air and then live in them. The contrary beliefs that life is simply drift or that iron laws of nature govern the future leave the individual prey to either the reactionaries on the one hand or the Marxists and kindred totalitarians on the other.[71] What mattered most for Americans was to realize the uniqueness of their New World tradition and the freedom of action it proclaimed.

The contrasting view of American tradition as part of a more ancient European tradition was presented with passionate force by the novelist and social critic Waldo Frank. Frank's early immersion in European literature and philosophy gave him a special calling for the task. Born in 1889, the son of a serious and prosperous Jewish businessman, Frank spent his childhood in the genteel isolation of the Upper West Side of

New York. His father stressed rational, intellectual values and in that spirit abandoned Judaism for the more worldly doctrine of Ethical Culture. Yet even he was alarmed at the ferocity with which young Waldo devoured the writings of European and American philosophers, psychologists, social reformers, and novelists and then proclaimed original, nonconformist doctrines that he intended to elevate into personal philosophies.

After graduating from Yale in 1912 with a strong academic record and the manuscript for a book on French literature, Frank went to Paris not to escape but to work at becoming a professional writer. Significantly, he chose to move in wholly French circles rather than within the orbit established by Gertrude Stein, Ezra Pound, and others of the early American expatriates.

Frank returned to New York in 1913 with an idea of becoming a playwright. But he soon abandoned that ambition to join the invigorating work of cultural renewal he found expressed in the famous Armory Show of modern art and several new journals of ideas. They were "days of the Phoenix," as Frank's friend, Van Wyck Brooks, recalled them, and Frank had chosen to help raise American culture up from the ashes.[72] In Paris he had listened to expatriates gibe at America's low stature. He also heard the judgment of the ancient Anatole France that Europe was all past and America all future and decided that France was right. America was at "sea level," ready to ascend, and Frank concluded that his great opportunity waited at home.

With that formidable vision before him, Frank joined with Van Wyck Brooks, Randolph Bourne, and others on the *Seven Arts* and found exhilaration in his own writing and in helping advance the careers of such writers as Sherwood Anderson, John Dos Passos, Eugene O'Neill, and D. H. Lawrence. Frank also drew inspiration from the studio of the great photographer and art impresario Alfred Stieglitz. Apparently Stieglitz exerted a force of personality that only those who knew him could fully appreciate. But to the extent his great presence derived from a fusion between his own being and the finest possibilities obscured in the tumult of American life, his artful photographs indicated the scope of his achievement. Stieglitz' beautiful work showed how one might use the machine to express a personal artistic vision and showed also, as part of the same transformation, how the plain facts of life could be rendered into art. Stieglitz served the unifying purposes of the liberal traditionalists by capturing photographically—not abstractly—canons of universal human excellence in America that might with dedicated effort be made the conscious guides of social policy.[73]

The yield from Frank's associations was distilled in *Our America* (1919). There Frank argued against American Puritanism as a corruption of the original Reformation desire to reach mystical accord with a personal God. Under frontier conditions, Frank charged, the pioneer was pressed to abandon his old unifying religious mission in order to meet the many demands of survival. "He had to abhor Wholes, in order to be equal to the infinite detail of his existence."[74] And as the commitment to an organic culture faded amid fragmented effort and ambition, practical reason became king. Culture reemerged as a commodity—the five-foot shelf—and pragmatism became the official American philosophy. Frank did not scorn pragmatism, just as he never rejected America the way many of the more romantic and shallower intellectuals of the day were inclined to do. He granted pragmatism's liberating effect in refuting the stuffy pretensions of the genteel tradition. "But when it came to the next task of creating values of our own," Frank continued, "[pragmatism] emerged from its panoply of liberal phrases as a mere extension of the old pioneering mood. . . . Reason becomes the ding an sich, the absolute that the pragmatists pretend so piously to abhor. Desire—the emotional and esthetic and spiritual capacity of man—is Reason's servant."[75] And in the end, pragmatism was used to support unworthy ends. "The backswoodsman needed a rationale for pressing on: He needed to make the bitter sacrifice of self, the sacrifice of culture, in order to carry through the job of his Age—the unfolding of the American empire."[76] With variations of intensity and objects of concern that judgment of American tendencies remained the key to Frank's critical outlook.[77]

A series of novels in the 1920's, which Frank termed "lyrics," developed Frank's mystical sense of tradition.[78] His point of view— essentially a Neoplatonic belief in the oneness of humanity—emerged at an inauspicious time. Frank's summary analysis of American culture, *The Rediscovery of America*, was published in 1929, at a time when intellectual interest centered on the contest between the prevailing Babbitt spirit of business boosterism and the opposing radicalism, with strong overtones of Marxism, that was just beginning to gather momentum. In the face of totalitarian danger ten years later, Frank's appeals to tradition had bite. But in the sleek twilight just before the Crash he had little success in persuading his countrymen to exchange a pragmatic, materialist outlook for belief in a great spiritual tradition standing as the source of all social wisdom. Still, for those who would notice Cassandra, there were useful premonitions. Frank warned against the tradition of violence being fostered by repression of minorities and by an excessive dependence on material goods. Society, he concluded, "is being prepared, in the inevitable day when prosperity droops or trouble rises, for violence against itself. A folk that learns no control *except the economic* will lose all control when the economic security for some reason falls. That is why I say that we are literally sowing a whirlwind of blood." [79]

Sidney Hook, whose philosophic and political views were an amalgam of the two strains of thought that dominated the thirties, Marxism and Deweyan pragmatism, criticized Frank's view of the whole as culturally illiberal: It sought a single standard of patriotism that would obliterate minority differences, and by urging an overriding attention to the needs of regenerating the inner self, it would cripple attempts to provide collectivist reforms.[80] Frank, in rebuttal, pointed to the key difference between his liberal traditionalism and the pragmatic rationalist social planning approach. The planners stressed economic security and equality of opportunity as the base from which individual development would proceed. Frank insisted that the transformation of individuals must come first. "To believe that society can be transfigured without transfiguring the dead psychic patterns which have evolved the social structure which makes revolution necessary is naïve Utopianism." [81]

Frank's doctrine of the Whole placed him in explicit opposition to the concept of the melting pot, which he considered a weak surrender to conformism, and Kallen's doctrine of cultural pluralism, which he believed to be divisive. Kallen, like Frank, spoke of the need to "symphonize" America's motley population but, in Frank's view, Kallen failed to appreciate the need to have an overriding doctrine to conduct the symphony." [82] Lacking a clear idea himself of exactly what form that overriding doctrine should take in America, Frank spent the decade of the 1930's in a restless search that helps illuminate the difficulties the Great Traditionalists had in clarifying their views.

The economic crisis inspired Frank to become socially active and responsive to the Communist appeal. In 1931 he marched with intellectuals and Communists protesting mining conditions in Harlan County, Kentucky, and returned home battered and bandaged after a beating by mineowners' hired toughs. That same year, in the wake of considerable publicity given him by the press and the Communists for his battle scars, Frank left for a tour of Russia. His account of the Soviet Union in *Dawn in Russia* (1931) showed the ambivalent view toward official Soviet Communism that characterized all his relations with the Communists until he broke with them at last toward the end of the decade. Frank admired the Marxian ideal of communal oneness and equality. But he showed dismay over the officious Soviet interference with every aspect of the citizen's life and the insistence on rigid adherence to the party line.

Frank's own hopes for Communism were unique and rather romantic —departures from hard Leninist doctrines that, like many other deviations by American fellow travelers, found brief tolerance while the Popular Front prevailed. In 1933 Frank first outlined his rather remarkable views. He wished to fuse the wisdom of Marx and Spinoza into one program. First, using the economic warfare detailed by Marx, the oppressed lower classes would enact a social revolution to establish an equitable society. Then, with material conditions rectified, Frank would have society turn to Spinoza's vision of godliness to fulfill spiritual needs.[83] That affinity between Spinoza and Marx had been stressed by Frank as far back as his *Our America* (1919). He believed that there was a Jewish paradox which Spinoza and Marx symbolized in powerful terms: "God is infinite, and man is lost in Him, yet God must be contained within the consciousness of man. The first clause satisfied the need of abnegation, the second the need of power." Spinoza then provided a philosophic vista on life and the ways of God lying beyond, while Marx appeared to give the vision "form, substance, the passion of organic hope."[84]

Frank's dual concept was far more an expression of loyalty to the idea of a controlling Great Tradition than to Marxism. He showed faith that the ideas of Spinoza—which Frank considered a distillation of the noblest elements of the Western tradition—could make even such a powerful ideology as Marxism its agent. Nevertheless, Frank's militancy in urging Marxist means to attain a spiritual end had pushed him some distance from his earlier insistence that internal regeneration should precede social reform. "The Revolutionary proletariat cannot trouble about God," he stated boldly. "There are good functional reasons for the atheism of the Marxists. The word God has been monopolized so long by the apologists of the class of exploitation: theologians, philosophers, poets!"[85]

Frank's diminished emphasis on contemplation reflected concern over the economic crisis and the threat of Fascism. Further, a dormant sense of Jewishness rose to color his conception of the Great Tradition and to provide vision for a social revolution that must have recourse to distasteful direct action. The long, dark history of persecution seemed to Frank to have left the Jews uniquely fitted to provide guidance. "To be a Jew," Frank declared, "has always meant *to live a certain way:* a way which, evolving with the ages and with the cultural-economic conditions of the lands, was yet an organic growth from a single tradition."[86] Jews have shown an ability to retain a communal tradition in the midst of trying times.

Frank's involvement with the American Communists reached a peak in 1936 when he accompanied Earl Browder on his campaign tour for the Presidency. At that time he made his strongest statement in behalf of the Communist movement in a foreword to André Malraux's fictional attack on Nazism, *Days of Wrath.* Communism, Frank suggested, was the logical expression of the Judeo-Christian concept of equality before God. By contrast, idealization of the free, unaligned individual was the great defect of nineteenth-century liberal thought. That Faustian man—borrowing Spengler's phrase—is "the anarchic false 'atom' released from the break-up of the Medieval Christian synthesis, whose creation (rotten ere half ripe) has been the culture of bourgeois industrial democracy."[87] In that spirit Frank entered the second half of the decade. The tragic events in Spain and the approach of general European war had yet to exert their full force in making reformers reconsider the spiritual and practical nature of their collectivist hopes.

4. The Approach to War

As the world moved toward total war after 1936, liberal traditionalists moved away from enthusiasm for particular collectivist programs and began to show a larger and vaguer concern for the national welfare. They became at once more conservative, more troubled about the protection of individuals against the threat of mass power, and increasingly anxious to fuse the elements of America's past into a force that could successfully combat Fascism. Regionalism and cultural pluralism, as they became more national in scope, relaxed their emphasis on the particular traditions, customs, and qualities of subgroups within American society. Their enthusiasm for pluralism declined, and with it went their programs for federative reforms.

The Distributist movement was the most emphatic casualty, disappearing entirely between 1936 and 1941. Allen Tate, who came into the movement from an earlier commitment to separatist Southern sectionalism, lost his faith in the possibility of any form of collectivist reform and moved on to an absorbing interest in esthetic literary criticism that weighed the merits of writing with almost no reference to its social import. Herbert Agar published infrequently in the time from *Who Owns America?* down to the outbreak of war in 1939. Then he began an active career of urging active American support for the Allied cause.[88] Distributism vanished as a firm and separate program in his writings. What vestiges of it remained were intended to help guide the preservation of democratic practices, not to lead a social reformation.

Agar's most noted book, *A Time for Greatness* (1942), summarized his mellowing views. Not radical change, but fealty to traditional American and Christian virtues on an international scale gave the greatest promise for rebuilding the world on a sound basis after the war. The great error of intellectuals in the 1930's, Agar charged, was to reject the possibility of extending liberal democracy throughout the world merely because Wilson's efforts to do so were such a demoralizing failure. Now the time had come to exalt the spiritual over the material, to shake free of the cynical toughness of the economic determinists and the planners. We must recognize, repentantly, that "the idea that our great culture—freedom and science and respect for the divine in man; Judaism and the Christian Church and the classic passion for clarity—the idea that all this is a by-product of economic progress is the heresy that helped bring Nazism and the Axis barbarity into our world."[89]

Planning, within the context of Agar's heightened sensitivity to individual and spiritual considerations, took on a somewhat sinister aspect. "The men who once believed in NRA," he declared, "have either abandoned the idea of over-all planning in a democracy, or they have accepted the doctrine of compulsion—even if they dare not admit to themselves what compulsion means."[90] Agar still held to the value of democracy based upon widely distributed property. He pointed to the hysteria of the American upper classes in time of crisis and contrasted that to the calm of the British upper classes as evidence that the latter, with their social positions based upon traditional landholdings, had a far firmer basis for feeling secure and self-respecting than did their American counterparts, whose lives were propped up on foundations of paper finance. But Agar no longer called for a Jeffersonian social revolution. Rather, he contented himself with supporting moderate regulation of industry along the lines set down by Thurman Arnold and Leon Henderson in the TNEC reports.

Howard Odum at the end of the decade showed a similar willingness to dissolve specific, novel programs within a larger and vaguer expression of concern for the national welfare. His book *American Social Problems* (1939) went further toward fixing all of America in its regionalist sights than his earlier study, *Southern Regions of the United States*, had done. Notwithstanding its massive compilation of data, *American Social Problems* proved to be less specific in suggesting remedies for social ills. In *Southern Regions* Odum had mapped out a plan for regional planning coordinated through a centralized federal planning commission. In the later book he announced in general terms that "one implication of regionalism may well be the opposite of the present tendency toward urbanism, centralization, and the concentration of power and wealth. If, as we have pointed out, cultures grow from beginnings outward, the margins of bigness are the occasion for redistribution."[91] Odum expressed alarm over the growing threat of irrational mass society of the sort decried by Ortega y Gasset in *The Revolt of the Masses*. Hitler, like the Russian revolutionaries earlier, was showing the dismaying possibilities for wielding peasants into a power base through adroit propaganda and terror. In the United States, Odum warned, a comparable mass of farmers and workers was stirring restlessly. Better educated and more alert than the European lower classes, these people nonetheless, in view of their wide diversity and earlier silence, raised valid questions: "Who and of what sort are these people whose voices are being raised more and more, oftener and oftener, in an ever-extending range of inquiries and complaints; and whose patronage becomes increasingly important for ruler and leader; and whose restlessness appears itself as a major social problem in many parts of the world?"[92] Quite logically, Odum concluded that most "pressing and vivid in the midst of all the dramatic episodes of world events of the 1930's and especially in the American scene is the perennial question as to whether democracy will survive, whether the democratic nations can hold their own in a world threatening dictatorship, and whether society can find the happy margin between governmental control and governmental service."[93]

Odum shaped *American Social Problems* on the assumption that America was in the midst of a transition so sweeping as to have thrown all aspects of American life into confusion. "The hypothesis of this discussion," he announced flatly, "is that the present gross inequalities and chaos are due to failure to achieve orderly transition from the old America to the new, and that in all probability the motivation and the attainment of such orderly transition in the present period will constitute the sole definitive democracy of the next few years."[94] Odum saw several exits that Americans might conceivably take from their predicament. At one extreme is the possibility of violent revolution. "In America the catalogue of possible constituents here is relatively long. In the nation at large there are agrarian discontent, labor restlessness, minority groups, and the intellectual discontent of the professional agitator. In the regions roundabout there are the Negro, other minority groups, the disinherited tenant or miner, the industrial worker, the local demagogues, and the extra-regional agitator." Then, he continued, "on the other side is the movement toward fascism and dictatorship."[95] The appeal pragmatic rationalists had been making for a third road Odum dismissed as a "mass and messianic current which sweeps along a mixed company of idealists and discontents, . . . playboys, super-technologists, who seek new experimentation every morning, new games of human direction every night. With little economic or cultural back-ground, they appear oblivious of the fact that there has been a past, or that society evolves through equilibrium and balance."[96] Odum con-cluded with an appeal for moderate, decentralized regional planning. Unhappily, "the exact form of democratic organization strong enough to meet the needs of our present confused American civilization does not now exist. It is, therefore, the task of the social sciences and their techniques to help discover the basis and form for such organization."[97] Even with that endorsement of social science, Odum's suggestions for planning made at various points throughout the book seemed defensive, a hope for carefully constructed barriers to protect citizens against an engineered society. He closed on a doubting note, stating that "the technological backgrounds from which many of our social problems arise may be approached by stating that the complaint is frankly against the dominance of technology and bigness over human welfare and social evolution."[98]

Odum's subsequent research, resulting in *Race and Rumors of Race* (1943), further illustrated the increased stress he, in common with other liberal traditionalists, was placing on individual rights. More and more reformers were declaring the need for caution in large-scale planning lest the reforms effected by radical change amount to less than the havoc caused by disrupting settled customs. While berating Southerners for their cruel efforts to keep the Negroes down, Odum showed alarm over the attempts of outsiders in recent years to invade the South and force drastic changes in the race relations of that area. Such militancy, Odum felt, would only hamper the work of responsible white Southerners and conscientious Negroes to make beneficial changes within the bounds of a social system worth saving for the depth and intensity of the communal bond it sustained. Of course, Odum's plaint could be considered that of one more white Southerner of his generation resisting substantial change. But it is of larger interest because it was markedly more conservative in its approach to equality than the strong disclaimer of racial prejudices that he had made in *American Social Problems*. Furthermore, Odum's shift of direction from economic and political questions to an analysis of the sensitive human questions of Negro life indicates closer attunement to matters of individualism and tradition.

When he did resume writing on regionalism in *The Way of the South* (1947), his discussions of economic and political issues was strongly tempered by a romanticized regard for the individuals comprising the regions under scrutiny. In a lyric tone he had not displayed in his sociological writings before, Odum closed the book with an assertion that "if we have mixed the swing and rhythm of *Rainbow Round My Shoulder*, *Wings on My Feet* and *Cold Blue Moon* with the hard reality of regional development and social theory, this still reflects the mixtures of 'the fruits of society . . . the wrestle of evil with good . . . the models departed, caste, myth . . . the sounding and resounding,' of 'what all sights, North, South, East, and West, are,' to recall again the universalism of Walt Whitman."[99]

When war drew near, the advocates of the Great Tradition proved to be the most belligerent of all the liberal traditionalists in confronting Fascism. Partly that may have been because they were not as fully absorbed with domestic economic and political concerns as the regionalists; nor were they as defensively minded as the cultural pluralists, whose primary task had been to find a safe haven for the nation's minorities. In any case, they involved themselves vigorously in the great debate over whether the United States should actively intervene in the European war. The major issues at stake were directly in line with their primary concerns: What were the ideals and interests to which the nation should devote itself? Do any of them merit war for their defense?

The two most important organizations that sought to answer those questions and guide America's response to the war were, on the side of intervention, the Committee to Defend America by Aiding the Allies, organized by William Allen White in May, 1940, and on the side of the isolationists the America First Committee, featuring Charles Lindbergh as its most impressive spokesman. Many of the liberal traditionalists were attracted to the White committee, including Waldo Frank, Herbert Agar, Lewis Mumford, and Louis Adamic. Most of those individuals, however, were more militant than White and his closest associates, who tended to be enmeshed in relatively cautious governmental and business circles. The Committee to Defend America made it clear that its intention was to avoid direct American participation in the war.[100] By rushing all aid short of war to Britain, they hoped to be able to save that bulwark against Fascism or, at least, to buy enough time for America to prepare an adequate defense. Although Congress hesitated to follow the committee's recommendations, public opinion seemed to be strongly inclined toward White's position. In May, 1940, polls showed 73 percent of Americans in favor of all aid to Britain short of war. At the same time —paralleling the committee's viewpoint—93 percent were opposed to an immediate American entry into the war. Only 19 percent were in favor of American entry if it became apparent that otherwise the Allies would collapse.[101]

Many liberal traditionalists who were involved with White's committee were not satisfied with the seeming passivity of attempting to hide behind a British shield. In June, 1940, Agar and Mumford joined a citizens' group of thirty in a statement widely distributed to the newspapers urging that America declare war on the Axis at once.[102] White recoiled from that radical suggestion. "By advocating the declaration of war you get about four jumps ahead of my group," he complained. White refused to consider endorsing the statement, protesting that "I cannot afford to seem to be crowding my own mourners at the funeral." [103]

The appeal for direct action resulted in the formation of the Fight for Freedom Committee in 1941. Liberal traditionalists Adamic, Agar, Mumford, Frank, and Van Wyck Brooks lent support to the undertaking, and toward the fateful end of the year Agar set out on a nationwide speaking tour to promote American intervention.[104]

Although not an active member of any of the interventionist committees, Archibald MacLeish provided one of the strongest expressions of the liberal traditionalist position. MacLeish became deeply involved in the drive to invigorate the Great Tradition as an antidote to Fascism at the time when the Spanish Civil War erupted. In 1937 he wrote a vehement appeal to Americans to realize that Fascism was, by the very nature it had displayed in Spain, the mortal enemy of democracy. "As to the argument . . . that those who make common front against fascism are themselves warmakers, indistinguishable from the warmakers of 1917, . . . the answer," MacLeish exclaimed, "is that the war is already made. It is made in Spain." The great error of most critics of intervention is their failure to perceive that this conflict involves civilization itself and has dispensed with the usual rules of diplomacy. Isolationists wrongly "decide that because there have been no declarations of war and because the nations of Europe have not yet mobilized their armies, the Spanish war cannot be the real war against fascism which is foreseen. . . . The weakness of this argument lies in its assumption that the pattern of 1914 fits the facts of 1937. . . . In 1914 the methodical and murderous shelling of the civil population of a Spanish seacoast town by a German fleet would have been an act of war. In 1937 it is not an act of war. . . . The wars of 1937 are not fought by declarations and mobilizations. They are fought in the back streets like the assassinations of gunmen. And for an excellent reason. For they are the assassinations of gunmen." [105]

MacLeish dramatized his concept of the need and ability of democratic peoples to crush Fascism in two verse plays and a movie about the Spanish War that he helped to write with John Dos Passos and Ernest Hemingway. In the play *The Fall of the City* (1937) MacLeish pictured the inhabitants of a nameless European city fearfully awaiting the invasion of a mysterious and, by all accounts, invincible dictator. At last he appears, encased in a terrifying suit of armor. The people grovel before him. Then the narrator who has been relating the train of events discovers the dictator's shocking secret: "The helmet is hollow!"

The metal is empty! The armor is empty! I tell you
There's no one at all there: there's only the metal:
The barrel of metal: the bundle of armor. It's empty!
The push of a stiff pole at the nipple would topple it. [106]

MacLeish amplified his attack on pacifism and defeatism in *Air Raid* (1938). Another mythical city, harmlessly set in a remote mountain region, receives warning of approaching enemy bombers. But the inhabitants scoff at the alarm, reminding the official who urges them to take cover that their city cannot possibly be threatened. It is of no strategic importance. Moreover, all the men of fighting age are away at the time. In the end, of course, the bombers drone overhead and destroy the helpless city. Fascism, MacLeish was reiterating, follows no civilized rules and spares no one.

In the spring of 1940, just as France was collapsing before the Germans, MacLeish unlimbered his heaviest and most famous barrage in the pages of the *Nation*. Titled "The Irresponsibles," his article berated writers for shrinking from their social duty of opposing Fascism. "The men of intellectual duty," he charged, "those who should have been responsible for action, have divided themselves into two castes, two cults—the scholars and the writers. Neither accepts responsibility for the common culture or for its defense." [107] The problem, as MacLeish saw it, was that the experiences of the past had been divorced from the concerns of the present as scholars had retreated from playing active roles in society. "Past is the scholar's country: present is the writer's. The writer sees the present on the faces of the world and leaves the past to rot in its own rubbish. The scholar digs his ivory cellar in the ruins of the past and lets the present sicken as it will." [108]

MacLeish's plea for devotion to a unified, active tradition evoked a vehement response. Reinhold Niebuhr and Stephen Vincent Benét, both believers in the salutary presence of tradition, praised him for his efforts to rally the American people. [109] The chief reviewer for the *New Republic*, Malcolm Cowley, who was at that time undergoing the anxieties of withdrawal from Marxism, insisted that MacLeish had wrongly laid the blame for world crisis at the doorstep of the intellectuals. Many writers had for years vainly tried to stir up support for anti-Fascism, Cowley insisted, only to be defeated by adverse social conditions. In just the mood of defeat that MacLeish found culpable, Cowley concluded that "as a political force, the intellectuals have probably been defeated for this generation, but that is no reason for despairing of the world; it will go on without them." [110] Max Lerner, a democratic collectivist with a milder past infusion of Marxism, joined Cowley in criticizing MacLeish's attack on writers for evils that arose out of iniquitous social conditions. [111]

Another group of critics who were neither Marxist nor conservative isolationists berated MacLeish in bitter terms. Their harsh criticism provided a glimpse at a significant trend toward defensive individualism. Far from "rugged," this individualism was based on disillusionment and sought escape from social commitments. Mary Colum and Burton Rascoe, representative of many who had swung sharply away from an earlier enthusiasm for collectivism, accused MacLeish of trying to promote a new lockstep culture. [112] Instead they urged intellectuals to retain their purity in the midst of increasing conformism by withdrawing into critical freedom.

Waldo Frank agreed with MacLeish's thesis of irresponsibility among artists and writers. But he felt that MacLeish had not penetrated beyond the symptoms. Underlying the failure of nerve in the modern world, in Frank's view, was a general belief in "empirical rationalism." The modern bloodless faith in science and calculating reason had produced schemes for social planning in great number; but when scientific collectivism failed, it carried that bloodless faith down with it. The Marxists, planners, Technocrats, and others of like mind had failed, in their concentration on purely material concerns of the moment, to provide a sustaining sense of unity with an organic past.[113]

In 1940 Frank published a gloomy article attacking liberals for having foisted a simplistic belief in "facts" upon the American mind. Dewey and the pragmatic rationalist social engineers gathered about him were the chief villains in the piece. By failing to appreciate that an intuitive awareness of one's existence and a set of culturally imposed attitudes precede rationality in an individual, the Deweyans dealt in spurious logic that was little better than "a word religion, as fantastic, as exclusive of the organic real and of its experience, as that old Kabala doctrine which made of the letters of the magic name of Jahweh the world's elements. . . . Every great religion, every great culture, . . . were premised on myths that embodied the organic intuition of the race and of the whole man of the race."[114] The most sinister aspect of empirical rationalism, Frank felt, was the encouragement it gave to Fascism by denying the existence of a unified human tradition and, consequently, a sense of moral involvement in the fate of others. What remained was simply a mechanistic interest in the present. Dealing with social issues from such a position could only be a form of aimless tinkering. For that reason Frank was disturbed that the New Deal had not resisted empirical rationalism more vigorously. "The New Deal under Mr. Roosevelt," he charged, "has furthered the collectivizing trend of machine economics; it has done very little . . . to ensure that the bureaucratic control remain with the people. And what of our people? Is their education . . . a sure safeguard against their becoming, when really hard times strike us, the dupes of demagogues?"[115]

In *Chart for Rough Water* (1940) Frank joined the militant interventionists in urging American participation in the war against Fascism. Like them, he insisted that neutrality was impossible. It represented the myth of "rugged individualism"—one of the many myths that swirl through the air in America, which Frank considered "the most idealistic, the most unrealistic nation in the world." Americans must realize that "the world crisis is a revolution and that we are in it." And that involved recognizing that Fascism was a spiritual as well as a military threat. "The truth is," Frank warned, "that the United States has as yet no strong integral resistence to the contagions, economic and ideologic, that lead to war—not as strong resistance as many of the peoples of Europe. The truth is that the United States has as yet no economic-social system, no ethical-intellectual-religious discipline—no WAY OF LIFE to immunize us from the disasters of the present world crisis. The truth is that in our values of business as in the values of humanity by which we actually live, we are not separate from Europe. We have not achieved a true birth, a true independence from the swarming death of Europe." [116]

Frank showed the increasing reaction against collectivism, as well as his concern over America's lack of a firm sense of tradition, in his summary critique of the New Deal:

> During the past seven years the accelerated pace of our revolution has been guided by a gentleman of good will and liberal thoughts named Franklin D. Roosevelt. If a man of the Hoover type had been President, the main steps of the New Deal (including the unbalanced budget) would still have been taken, but perhaps under uglier names. And that might have been a blessing. For Mr. Roosevelt's pleasant ways have misled most of us. He has furthered the collectivist trend of our business and cultural life. . . . He has created no instruments to guarantee that the new forces of control remain permanently in the hands of the people. . . . That would have meant a revolution in *depth*— a growth of the spirit. . . . What Mr. Roosevelt has talked is certain cant phrases of the Great Tradition. What his talk has done is to create a delusion that America was moving organically toward wider social freedom. What his acts have done. . . was to implement government with powers of centralization and collectivization. [117]

At the close of his book Frank offered a spark of hopefulness. Though the prospect of war was frightful, it might provide the shock required to bring radical reform. He was even optimistic enough to talk of a new third party, though in highly tentative terms, disclaiming any strong qualifications as a political prophet. He envisioned a "political party which shall understand Blake's deep dictum that true politics is religion. . . ." Its dedication to the Great Tradition and to a cooperative economy, rather than capitalism, would be deep and binding. Anti-Communist, anti-Fascist, anti-capitalist, the party would be a "synthesis of many political tendencies in our past decades, all of them generous in intention, all of them ineffective because of their shallow sense of man." Idealistic refugees from the discredited leftist parties would be potential recruits. "And among the conservatives, too, there is material for our new political party: those folk sensitive to the organic corruption of the bourgeoisie whose blood is the misery of the poor, who have been unable to go to the left because of the left's arrogant flouting of their religious intuitions."[118] However rhetorical Frank's call for a new party might have been, yet it reflected the feeling among liberal traditionalists at that time that significant change was occurring. Indeed, a new era, displacing the scientific rationalism and materialism of the thirties in favor of intuition and deference to an individualistic tradition, was due to begin.

IV. Lewis Mumford: A Liberal Traditionalist Conscience

Lewis Mumford: A Liberal Traditionalist Conscience

In his long and intense career as a social critic Lewis Mumford has fused many of the elements of liberal traditionalism into a challenging point of view.

A self-made authority on architecture and community planning, he has been a vigorous advocate of regionalism, urging that town and country be tied together into organic units insuring the best use of the resources of distinct geographic areas. In concert with that regional outlook he has shown an impressively realized appreciation of the traditions of Western civilization. In a manner redolent of Henry Adams' homage to Mont St. Michel and Chartres, Mumford has admired medieval culture for the sense of organic unity it imparted to all members of society. Like others of the liberal traditionalists, he has sought to instill some sense of such an organic tradition in America by harking back to the "Golden Day" of American life—the years before the Civil War—when the Transcendentalists and kindred souls were importantly advocating the primacy of spiritual union over the practical, more selfish concerns of the marketplace.

In addition, Mumford spoke for many liberal traditionalists in his criticism of the New Deal as a pragmatic, compromising movement more interested in saving competitive capitalism than in pressing for a new, cooperative social order.

And at the close of the decade Mumford's plea for America to pit itself actively against Fascism echoed the feelings of Herbert Agar, Archibald MacLeish, Waldo Frank, Van Wyck Brooks, and other liberal traditionalists who considered that the issue was primarily moral and did not admit, in good conscience, of any retreat into isolationism.

The ethical questions posed by the Fascist menace seemed to Mumford to display the most glaring weakness of pragmatic rationalism: a selves half blindly to what men *do*. They failed to examine the elements of humane values that surround human events and that, in the final judgment, outweigh them in importance. Consequently, they could accept neither the rigors of war, with all its horrific, irrational trials, nor the alternative of Fascist conquest. Calm reason failed to answer the needs of the situation. And the pragmatic rationalists possessed no firm traditional principles to underwrite the cruel means required by a morally sound end. Mumford closed the Depression period, as America was edging into war, proclaiming to an increasingly receptive nation the need to forge a national unity out of traditional allegiances that overrode any of the claims of science or of sheer reason.

1. Early Years

Mumford was born in Flushing, New York, in 1895 and grew up in modest circumstances on the West Side of New York City. Intense and of an independent mind, he valued his education on the streets, among the habitués of the West Side Tennis Club, and in various city haunts where aspiring writers and assorted intellectuals met, more than his formal training. He attended City College of New York for a time but rapidly became bored with the routine and with course offerings that seemed elementary to his already well-stocked mind. Without ever gaining a degree, he later attended classes at Columbia and then at the New School for Social Research. There he acquired a lifelong admiration for the social analyses of Thorstein Veblen.

At nineteen his discovery of the writings of the Scottish biologist and regional planner Patrick Geddes seemed to him a revelation. Geddes' insistence on the prime virtue of organic unity in human life—the need to fuse intellectual effort with full development of the senses—remained at the center of Mumford's thought. That conviction helped make him wary of abstract rationalist schemes, of ideologies, and of simple creeds that stressed one side or the other of man's nature. Mumford's skepticism about narrow-gauge doctrines reinforced the tendency of his intense character toward isolation and skepticism. Thus, not surprisingly, although he has exercised great influence over contemporary American social thought, he has stood apart from mass movements, as if fearful that subscribing to the thinking of any single group would compromise the integrity of his own all-embracing cast of thought.

Mumford's first writings, in the 1920's, displayed both the regionalism he imbibed from Geddes and a large measure of disillusion with contemporary Western society, such as plagued many in the post-World War I generation. His contribution to the sharp critique of American society edited by Harold Stearns, *Civilization in America* (1922), was not as caustic as many of the other selections, but it did level an attack on the dreary capitulation of city planning to the profit motive.[1]

In the same year Mumford published *The Story of Utopia*, a provocative survey of man's unsuccessful search for the ideal society. Mumford's criticism of past Utopias typified the blend in him of skepticism and radicalism. He was impatient with the romantic impracticality of many Utopian thinkers. But he did not disapprove their efforts because they had gone too far in their prescriptions for change. Rather, "if the story of utopia throws any light upon the story of mankind it is this; our utopias have been pitifully weak and inadequate; and if they have not exercised enough practical influence upon the course of affairs, it is because . . . they were simply not good enough."[2]

In his distinction between the two basic types of Utopias that had been proposed throughout the history of the West—the Utopia of reconstruction and the Utopia of escape—Mumford suggested a theory of historical change that he was to outline more thoroughly in later writings. During the Middle Ages, he claimed, Utopian thought was incorporated into the normal proceedings of society in the form of the dominant Christian theology. Man's imaginative life, his hopes, and his workaday place in the world were united into an organic pattern of life.

The Utopias the medieval man envisioned would join elements of prevailing reality that he observed in this world with imagined elements that he believed were equally real facets of the supernatural realm of God. Although they directed men's eyes beyond their own physical surroundings, those Utopias were not escapist. They comported with the facts of the universe, as the medieval mind conceived it, and thus sought to reconstruct the world, not deny it. Vaulted, like the cathedrals it decreed, the religious imagination of the Middle Ages could contain soaring hopes within a mood of practical realism.

But as Europe moved into the Renaissance and men more and more came to make sharp distinctions between the various aspects of life and thought, Utopian ideas became detached from everyday existence. Division complicated a number of key areas: The life of the mind came to be considered distinct from the life of the senses; similarly, the *natural* was abstracted from the *supernatural* and personal concerns separated out from social concerns.

One response to that disturbing dissociation was an emphasis on

Utopias that would remake society, seeking in a new form the organic unity that characterized the Middle Ages. Necessarily, such Utopias required inventive minds to devise them. That necessity acted as a spur to the great scientific revolution of the sixteenth and seventeenth centuries and cast the mantle of Utopian leadership on the shoulders of the leading scientific figures of the age. Mumford found the Renaissance Utopias impressive, though a little disturbing in their mechanistic overtones: "Campanella with his dream of powerful mechanical inventions, in which he had been anticipated by Leonardo, and Bacon with his sketch of scientific institutes—with these two utopians we stand at the entrance to the utopia of means; that is to say, the place in which all that materially contributes to the good life has been perfected." Well and good. But "the earlier utopias were concerned to establish the things which men should aim for in life."[3]

The final stage of Utopian development, however, seemed to Mumford far more disturbing. The disintegration of organically unified life during the Renaissance moved Utopian thinking from the plane of actual existence to the realm of hope; the industrial revolution moved Utopian thinkers on into despair. "There is a gap in the Utopian tradition between the seventeenth century and the nineteenth. Utopia, the place that must be built, faded into no-man's land, the spot to which one might escape. . . ."[4] The few remaining prophets of Utopias designed to reconstruct society lacked the vision to realize they must transform the dreary, regimented style of life that characterized the new industrial order. Instead, they concentrated on merely changing the system of distributing the material benefits industrialism had to offer. From Marx to Samuel Smiles, "all the utopias of reconstruction had a deadly sameness of purpose and a depressing singleness of interest; and although they saw society whole, they saw the problem of reconstructing society as a simple problem of industrial reorganization."[5] The need to provide nourishment for man's esthetic and moral senses went unnoticed.

European Socialism, Mumford felt, had drawn disastrously on the inadequate notions of these nineteenth-century Utopianists. It failed, as a result, to offer any radically different alternatives to present conditions. Short of advocating revolutionary expropriation and redistribution of property, which few people were willing to undertake, and which the ruling industrial order had been able to thwart by engaging in a limited redistribution on its own, Socialism presented little but slogans and wishful thinking. "It seems plain enough that our radical programs have had simply a sentimental interest: they moved people without giving them a specific task, they stirred them emotionally without giving them an outlet, and so, at best, they are but partial utopias of escape, using the powers of organization, collective meetings, and pronunciamentos to take the place of the emotional stimuli which the avowed utopia of escape, like *News from Nowhere*, supplies by introducing a beautiful girl." Mumford included moderate American political programs in his indictment: "In this aspect, the Socialist Party, with its revolutionary demands, did not differ in its psychological performance from the Republican Party, which specialized in the rhetorical device of the full dinner pail; nor did it differ in any fundamental way from the defunct Progressive Party, which for a time believed in a new heaven and earth to follow the initiative, referendum, and recall with an intensity of moral conviction beside which the social revolutionist was positively tame."[6]

Having sketched the shortcomings of Utopian thinking, Mumford posed a need for educating the public into willingness for radical changes. In that assertion Mumford echoed the widespread skepticism of the 1920's about the level of the common man's ethical and mental powers. Walter Lippmann's *Public Opinion* (1922), following in the wake of Pavlov's famous stimuli-response experiments and the indication by World War I Army intelligence tests of widespread mental deficiency, made a great impact on American social critics by contending with shrewdly reasoned pungency that "at the level of social life, what is called the adjustment of man to his environment takes place through the medium of fictions."[7] Lippmann went on to say that "what each man does is based not on direct and certain knowledge, but on pictures made by himself or given to him."[8] The issue to Mumford was not to free men from such symbolic dependence, which would be impossibly difficult, but to see that the guiding principles proposed were worthy. Society should consider well "whether these images shall be provided by patrioteers, hack editors, politicians, advertising men and commercialized 'artists' or whether they shall be created by genuine playwrights and poets and philosophers. . . ."[9]

That catechistic idea of unity remained an important element in Mumford's thought, recurring mildly or fervently in his various writings depending on the dangers worthy ideals seemed to be facing at the time.

As we shall see, the menace of Fascism provoked Mumford to his strongest appeals for national reinforcement of traditional values, drawing from him bitter insistence that the nation brook no opposition to the maintenance of its Judeo-Christian and democratic ideals and symbols.

Mumford applied his cultural yardstick to the United States during the 1920's in two critical works. The first, *Sticks and Stones* (1924), assayed American culture by examining the nation's architectural record. The second book, *The Golden Day* (1926), followed the more conventional mode of literary and social commentary.

In explaining the unusual avenue of approach taken by *Sticks and Stones*, Mumford paid one of his many acknowledgments to the great influence the literary historian and critic Van Wyck Brooks had upon him. "While a new generation of literary critics, headed by Mr. Van Wyck Brooks, was awakening American interest in the unsuspected richness of our literary past, no equivalent movement was yet visible in architecture."[10] For the task suggested and left open by Brooks, the inspiration of Patrick Geddes was central to Mumford, prompting his observation that discussions on architecture up to that time had failed to convey the full significance of their subject because they had simply taken each work of construction as an isolated example rather than as a part of an organic communal matrix. Mumford aimed instead to study various key societies according to the pattern of buildings they had seen fit to provide for their members. "For this purpose," he stated, "my training had perhaps prepared me better than that of most of my contemporaries. . . ." But he did not neglect to recognize other Americans who were pursuing a similar path. He acknowledged that "my insight into the processes of building was constantly sharpened by association with the remarkable group of architects, engineers, planners and 'geotects'—as our beloved Benton MacKaye likes to call himself—who in 1923 formed the Regional Planning Association of America."[11]

Mumford conceived of American architectural and, by inference, social history as a condensed analogue to the cultural history of Europe that he had traced in *The Story of Utopia*. In his discussion Mumford displayed the antagonism to capitalism and industrial society that was a large part of the motivation behind his career as a social commentator. He divided American history into several periods, distinguishable in character largely by the degrees to which they incorporated a hateful acquisitive spirit and an emphasis on competitive individualism. The analogies to more generally accepted labels for phases of European history were designed to make the distinctions more vivid. At the same time, those analogies were intended to link the development of American life to the unfolding of European values and ideas and so to bring together all relevant elements, American and European, within a single Western tradition. He began with praise for the early organic village pattern of New England in a chapter entitled "The Medieval Tradition." In the following chapter, which he called "The Heritage of the Renaissance," he described the disintegrative effect of growing urban, commercial interests. The typical American settlement after 1800 was no longer a "City on a Hill," animated by desire for communion with a stern God, but an entrepôt for self-seeking traders and manufacturers. In the end "the common concerns of all the townsfolk took second rank: the privileges of the great landlords and merchants warped the development of the community."[12]

By 1890 the class-splintering acquisitive spirit had reached its peak and inspired what Mumford termed "The Imperial Façade." Drawing on Frederick Jackson Turner's analysis, Mumford argued that "by 1890 the frontier had closed; the major resources of the country were under the control of the monopolist; it became more important to consolidate gains than freshly to achieve them."[13] Reformers abandoned pleas for the simple, natural life in isolation, or in small cooperative communities, and accepted large-scale industrialism as an irreversible fact. "The defeat of Henry George as a political candidate was symbolic," Mumford declared: "by 1888 a humane thinker like Edward Bellamy had already accepted the defeat, had embraced the idea of the trust, and conceived a comprehensive utopia on the basis of letting the process of monopoly go the limit, so that finally, by a mere yank of the levers, the vast economic organizations of the country would become the 'property' of the people."[14]

In 1893 a style befitting the new imperium of wealthy monopolists established its dominance at the Chicago Exposition. Newport "summer cottages" sprang up in the imposing form of Roman villas; and in the cities banks, railroad stations, and assorted public buildings were constructed along the even more massive lines favored by the Emperor Augustus when he rebuilt the Forum. The architects of the time "divined that they were fated to serve Renaissance despots and emperors with more than Roman power, and unerringly they chose the proper form for their activities." [15]

Mumford deplored that classical trend as a form of subordinating human needs to materialist whims. Just as the mechanized industrial order of the nineteenth century enslaved workers to their machines, so the imperial style of architecture imposed standards upon the nation without regard to whether they were congenial to the life-styles of the various regions. "Our imperial architecture," Mumford concluded, "is an architecture of compensation: it provides grandiloquent stones for people who have been deprived of bread and sunlight and all that keeps man from becoming vile." [16] The same materialist divorce from a living state of nature showed itself in the late-nineteenth-century mania for collecting. "The museum," Mumford noted, "is a manifestation of our curiosity, our acquisitiveness, our essentially predatory culture; and these qualities were copiously exhibited in the architecture of imperialism." [17]

Although Mumford observed that the twentieth century has witnessed an emergence from the most flagrant callousness toward human needs shown by the dingy, begrimed nineteenth-century industrial centers, contemporary buildings still betray a lack of wholesome connection with human nature. "It is enough to point out that the virtues of the sky-scraper are mainly exercised in technique," Mumford commented in discouragement. "They have precious little to do with the human arts of seeing, feeling, and living, or with the noble architectural end of making buildings which stimulate and enhance these arts." [18]

Any possible breakthrough to a truly admirable plane of life would still involve, in Mumford's reckoning, a radical, even revolutionary change in social concepts and structure. That drastic requirement had cowed most reformers in America. Mumford rebuked them for having sought merely "to work a change of heart or to alter the distribution of income. . . ." [19] "To see the interdependency of city and country," Mumford went on, "to realize that the growth and concentration of one is associated with the depletion and impoverishment of the other, to appreciate that here is a just and harmonious balance between the two —this capacity we have lacked. Before we can build well on any scale we shall, it seems to me, have to develop an art of regional planning, an art which will relate city and countryside in a new pattern from that which was the blind creation of the industrial and the territorial pioneer." [20]

Mumford closed *Sticks and Stones* with a harsh summation of American society. "The pioneer inheritance of the miner," he declared, "coupled with the imperial inheritance of the hunter-warrior, out for loot, lie at the bottom of our present-day social structure; and it is useless to expect any vital changes in the milieu of architecture until the miner and the hunter are subordinated to relatively more civilized types, concerned with the culture of life, rather than with its exploitation and destruction."[21]

The Golden Day (1926) carried the negative side of Mumford's view of America to its peak. Focusing upon literature and art, he drew the bonds between American and European culture even tighter than he had in *Sticks and Stones*. At the same time he showed traces of the idea fostered most conspicuously by H. L. Mencken, Sinclair Lewis, and Van Wyck Brooks that America was a uniquely vulgar land. He castigated America for having adopted the worst features of the Reformation— that dread phenomenon which dominated the last phase of the Renaissance with its cold, clumsy, abstract thought. "The meagerness of the Protestant ritual," Mumford intoned, "began that general starvation of the spirit which finally breaks out, after long repression, in the absurd jamborees of Odd Fellows, Elks, Woodmen and kindred fraternities."[22]

In Mumford's mind those grotesques were not uniquely American but part of an international congregation that had withered under the doctrines of Protestant Christianity. Their features appeared vividly in the persons of the two masters of "Coketown" whom Dickens so bitterly satirized in *Hard Times:* Josiah Bounderby, a pious hypocrite who equated the glory of God with rising profits and did not scruple to sacrifice any number of workers in his factory to such a divine end; and the schoolmaster, Thomas Gradgrind, who had been fashioned, like a piano leg on a lathe, into the perfect design for teaching Coketown's children to accept their bleak environment by fixing their minds solely upon "facts."

Despite his chilly view of nineteenth-century Protestantism, Mumford did not see the development of the American frontier that took place under the auspices of Protestant values as entirely a disaster. For a brief period—"The Golden Day" of American culture—the new nation hung in an exciting balance between the intellectual heritage of Europe and the wild, unknown promise of a new continent. At the height of that brief interlude, the years approximately from 1830 to 1860, "an imaginative New World came to birth . . . , a new hemisphere in the geography of the mind. That world was the climax of American experience."[23]

Emerson, Thoreau, Whitman, and Melville were the leading figures of that American renaissance. They sought a synthesis between the wisdom of the Old World that was becoming increasingly abstract and complex and the brute fact of a New World where thought could not be widely separated from its physical surroundings. Mumford stressed the gap of intellectual complexity between the Old World and the New. He might well have included more extended discussion of the role romanticism, at its peak in the 1830's and 1840's, played in conditioning the American renaissance. Romanticism involved a flight from the growing complexity and abstraction of European culture, which opened a different sort of gap from the one Mumford depicted between Old World sophistication and frontier rudeness. The American romantics consciously, with intellectual depth and conviction, sought to break their ties with Europe and the past in the interests of an uncompromised commitment to their own circumstances.

In Mumford's view, the essence of the admirable work of those directing the American renaissance was mediation. Consequently, "those who really faced the wilderness, and sought to make something out of it, remained in the East. . . ."[24]

The mood of hope of those early days darkened later for two crucial reasons: the Civil War and the fact that the actual process of clearing the American wilderness proved, in its harshness, to have a brutalizing effect on the pioneers involved. That struggle advanced Calvinist materialism at the expense of more humane, esthetic ideals. "In short," Mumford lamented, "protestantism triumphs in a crisis; but it is tempted to prolong the crisis in order to perpetuate the triumph. A humane life does not demand this digging and dogging at the universe; it prospers as well in Eden as it does in the rorty wilderness outside."[25]

In the crass society that developed after the Civil War Emerson, Whitman, Melville, and others who survived from the Golden Day were spiritual exiles. Pragmatism and the apologists for the new industrial order prevailed. "As it turned out," Mumford summarized, "the war was a struggle between two forms of servitude, the slave and the machine. The machine won, and the human spirit was almost as much paralyzed by the victory as it would have been by the defeat."[26] The higher qualities of imagination and spiritual idealism were forced out. For "what is valid in idealism is the belief in this process of re-molding, re-forming, re-creating, and so humanizing the rough chaos of existence. That belief had vanished." The prevailing motto then was: "We must idealize the real." "There," Mumford continued, "was the work of a Howells, a Clemens, a James. It was an act of grand acquiescence."[27]

Acquiescence not only blighted the creative imagination during the Gilded Age but also crippled reform programs. Advocates of a Socialist state suffered from "the assumption that modern industrial society possessed all the materials essential to a good social order."

> On this assumption, all that was necessary was a change in power and control: the Social Commonwealth would simply diffuse and extend all the existing values. These writers accepted the trust, and wanted the principle of monopoly extended: they accepted the bloated city, and wanted its subways and tenements socialized, as well as its waterworks; there were even authoritarian socialists, like Daniel De Leon who believed that the corporate organization of workers, instead of being given added responsibility as guilds, would disappear entirely from the scene with the Socialist State.[28]

In a return to his criticism of the halfway nature of most Utopian thought in history, Mumford insisted that "what was lacking in such views was a concrete image of perfection: the 'scientific' socialists distrusted utopias, and so made a utopia of the existing order."[29]

If anything, in Mumford's eyes, the situation after the Gilded Age, which William James reflected in thought, became worse. James came to maturity in the late nineteenth century as the pioneer spoliation of the West was reaching its crescendo. By the end of the century, when the frontier had finally been exhausted and a period of consolidation had gotten under way, the industrial system was fastening its grip on a population with fewer and fewer avenues of escape, even to the lusty barbarism of pioneer life. "The pioneer, at worst, had only been a savage," Mumford remarked, "but the new American had fallen a whole abyss below this: he was becoming an automaton."[30]

The drift toward mechanized living displayed itself in the writing of twentieth-century social critics. "William James had a style," Mumford conceded. In contrast, "Dreiser and Dewey, the commanding writers of the Chicago school, . . . had no style: they wrote in a language which, however concrete its objects, was as fuzzy and formless as lint. . . ."[31] The implications of such esthetic numbness were tragic to Mumford, suggesting an inability to experience the whole of life. "Style," Mumford declared, "is the indication of a happy mental rhythm, as a firm grip and a red cheek are of health. Lack of style is a lack of organic connection: Dreiser's pages are as formless as a dumpheap: Mr. Dewey's pages are as depressing as a subway ride—they take one to one's destination, but a little the worse for wear."[32]

Despite his scorn for Dewey's style, Mumford reckoned him a major figure in American thought—and a perplexingly many-sided one. He felt that "Dewey's philosophy represents what is still positive and purposeful in that limited circle of ideas in which the American mind was originally born; he is at home in the atmosphere of protestantism, with its emphasis upon the role of intelligence in morals. . . ."[33] To be sure, Dewey was woefully deficient in matters of feelings and aesthetics. "This aspect of Mr. Dewey's instrumentalism is bound up with a certain democratic indiscriminateness in his personal standards; a Goodyear and a Morse seem to him as high in the scale of human development as a Whitman and a Tolstoi. . . ."[34]

And yet, "in spite of all these opacities, it would be absurd to ignore the great service that instrumentalism has performed; for it has crystallized in philosophic form one of the great bequests of science and modern technology: the respect for cooperative thinking and for manual activity —experiment and invention. . . ."[35] In his grudging praise of Dewey, Mumford stressed the moral aspects of technology's relationship to science. Technology was wholly neutral, capable either of notable service or notable destruction. Those who aspired to leadership in science were like the sorcerer's apprentice, with a great, witless servant on hand whom they had to train to serve man's true interests.

But what, to get to the heart of Mumford's case, comprises the true interests of humanity? Mumford's answer to that question, never directly given, can be discerned by drawing several of the strands of his thought together. The fact that those strands will not completely mesh is significant indication of an ambiguity, bordering on contradiction, in his judgment of society and values.

Mumford's first appraisal of contemporary technology, in an article entitled "Machinery and the Modern Style" (1921), gave a cautious endorsement to the prevailing uses of the machine. He joined many who believed that the World War experience in effectively mobilizing industry to achieve large goals, albeit destructive ones, could be translated into peacetime mobilization to raise the general standard of living. Many American economists cheerfully entertained the same notion. And even the speculative philosopher Horace Kallen was moved temporarily to leave his concern for cultural relations between minority groups to praise the direction business and technology seemed to be taking in postwar America. [36]

But after his association with Patrick Geddes in New York in 1923 and studying machine-ridden civilization, with Geddes' aversion to it in mind, Mumford adopted a very critical tone toward the role of technology. [37] His former optimism did not altogether dissolve, however, and his subsequent comments on the problems of technology in society fluctuated ambivalently between drastic attacks against the mechanization of life that had proceeded from late-nineteenth-century industrialization to pleas for the increased fusion of technology with human life for the purpose of enhancing human control over nature. The latter approach had an element of stoicism in it. When he proposed a greater infusion of technology into human life, Mumford was arguing not simply for greater efficiency but also for recognition that great technological complexity was the inevitable lot of modern society and should be realistically adjusted to.

So, in short, Mumford moved restlessly back and forth between two classic poles: distrust of technology as a distorter of human values, in the style of Ruskin, and on the other hand, belief in the natural harmony between technology and creative human instinct, as Veblen preached. At no point did Mumford stake out a firm claim at a definite point on the ground between, though Geddes' influence drew him strongly toward the Ruskin extreme.

From the time of his first book on architecture and regional planning, *Sticks and Stones* (1924), Mumford persistently charged that the acceleration of technological change has been accompanied by the use of that change to lead human society away from the natural workings of the environment. True science, developing its corpus of wisdom by observation of nature and experimentation, as Dewey implored, would seek to keep human beings within a close organic connection with nature. Full organic connection, Mumford insisted, required cooperative understanding; and that quality necessarily worked to restrict selfish gain and the oppressive control over others that was its partner in crime.

Relating his view of proper harmony among science, technology, and environment to American culture placed Mumford in a rather awkward critical stance. In *The Golden Day* (1926) he lauded the achievements of the New England renaissance of the 1830's and 1840's. Five years later in *The Brown Decades* he reiterated that praise, likening those years to a "few warm weeks" of "leafing and efflorescence" between the bleak wintry Puritanism of America's early years and the brown, sordid autumn of the years after the Civil War when the nation was subjected to rapid industrialization.[38] But Mumford's culture heroes of pre-Civil War America were not advocates of an organic unity based on the proper use of science and technology. Rather, they were closer to the classic Romantic position, urging the achievement of personal integrity primarily by the use of intuition rather than the scientific methods of observation and experiment. They sought to resist the collectivist tendency of the machine, along with the eighteenth-century rationalism that lay behind it. Emerson scorned the tendency of refined societies "to detach the beautiful from the useful." But his contrary hopes for organic unity related to art and nature, not to complex technology, which he seldom discussed except in terms of its distortion of what existed freely in nature. Mumford could only take the spirit of Emerson's organic hope, shared in slightly altered form by Thoreau and others of the Transcendentalists, and hope to accommodate it to the alien world of technology. Further, without examples of cooperative societies based on science and technology to draw from history, he could only suggest that such might be done in the future. Mumford's tenuous effort to tie the Emersonian spirit to his own vision of an unrealized utopia was further weakened by Emerson's individualism, which was often quite skeptical of communal reform. In one of his most celebrated decisions against communal enthusiasm the Concord sage once refused an invitation to join Brook Farm. To his friend George Ripley he defended his position simply: "I do not," he declared, "wish to remove from my present prison to a prison a little larger."[39]

Mumford was far from the cynicism of many other social critics of the time. His attacks on many aspects of American culture were sharp. But he tempered his criticism with hope for the future. Mencken and his camp followers sneered at the great, incorrigible American booboisie. Mumford, in contrast, got angry with stupidities because he expected better from the people who perpetrated them. Though he deplored the power industrial materialism exercised over the country, he could conclude, optimistically, about their philosophic pretensions that "the pragmatists have been defeated, these last few centuries, because they have not searched for the kingdom, the power, and the glory together, but have sought to achieve power alone. . . ."

> And our generation, in particular, who have seen them fall back, one by one, into commercial affairs, into administrative absorption, into a pained abandonment of "reform," into taking whatever fortune thrusts into their laps, into an acquiescence even more pathetic, perhaps, than that of the disabled generation which followed the Civil War—our generation may well doubt the adequacy of their complaisant philosophy.[40]

A final passage, aptly entitled "Envoi," foreshadowed the reformist enthusiasm that was to burst wholesale onto the American scene in the 1930's. Mumford saw long-smothered human hopes and emotions breaking through the dreary pragmatic acquiescence. Already hints of a possible new order, celebrating values akin to those of "The Golden Day," had appeared:

> Is Robert Frost the evening star of New England, or the first streak of a new dawn? Will the Dewey who is struggling to step outside his old preoccupations influence the coming generation, or will the more passive and utilitarian thinker continue to dominate? . . . What is the meaning of Lindsay and Sandburg and Mrs. Mary Austin? What is the promise of regional universities like Nebraska and North Carolina and New Mexico? May we look forward to a steady process of resettlement . . . ? Allons! the road is before us![41]

2. The 1930's

a. The Elaboration of Mumford's Theory of Civilization

Mumford's characteristic hopefulness surged upward after the Great Crash of 1929. The capitalist system and the pragmatic temper that supported it seemed to have failed, as he had predicted they would. The time for the sort of truly comprehensive Utopian thought that he had long advocated had arrived. In a statement of "What I Believe," written in 1930 for the *Living Philosophies* series in *Forum*, Mumford declared his radicalism. He had never been a liberal, he declared. Nor, for that matter, did the revolutionary doctrines then circulating arouse his enthusiasm: "If I cannot call myself a revolutionist now, it is not because the current programs for change seem to me to go too far: the reason is rather because they are superficial and do not go far enough. . . . It is a new life I would aim at, not simply a new balance of power. Such a life would leave less of the present world standing than Soviet Russia has left."[42] The new life would replace pecuniary aims with spiritual aims. Like ancient Athens and a host of unrealized Utopias, the community would supply basic creature needs with as much speed and efficiency as possible, thus leaving the greater part of life free for creative leisure. Life would be whole and moral. The moral fiber would hold the individual use of leisure within humane bounds. And the wholeness would lead men to make a vital provision in life for evil and misfortune as well as the happier aspects of life. Mumford made a special point of stressing the force of evil in human life in order to dissociate himself clearly from the naïveté that he considered the curse of many reformers who sought to insulate their efforts from the sordid realities of life. In "What I Believe" Mumford advised a creative use of evil and misfortune to enhance an understanding involvement in life in all its fullness. The utilitarian doctrine, which he accused of equating perfection with satisfaction of animal needs, Mumford condemned as materialistic to the point of being inhuman. His view, strongly colored by Geddes, that the emotions and the mind must be joined, that the entire human personality, not just its rationally justifiable needs, must be served by social reform led him to distrust the pragmatic rationalist emphasis on scientific social engineering. Eventually it lent him support in his decision to join Reinhold Niebuhr, Archibald MacLeish, Van Wyck Brooks, and other interventionists urging American entry into the struggle against Fascism. With his view of the limited place of rationality in human life, he was not utterly shocked to discover that the Fascists could not be approached by reason. Sternly self-assured, he heaped scorn on those who would have America avoid involvement in war as a compromise with evil and unreason regardless of the consequences of allowing a Fascist conquest by default.

Mumford operated vigorously on two levels during the 1930's. Like most intellectuals, he threw much of himself into debating the crucial social problems of the time and suggested solutions for them. At the same time, unlike many of his colleagues, he made provision for continuing creative work that was not contingent on current issues.

Mumford's great enterprise was a series of writings entitled "The Conduct of Life" designed to systematize his ideas on human society into a unified account of the development of Western civilization and a prescription for humane living. True to his training and previous writings, he used architecture and technical innovations as the threads from which to hang his story. The first volume of the series, *Technics and Civilization* (1934), formulated the key theory that modern Western civilization had unfolded in three stages.

The first stage, which Mumford termed eotechnic, lasted from approximately the tenth century up to the eighteenth century. It was the time when the majority of technical inventions basic to industrialism were devised, at least in embryo. Extending from the close of the medieval period through the Renaissance, the eotechnic era was a brilliant chapter in human history. It was also, however, as Mumford had pointed out in earlier works, a time of disintegration. The medieval unity of all phenomena gave way to scientific abstractions that sought to separate existence into small, discrete units that could be conveniently studied and defined.

The physical sciences, so astonishingly advanced by Newton, Copernicus, Bacon, and a great many more notables appearing in climactic profusion in the seventeenth century, contributed most heavily to the abstractive process:

> The method of the physical sciences rested fundamentally upon a few simple principles. First: the elimination of qualities, and the reduction of the complex to the simple by paying attention only to those aspects of events which could be weighed, measured, or counted, and the particular kind of space-time sequence that could be controlled and repeated—or, as in astronomy, whose repetition could be predicted. Second: concentration upon the outer world, and the elimination or neutralization of the observer as respects the *data* with which he works. Third: isolation: limitation of the field: specialization of interest and subdivision of labor. In short, what the physical sciences call the world is not the total object of common human experience: it is just those aspects of this experience that lend themselves to accurate factual observation and to generalized statements.[43]

The implications of that highly practical scientific method seemed clear to Mumford:

> By confining his operations to those aspects of reality which had, so to say, market value, and by isolating and dismembering the corpus of experience, the physical scientist created a habit of mind favorable to all those forms of art for which the secondary qualities and the individualized receptors and motivators of the artist were of fundamental importance.
>
> Machines—and machines alone—completely met the requirements of the new scientific method and point of view: they fulfilled the definition of "reality" far more perfectly than living organisms.[44]

Underlying the great scientific advance toward a machine world, however, was a more basic development. True to the spirit of the 1930's, Mumford identified capitalism as the impetus behind eotechnic development: ". . . to think in terms of mere weight and number, to make quantity not alone an indication of value but the criterion of value—that was the contribution of capitalism to the mechanical world-picture. So the abstractions of capitalism preceded the abstractions of modern science and re-enforced at every point its typical lessons and its typical methods of procedure."[45]

Thus, in opposition to the general opinion that gave the Renaissance its favorable reputation, Mumford judged that "the Renascence was not, socially speaking, the dawn of a new day, but its twilight. The mechanical arts advanced as the humane arts weakened and receded, and it was at the moment when form and civilization had most completely broken up that the tempo of invention became more rapid, and the multiplication of machines and the increase of power took place."[46]

Mumford was most expressive in describing the next period in his progression—the paleotechnic era, which he located roughly between 1700 and the late nineteenth century. That impressed Mumford as a time of consolidation in which the scientific advances of the eotechnic period were translated into industrial machinery and processes. The tendency toward abstraction, begun in the physical sciences, now reached into the organization of society itself. With environment treated as a mere abstraction, concern over the living conditions of those who toiled in the mushrooming cities was slight. Profit and productivity were the guiding abstractions. What remained of humane conscience was largely rationalized away by the doctrine of progress. Since the world is steadily becoming better (is it not?), the argument ran, are the new, booming factories not necessarily good and tending toward greater general happiness?

The self-righteousness, competitiveness, and greed running paleotechnic society had alarming effects, Mumford asserted. Those who questioned the central doctrines were cast into social limbo. Such men as Ruskin, Nietzsche, and Melville, all of whom Mumford greatly admired, were plunged into continually deeper isolation and despair.

Mumford's own appraisal of paleotechnic society was as dark as that of his fallen heroes: "The state of paleotechnic society may be described, ideally, as one of wardom. Its typical organs, from mine to factory, from blast-furnace to slum, from slum to battlefield, were at the service of death. Competition: struggle for existence: domination and submission: extinction."[47] When World War I occurred, it was greeted almost with relief as an end to the great suspense that had hung so long over Europe.

But however grim the dynamics of paleotechnic society may have been, Mumford believed that the system held within it the seed of positive change. Large-scale machine production, he contended, is inherently cooperative in its operations. And in its tendency to shape and use materials with precision and efficiency it is a creator of beauty. Thus:

What remains as the permanent contribution of the machine, carried over from one generation to another, is the technique of cooperative thought and action it has fostered, the esthetic excellence of the machine

forms, the delicate logic of materials and forces, which has added a
new canon—the machine canon—to the arts: above all, perhaps, the
more objective personality that has come into existence through a more
sensitive and understanding intercourse with those new social instruments and through their deliberate culture assimilation.[48]

Following Veblen, but more sanguine than that dour critic, Mumford
posed an antithesis between the natural tendency of the machine toward
efficiency and craftsmanship and the desire of factory owners for profits.
Mumford accepted Veblen's contention that the lords of production had
not hesitated to sabotage production and induce irrational buying in
order to maintain high demand. But, he added, "this warfare between a
sound machine esthetic and what Veblen has called the 'requirements of
pecuniary reputability' has still another side. Our modern technology
has, in its inner organization, produced a collective economy and its
typical products are collective products. Whatever the politics of a
country may be, the machine is a communist. . . ."[49]

Mumford felt that the powerful natural tendencies of the machine
had proven stronger than paleotechnic values. Hence, a new era—the
neotechnic era—has, since the late nineteenth century, substantially displaced the bleak paleotechnic culture. "With the neotechnic phase,"
Mumford explained, "two facts of critical importance become plain.
First, the scientific method, whose chief advances had been in mathematics and the physical sciences, took possession of other domains of
experience: the living organism and human society also became the
objects of systematic investigation. . . ."[50]

Mumford hailed the way the neotechnic penchant for efficiency
promoted the coordination of rural and urban interests: "This marriage
of town and country, of industry and agriculture, was constantly present
in the best minds of the nineteenth century, although the state itself
seemed an astronomical distance away from them: on this policy the
communist Marx, the social tory, Ruskin, and the anarchist Kropotkin
were one. It is now one of the obvious objectives of a rationally planned
economy."[51]

Mumford sided with Odum, Herbert Agar, and others who would
concentrate on unified, scientific planning, rather than with those who
sought romantic isolation in an idolum of the past. "The besetting weakness of regionalism," Mumford contended, "lies in the fact that it is in
part a blind reaction against outward circumstances and disruptions, an

attempt to find refuge within an old shell against the turbulent invasions of the outside world. . . ."[52]

Neotechnic values not only clashed with reactionary regionalism; they also undercut the capitalist system. "We are now entering a phase of dissociation between capitalism and technics," Mumford declared; "and we begin to see with Thorstein Veblen that their respective interests, so far from being identical, are often at war. . . ."[53]

Mumford underscored the criticism of capitalism with a bitter blast at the famous report issued by President Hoover's Research Committee on Economic Changes, *Recent Social Trends in the United States* (1933):

> The dogma of increasing wants, and the division of consumption into necessities, comforts, and luxuries, and the description of the economic process as leading to the universalizing of more expensive standards of consumption *in terms of machine-made goods*—all these beliefs have been largely taken for granted, even by many of those who have opposed the outright injustices and the more flagrant inequalities of the capitalist economic system. The doctrine was put, with classic fatuousness and finality, by the Hoover Committee's report on Recent Economic Changes in the United States. . . .
>
> Horrified at the "utopian" notion of limited and normalized wants, and proudly proclaiming on the contrary that wants are insatiable, *capitalism has not come within miles of satisfying the most modest standard of normalized consumption.*[54]

Mumford's plan for society—which he felt to be consonant with, if not the inevitable result of, the ideals of regionalism, efficiency, and organic cooperation that the neotechnic culture promoted—embodied what he called "basic communism."

> For the better part of a thousand years, widows, orphans and prudent sedentary people have been living at ease, buying food, drink, and shelter, without performing any work for the community. . . . No capitalist talks about this system as one that demoralizes or undermines the self-respect of those who are so supported: indeed, the small incomes of the rentier classes have been an obvious help in the arts and sciences to their recipients. . . .
>
> The extension of this system to the community as a whole is what I mean by basic communism. In recent times, it was first seriously proposed by Edward Bellamy, in a somewhat arbitrary form, in his utopia, *Looking Backward*; and it has become plain during the last fifty

years that an efficient mechanized system of production can be made serviceable to humanity at large in no other fashion. To make the worker's share in production the sole basis for his claim to a livelihood —as was done even by Marx in the labor theory of value he took over from Adam Smith—is, as power-production approaches perfection, to cut the ground from under his feet. In actuality, the claim to a livelihood rests upon the fact that, like the child in a family, one is a member of a community: the energy, the technical knowledge, the social heritage of a community belongs equally to every member of it, since in the large the individual contributions and differences are completely insignificant.

Differentiation and preference and special incentive should be taken into account in production and consumption only after the security and continuity of life itself is assured. Here and there we have established the beginnings of a basic communism in the provision of water and education and books. There is no rational reason for stopping short any point this side of a normal standard of consumption.[55]

Mumford emphatically distinguished his form of "communism" from those proposed by Marx on the one hand and the apostles of industrial management Utopias—men such as Robert Owen and Charles Fourier —on the other. Mumford wanted no part of ideologies. Rather, he considered his recommendations merely the empirical result of looking at the specific needs of men and at society's commitment to machine technology. Mumford's aloofness from ideological systems at a time that made so much of ideology was characteristic of liberal traditionalists and pragmatic rationalists both. His collectivist planning proposals were, similarly, in line with those of other independent liberals of the time. Generally, they sought a unitary state founded on some natural principle —scientific efficiency, coordination of regional resources, ethnic harmony, or the common inheritance of an ancient Western culture—rather than upon an intellectualized system of thought. The abstract absolutism offered by such as the Communists and the Fascists, and, for that matter, by the Liberty League, repelled them in its form as well as in its doctrines.

In that spirit Mumford declared that "basic communism, which implies the obligation to share in the work of the community up to the amount required to furnish the basis, does not mean the complete enclosure of every process and the complete satisfaction of every want in the system of planned production."[56] Mumford saw no need for total central planning. One might well also suspect that he felt an uneasiness about an all-embracing central agency that could make men slaves to its directives, as they had been slaves to machines in the paleotechnic era. Mumford's faith in organic wholeness did not sit well with the rigid living conditions that an engineered society implied. "It is no accident," he bade his readers remember, "that the epic of Moby Dick was written by a common sailor, that *Walden* was written by a pencil-maker and surveyor, and that *Leaves of Grass* was written by a printer and carpenter. Only when it is possible to move freely from one aspect of experience and thought and action to another can the mind follow its complete trajectory. . . ."[57]

That task of unity involved, in Mumford's mind, "a new political and social order, radically different by reason of the knowledge that is already at our command from any that now exists. . . ." As he was to reiterate frequently, and often harshly, in rebuttal of purely rationalist hopes, "to the extent that this order is the product of scientific thought and humanistic imagination, it will leave a place for irrational and instinctive and traditional elements in society which were flouted, to their own ultimate peril, by the narrow forms of rationalism that prevailed during the past century."[58]

Mumford echoed the general fear of reformers at the time that the transition to noncapitalist collectivism would arouse the dual opposition of Fascism and the lords of finance. He conceded the possibility that Fascism and capitalism might merge into a brutal phalanx of resistance. But he remained more hopeful than many observers, particularly those most enthralled with the Stalinist concept of Fascism as the last stage of capitalism, in supposing that leaders of the present order might voluntarily accept leftward change. Monorail belief in economic determinism was, to him, bleak and unconvincing. By the same token, holding to his Emersonian view that the paths of humanity to any good end were many and often hidden from one another, he denied all visions of one inevitable sort of social crisis heralding the final reform solution. Unquestionably, the situation demanded a "revolution." But "whether it shall be humane or bloody, whether it shall be intelligent or brutal, whether it shall be accomplished smoothly, or with a series of violent shocks and jerks and catastrophes, depends to a large extent upon the quality of mind and the state of morals that exists among the present directors of industry and their opponents."[59] They, not some chimerical laws of history, would determine how reform was to proceed. The way they chose to respond to the pressures for sharing their wealth and power with the rest of society would show what actions were needed.

The revolution Mumford contemplated was a rather conservative one. Unlike Dewey and kindred pragmatists, not to mention the more militant Marxists, Mumford felt that the great task of the times was to consolidate and refine the changes neotechnic values had already wrought. The pragmatists declared for constant change in human life. The Communists looked for a hitherto unknown classless society. But Mumford, displaying his respect for Turner's concept of an exhausted frontier, declared that "we are now faced with the period of consolidation and systematic assimilation. Western Civilization as a whole, in other words, is in the condition that new pioneering countries like the United States found themselves in, once all their free lands had been taken up and their main lines of transportation and communication laid out: it must now begin to settle down and make the most of what it has."[60]

At the close of *Technics and Civilization* Mumford outlined the three great requirements for a rationally ordered regionalist society: first, an equilibrium between man and nature, calling primarily for improved conservation controls to redress the paleotechnic era's wasteful exploitation of natural resources; second, an equilibrium between industry in order to place factories near the source of supply for their raw materials, to diffuse the great slum proletariats into more healthful surroundings, and to give rural inhabitants in areas unfavorable for agriculture opportunities close at hand to escape lives of scrub-farming poverty; and finally, an equilibrium in population. In that last area Mumford was particularly optimistic, echoing the common erroneous view at that time that the birthrate in Western countries would decline at such a rate that in the near future population would become stabilized at a permanent, manageable number.

Mumford repeated his vision of regionalist "basic communism" in the second book of the series, *The Culture of Cities* (1938). His scope in that work was narrower than in *Technics and Civilization*, being concerned with the pattern of city growth since the Middle Ages. But he showed, clearly, that his views on cultural development had remained constant. He restated his admiration for the organic concept of life, speaking in praise of the clean, well-planned cities of the medieval period. Ensuing patterns, particularly the neoclassic style, seemed to Mumford, as they had to Ruskin, somewhat sinister. Revered forms of antiquity, austere and uniform, dictated city planning, with human needs and wishes left to conform to the mold as best they could. Paleotechnic towns moved even further from affinity with human life. Failing to provide light, fresh air, or privacy, they embodied an insensate dreariness that could not fail to release the destructive potential in men.[61]

In reckoning the consequences of that history, Mumford showed a more direct concern over the menace of Fascism than he had earlier and, conversely, a stronger sense of identity with regionalist movements in America that were offering a viable alternative. Paleotechnic culture, Mumford declared, fostered a drive for power: Based on competitive industrial greed, shot through with brutalizing slums, the paleotechnic city stimulated a violent spirit. So constituted, "the metropolitan regime . . . subordinates life to organized destruction, and it must therefore regiment, limit, and constrict every exhibition of real life and culture. Result: the paralysis of all the higher activities of society: truth shorn or defaced to fit the needs of propaganda; the organs of cooperation stiffened into a reflex system of obedience: the order of the drill sergeant and the bureaucrat."[62] Nazi Germany, Mumford felt, with its regimentation and its absurd rationalizations of the bases on which the nation rested, was the ultimate caricature of the paleotechnic power drive.[63]

Regionalism, Mumford argued, was more urgently than ever the best answer to present dilemmas. "In its recognition of the region as a basic configuration in human life; in its acceptance of natural diversities as well as natural associations and uniformities; in its recognition of the region as a permanent sphere of cultural influences and as a center of economic activities, as well as an implicit geographic fact—here lies the vital common element in the regionalist movement. So far from being archaic and reactionary, regionalism belongs to the future."[64]

The state of the world impelled Mumford to stress the cooperative implications of regionalism more fully. The rise of aggressive Nazism, along with the airplane's elimination of inviolable frontiers, had made international cooperation essential. Mumford rebutted the antiwar touchiness of many during the 1930's by pointing out that the failure of Wilson's internationalist dreams lay in their faulty execution, not in the concepts themselves. Americans now had a chance—indeed, an imperative need—to assess those errors and set about to realize Wilson's hopes by more workable means. There, once again in the heat of his pleading

Mumford turned to prophecy. Since cooperative reform must come, he seemed to say, it will come. "Originating in this or that region, a local force will rise to universality: co-operation will spread throughout the world. . . ."[65]

Mumford's closer identification with existing regionalist movements showed itself in his praise of such partisans of the cause as Howard Odum, John Crowe Ransom, John Gould Fletcher, and, in a more strictly allusive, literary vein, Vachel Lindsay, Willa Cather, Carl Sandburg and Ellen Glasgow.[66] Perhaps Mumford's specific endorsements of such regional writers was also one sign of his growing attachment to American tradition. A glance at his commentary on American art and architecture, *The Brown Decades* (1931), indicates how his mood had mellowed since 1924, when he wrote *Sticks and Stones*, to a far more favorable estimate of American artistic life, especially as it unfolded in the years after the Civil War.

Though in *The Brown Decades* he still deplored the Protestant ethic and the industrial stampede that took place during the late nineteenth century, Mumford was less given to consider the artistic impulse of the period to have been tied to those forces. The architects Richardson and Sullivan, the artists Ryder, Eakins, and Homer, and such a fragile but resistant flower as Emily Dickinson showed that a drowned river of sensibility flowed beneath the muddy industrial waters. Hopefully the neotechnic period just coming into being would bring those vital forces to a dominant position on the surface.

b. Mumford's Social Activism

Mumford's involvement in the great reform tide of the 1930's was inhibited somewhat by his skepticism of ideologies and also by a tendency to hold himself aloof from other people. Early in his career he moved away from the New York City-suburban Connecticut axis where great numbers of social critics congregated to settle in the isolated upstate town of Amenia, New York. He delighted in the fact that his only son, Geddes, could feel so at home in the wild woodland surrounding the family's home. To outsiders he was difficult to approach. Archibald MacLeish, intellectually a kindred spirit, once remarked ruefully that he had known Mumford for many years but had never managed to ripen that acquaintance into friendship.[67]

At the same time Mumford succeeded in incorporating elements from the programs of many reformers into his prescriptions for society. He stood in the 1930's as the most complete exemplar of the liberal traditionalist position. To his basic commitment to regionalism Mumford joined a plea for basic communism that embodied parts of Rochdale cooperatism, Utopian socialism—in the Edward Bellamy and Henry George mold—and a deepening respect for American moral and esthetic tradition.

Mumford delineated his liberal traditionalist lines of disagreement with Marxism early in the decade in a debate with V. F. Calverton, the editor of the leftist *Modern Quarterly*, in 1931.[68] Mumford advised turning from Marx to a native genius, Henry David Thoreau, as a guide for reformist action movements. He agreed with Waldo Frank that individual regeneration must precede social regeneration and found Thoreau's translation of that premise into a program of civil disobedience to have proven its worth in Gandhi's social revolution in India. Moreover, America could not afford the sort of violent revolution that brought the Bolsheviks to power in Russia. As the pragmatic rationalists were fond of pointing out, Russia had little in the way of developed industry to lose through violent upheaval, whereas American society was delicately balanced on an industrial complex whose destruction in revolution would be a virtually irreparable disaster. America needed consolidation, not violence. In that belief, Mumford praised the constructive work of Americans who had stayed clear of radical shrines and dogmas: Stuart Chase in economics, John Dewey in education, and Benton MacKay in regional planning.

The following year Mumford tied his enthusiasm for native communal traditions to praise for Van Wyck Brooks. Brooks' *Life of Emerson* had appeared that year amid critical hoots from leftists who considered it a bland acceptance of the American past and a hindrance to development of a revolutionary spirit.[69] But Brooks, Mumford insisted, had long been an advocate of basic communism—in a form that was closer to Marx, in its emphasis on the development of the creative and humane springs in man, than the harsh Stalinism of the modern Marxian dogmatists. During the 1920's Brooks' appeals for cooperative communal living had been decried by intellectuals who were then promoting a mood of alienation. Now, Mumford pointed out derisively, many of those intellectuals had swung toward Brooks' position—or beyond it into the ideological gloaming to the left—with understandable resentment toward the man who had first seen the light.[70]

Mumford's basic communism was opposed to the New Deal, as were most of the programs of independent liberalism. An open letter to Roosevelt, appearing in the *New Republic* in October, 1933, accused the administration of indecisiveness, particularly in the crucial area of public works.[71] Optimistically, Mumford hoped that the New Deal would develop a new economic system replacing capitalism. Nothing, he felt, would better discredit capitalism than a vigorous, permanent program of public works geared to establishing a new regionalist pattern of production and distribution.

The following year Mumford published the massive *Technics and Civilization*, which, as we have seen, outlined the new neotechnic life Mumford hoped would displace the crumbling capitalist order. He welcomed a seeming ally in that enterprise the next year when the influential *New Republic* moved from the Progressivism of Herbert Croly toward a more socialistic position in harmony with the spirit of collectivism which was then at its peak.[72] The *New Republic*'s increasingly sharp criticism of capitalism led Mumford to hope that it would help lead the liberal forces, including the New Deal, into communism.

But the New Deal failed to become radical enough, and hopes for a new communal order dwindled away by the end of the decade. In 1936 Mumford published a plea to Roosevelt in the *New Republic*, cosigned by a number of other intellectuals including Suzanne La Follete, Lee Simonson, Thomas Beer, Rockwell Kent, Paul Rosenfeld, and Joe Spingarn, asking him not to dismantle the artists' projects sponsored by the WPA. "There has never been a place in our present industrial system for the artist," the letter protested in futile dismay, "except as a flatterer of the rich and idle, or as a mere servant of business enterprise. If the artist is effectually to serve his community, he cannot depend upon the private patron."[73] The demise of the artists' projects in spite of vigorous protests of their worth from artists and writers contributed to Mumford's disenchantment.

In 1939 Mumford repeated his disappointment with the New Deal's feeble efforts to reform capitalism.[74] But his critical attitude toward the state of affairs in America was far more sharply conditioned by the turn of world events toward war that became dramatically clear at the outburst of the Spanish Civil War in 1936. Mumford's fears of such a tragedy stretched back in apprehension to 1932, when it was becoming likely that Nazism would take control of Germany.[75] A suspicion that the seeds of Fascism lay within American society helped strengthen Mumford's concern for preserving the nation's organic connection with its past ideals. "We in America have had the social experience of Free Land and an Open Frontier and a Fresh Start," he pointed out. "We know the essential human decency of an ungraded community. . . . If we abandon our own revolutionary traditions of liberalism, we will not make matters easier for the orthodox Marxians: we shall simply put ourselves at the mercy of the fascists, who, promising to make every man a king, threaten to make each of us a slave to their childish despotism."[76]

In 1938, disagreeing sharply with the editors of the *New Republic*, whom he had warmly greeted a short time before, Mumford fired the opening salvo in that journal of his campaign to induce the United States to abandon its Neutrality Law shield and aim a strict nonintercourse policy against Fascist ambitions.[77] Mumford elaborated on that idea the following year in a book aptly entitled *Men Must Act*. Gloomily he declared: "There has probably not been a time when the outlook for humanity was so black since the fourteenth century of the Black Death."[78]

To drive liberals away from the paralysis of will that crept over them after the Versailles fiasco, Mumford argued that the ideal of a League of Nations was not only correct but, with all its operating flaws, had still helped to give the world a twenty-year breathing spell between wars. To insure that a new internationalist order would be even more effective he felt it necessary that considerable strength be added to its prerogatives. "One cannot finally do away with war as a mode of conflict without doing away with the pretentious legal myth of unlimited national sovereignty. This means providing both the administrative and judicial services necessary for adjusting national grievances: it also means implementing the decisions of these organizations with an international police force for each continent. . . ."[79]

Firmness at home seemed consonant with firmness abroad. Changing his emphasis somewhat from an earlier declaration of the natural linkage between liberalism and free thought and expression,[80] Mumford announced a policy of partial censorship. "By holding to the abstract principle of free speech without regard for political reality, a doctrinaire liberalism in fact proposes to commit suicide. . . . These abstract virtues are guiding points of the compass. But neither abstract freedom nor abstract honesty are good in themselves: they are good only in so far as they create good men and promote a good society."[81]

The threats posed to American ideals by elements within the Catholic Church—which had tragically allied itself with the Fascists in the Spanish Civil War issue—and certain state and municipal political machines should be forthrightly disputed by the moral authority of a strong federal government. Beyond that, "in cases where the laws of the United States and the safeguard of the Bill of Rights have been suspended by a local fascist organization—as happened originally in Louisiana under Huey Long and has come about again in Jersey City under Mayor Hague—the President of the United States should be specifically empowered by the Congress to declare a state of emergency, and to restore, under martial law, the regular processes of constitutional American government. . . ."[82] Mumford's call for regulation of expression clashed disconcertingly with his earlier pleas for release of human emotions as part of the reform that would reconstruct America. That turn away from openness to restriction illustrated a disturbing aspect of the case for allowing emotion a part in guiding society: What one man *feels* to be truth and virtue may be another man's poison. Mumford made no clear provision for reason to arbitrate such differences. Surely, to the individual caught in shifting currents of emotion that hold him now in, now out of favor, Emerson's dictum that "a foolish consistency is the hobgoblin of little minds" could offer scant solace.

Mumford rejected the idea of a Western Hemisphere economic autarchy being promoted just before America entered World War II by Jerome Frank, Stuart Chase, and other liberals as sheer ostrichism.[83] The days when isolation was practical were over, Mumford contended. Economic complexity had ended the hope of self-sufficiency, and the airplane had opened all formerly defensible frontiers. Moreover, the idea of pulling away from the European battleground where civilized values were in mortal combat with Fascism seemed immoral. Even if America were able to remain aloof, a Fascist victory in Europe would break the spine of Western civilization and leave America a disconnected, atrophying relic.

Mumford's writing during the next year, culminating in the highly charged book *Faith for Living* (1940), pressed his program of anti-

Fascism forward. An article in *Current History* suggested a link between bigness and oppression along Fascist lines. Citing Jefferson, Mumford noted that democracy flourishes best in small areas where neighbors know each other and each other's concerns. [84] Regionalism would diffuse social production and control so as to realize the ideal of localized democracy and would, thus, act as a foil to the threat of Fascism. In "The Menace to the American Promise," an article published the same year, Mumford stressed the traditional factor in his program. "That we have a living tradition is beyond doubt," he proclaimed; "it is that of Thoreau and Whitman and Melville in literature, that of Richardson and Sullivan and Olmsted and Wright in the constructive arts, that of Ryder and Homer in painting, that of Emerson and Peirce and James and Dewey and Royce—the Royce of the philosophy of Loyalty—in philosophy, with a no less redoubtable tradition in the sciences, beginning with Franklin and Joseph Henry."[85]

Successive articles turned from promotion of his liberal traditionalist policy to withering attacks on its opponents. To understand liberalism, he asserted, "one must remember that liberalism has two sides."

> There is an ideal liberalism, deeply rooted in the example and experience of humanity: a doctrine that commands the allegiance of all well disposed men. And there is a transient doctrine of liberalism, the pragmatic side, which grew up in the eighteenth century out of a rather adolescent pride in the scientific conquest of nature and the invention of power machinery: this is the side that emphasizes the utilitarian aspects of life, that concentrates on purely intellectual issues, and that, in its exclusive concern for tolerance and "open-mindedness" is ready to extend its benevolent protection to those who openly oppose the very purposes of civilization.[86]

The social planners and pacifists of the 1930's, he complained, had relied overmuch on reason, discounting the clear evidence of the Christian religious experience, and of psychology since Freud, that emotions inevitably color actions and that evil is an inextricable element in human life. That mechanical one-sidedness, a characteristic result of a machine society where men's lives become matters of rationalized routine, has fostered isolationism.[87] It has relinquished cultural and moral values in favor of the purely material and rationalistic. Thus Mumford felt justified in concluding that "the isolationism of a Charles Beard or a Stuart

Chase or a Quincy Howe is indeed almost as much a sign of barbarism as the Doctrines of a Rosenberg or a Gottfried Feder."[88]

Mumford reached the emotional peak of his traditionalist appeals in *Faith for Living*. By then the war had begun, and the argument over intervention was underway in earnest in America. Mumford quickly joined William Allen White's Committee to Defend America by Aiding the Allies and in 1941 joined the more militantly interventionist Freedom House.[89]

Faith for Living was a companion piece for Waldo Frank's *Chart for Rough Water* and Archibald MacLeish's "The Irresponsibles," with the addition of Mumford's own special emphasis on the pernicious tendency of machine civilization toward war. Mumford, in his anxiety over the precarious state of affairs, adopted a tougher line than either Frank or MacLeish. "If democracy is to preserve its very existence," he warned, "the majority must not scruple to use any necessary amount of coercion upon minority groups who might, if the danger were less, be converted by the slow process of reason, or blandly ignored."[90]

His proposals for national unity had a regimentative ring to them. "First," he declared, "we must erect a common goal of living, sufficient to stir the young out of their lethargy and cynicism and to give new meaning to every life in our democracy. And along with this must go a readiness to scrap swiftly every institutional arrangement, every habit of thought and action, that does not contribute either to the safety of our country, or to the intensification and enlargement of human life."[91] To make such unity functional "there must be a focus for communal attachment, bigger than the family or the city, smaller than the country or all mankind; and the surest source of that sustaining kind of patriotism is the region."[92]

Enthusiasm of such pervasive strength requires an extraordinary attachment to the values involved. Mumford felt that a Civilian Conservation Corps enlisting the services of all youths for at least one year would be of great value in instilling that spirit. But beyond that, the citizenry must face an elemental fact:" In any organic democracy . . . public life must necessarily embrace nearly half of a citizen's existence, day by day, year by year. It cannot be otherwise."[93]

The closing pages of Mumford's book resounded with his view that the world crisis had revolutionized the condition of man. The Utopians with their foolish dreams of a world purged of evil, the pragmatic rationalists appealing only to the mind, the reactionaries wishing to cling to capitalism of the "rugged individualism" stripe—all had been confounded by events. A new era of traditional unity—or else destruction —loomed ahead. In a final thrust at the unenlightened, Mumford declared starkly: "I have made no attempt to trim this argument to meet the objections of those who do not know that a thousand years separate 1940 from 1930. . . ."[94]

V.   The End of an Era

1. Discouragements of 1936 and After

Franklin Roosevelt's smashing election victory in 1936 forced a major revision of hope upon liberals who stood aloof from the New Deal. The pragmatic rationalists felt the strain more keenly than did the liberal traditionalists because they had gone so far in promoting comprehensive formal alternatives to the administration's program.

The major organization of pragmatic rationalists, the League for Independent Political Action, retained its impetus until November, 1936. Other, more marginal groups had succumbed earlier to Roosevelt's steadily tightening grip on popular favor. Upton Sinclair's EPIC movement ran into disaster in 1934 when the support Sinclair hoped to get from Washington for his campaign for governor of California never materialized. At about the same time Technocracy failed as a national craze and declined into a small fringe movement, catering to the angry and disappointed who found in Technocracy's eccentric leader, Howard Scott, the Messianic figure their frustrations demanded.

The League for Independent Political Action, however, professed to find some cause for optimism in the events of 1934. Reviewing the election results, an editorial spokesman declared that the Republican Party had suffered eclipse and that the Democratic Party was being pushed toward a similar discard by the rising new third-party sentiment. Farm-Labor candidates had swept the boards in Minnesota and Wisconsin, and the independent liberal Bronson Cutting had gained election to the Senate in New Mexico by mobilizing reform support against both the Republican and Democratic machines. In California, Upton Sinclair had carried his independent reform banner down to defeat; and the editorial extracted a stern moral for third-party believers from the disaster: "As Sinclair was betrayed in California [by the Democratic Party], so will any other progressive who hopes to find a permanent home in either of the two old parties, be betrayed."[1]

But by 1936 spokesmen for the League had come to see the political wisdom of voting for Roosevelt. Norman Thomas's Socialist program seemed better adapted to America's needs,[2] but the anticipated progressive third party combining rational economic planning with Farm-Labor democratic concepts, had not materialized to give League adherents the reasonable chance for success—meaning at least a large minority of the popular vote—that they had foreseen.

After Roosevelt's victory the League journal, *Common Sense*, reflected widespread awe over the size of the Democratic sweep. A new party to challenge the New Deal now seemed even more remote and its shape more obscure. Perhaps eventually a moderate collectivist party like the British Labour Party would emerge from the wings offering "fumbling reform." Or perhaps a militant, class-conscious worker's party—tinged with Marxism—would come to the fore. Or, hopefully, the League program might at last be brought to fruition through patient education of the public.[3]

At bottom, though, the chances of a strong challenge to existing Democratic power seemed slim to most reform opponents. *Common Sense* suggested its own imminent decline, as well as that of the League, by stating the likelihood that "1940 will be quite similar to 1936, and the popular revolt that should be challenging capitalism itself, will continue to fritter away the time in futile reforms—until 'the Leader' appears."[4] Their words suggested a mood of Messianic despair; but the talk of a "Leader" would seem, in the absence of any effort to find some charismatic figure to promote the LIPA program, merely rhetoric, reflecting the current interest in strong men that Marxist doctrines and the examples of Stalinist Russia and the Fascist countries aroused.

As the third-party challenge was dying, the cause of consumer cooperation enjoyed a brief flurry of excitement. To some extent that enthusiasm filled the void left by the decline of third-party movements. Cooperation was more moderate—and now seemingly more possible —than the task of mounting a full challenge to the burgeoning power of the New Deal. In 1936 the journalist Marquis Childs issued his famous report *Sweden: The Middle Way*, extolling the consumer cooperation movement in Scandinavia. At much the same time Upton Sinclair produced *Co-Op*, a praiseful novel of life in a cooperative state; and a number of other books proposing cooperation appeared, notably *Consumer Cooperation in America* (1936) by Bertram Fowler, the leading publicist for the Cooperative League of the United States, and Horace Kallen's *The Decline and Rise of the Consumer* (1936). Discussion of cooperation was capped in 1937 when the *Annals of the American Academy of Political and Social Science* devoted its May issue to a symposium on the history and merits of consumer cooperation.[5]

But the flurry soon died down after engaging the allegiance of a very few economists and liberals and stimulating only a handful of cooperative enterprises, mostly in the agricultural hinterland where cooperatives had long been a device for small farmers to compete with large marketing concerns. After 1937 only a few scattered writings appeared to grace the sporadic efforts of the Cooperative League of the United States to arouse enthusiasm for consumer cooperation among an indifferent—and independent-minded—public.

The clear import of the situation was that many had come to feel it was no longer sensible to promote radical alternatives to the New Deal. Reform thought was shifting from anticapitalist, collectivist reconstruction to advocacy of moderate change. Significantly, in pragmatic rationalist literature reference to the patron saints of American radical reform, Edward Bellamy, Henry George, and Thorstein Veblen, was declining as more attention was being paid to the great adjuster, John Maynard Keynes.

Adding greatly to the discouragement the unbreakable strength of the New Deal imposed on hopes that collectivism would prove to be a practical reform approach, was the example of collectivism abroad running amuck. Were Americans really so different from Germans and Italians and Russians that they could establish collectivist social planning without power cliques forming at the center and the mass of the people becoming abjectly subservient to propaganda and terror?

The Spanish Civil War raised the first great furor in America over Fascist collectivism. Outside the Catholic hierarchy a near unanimity prevailed in judging the Fascists to be morally reprehensible aggressors.[6] The Socialists and Communists leaped to the forefront in urging American intervention on behalf of the Loyalists—or at least relaxation of the Neutrality Laws to allow shipment of arms to the ill-equipped Loyalists. Many liberals joined the clamor for aid to Spain, especially those who held a moral view of the issue as a contest between democratic values, represented by the Loyalists, and the dark oppression of Fascism. Most Americans, however, shied away from the idea of such involvement.

Traditional American isolationism and bitter memories of the defeat of idealist hopes after World War I left Americans skeptical of the value of engaging in war for any purpose. Roosevelt, though sympathetic to the anti-Fascist cause, kept the country on a noninterventionist course. Partly he was deferring to the isolationist temper, which he tested in his famous Quarantine Speech of 1937 in Chicago and found powerful enough to keep him from pressing his suggestions for sanctions against aggression.[7] He was also wary of relaxing the rigid terms of the Neutrality Laws out of practical political deference to the powerful Catholic support of Franco's cause.[8]

The Spanish War underscored basic differences between the pragmatic rationalist and liberal traditionalist outlooks. While Van Wyck Brooks, Lewis Mumford, and Waldo Frank admired the wholeness of the organic Spanish culture, which they felt the Loyalists were defending, and wished for vigorous American action against the Fascists, the pragmatic rationalists found in the Spanish situation a clear warning to Americans to intensify their efforts at noninvolvement. The exigencies of war dramatized the contrast. Waldo Frank rushed to Spain to volunteer his services and the moral support of his fame as a profound student of Spanish civilization, while at the same time the pragmatic rationalist Journal *Common Sense* ran a series of stern warnings against entering the trap of European war.[9]

A succession of European crises aggravated the tension within the American liberal community. The Moscow Trials produced heated disagreement over the character of the Russian state, as well as over the question of whether the accused were, indeed, guilty of treason. A commission to investigate the validity of charges made in the Moscow Trials against Leon Trotsky, headed by John Dewey, climaxed the debate and provided an issue that helped distinguish the various shades of liberal opinion on the touchy questions of Marxism and the meaning of the Soviet Revolution. Then in quick succession the Munich capitulation, the Nazi-Soviet Pact, and finally the invasion of Poland, precipitating general war, helped to discredit collectivism.

Beyond the great popular support of Roosevelt, events within America suggested the futility of collectivist hopes for radical reconstruction of the nation. Workingmen, avoiding class-conscious political and economic groups, advanced their fortunes through strengthening the collective bargaining power of established unions and by forming the

CIO for unskilled workers along the traditional guidelines established by the American Federation of Labor for the skilled. The leaders of these unions were militant in their efforts to forge their organizations into more powerful weapons to force economic concessions from management—even to the point where spectacular and violent confrontations took place—but there was little thought of turning unions into collectivist planning bodies that would shape the political and social structure of the country.

Similarly, signs of unwillingness to support radical reform appeared among other segments of the population. Robert and Helen Lynd, whose book *Middletown, USA* (1925) seemed to corroborate Sinclair Lewis's description of the drab and at times vicious conformism of small-town life, returned to Muncie, Indiana, their model city, in 1936 and found conditions surprisingly unchanged by the great Depression crisis. Reflecting the liberal sense of the urgent need of change, they warned that continued stagnation could lead to a form of Fascism.[10]

Contemporary comment on the New Deal showed the declining sense of urgency for collectivism. Before Roosevelt's reelection in 1936 leftists pressed the slogan "either Communism or Fascism," while persons of a more moderate cast cautioned that programs embodying as little basic change as the New Deal harbored the danger either of provoking a frustrated underlayer of deprived citizens to give power to Fascistic demagogues, or else of allowing the old, discredited capitalists to regain their dominance.[11]

But in the course of New Deal moderation these fears of radical terrors eased amid the growing sense that a pragmatic style of individualism prevailed in America and was in harmony with Roosevelt's compromise between experimental social planning and continued support of free enterprise.[12]

2. Pragmatic Rationalism Adjusts: The Drift Toward the Center

a. A Useful Sensibility

Pragmatic rationalist hopes for comprehensive social engineering faded along with collectivism's reputation. The pragmatic rationalists had banked on the existence of a reasonable, flexible public that would accept centralized management of the materialistic side of life in exchange for increased leisure and a higher standard of living. Dewey even went beyond that concept of a reasonable bargain. He agreed with Edward Bellamy's dictum that planning was essential for full human development in that it alone could provide the time needed for humane ends.

The relative calm with which the pragmatic rationalists took the decline of collectivism is partially to be explained by the strain of esthetic feeling that ran through them. They were far from the fanatic sort of fact-worshipers that Dickens described. With their interests in aspects of life extending beyond the wholly rational, they had a measure of consolation, a cushion to fall back on, as the hope for an engineered society died out. As we have noted, Dewey interwove an appreciation of esthetics through the entire skein of his philosophic writings and capped his efforts with *Art As Experience* (1934). On a less systematic plane, Stuart Chase showed a similar appreciation for esthetics. His description of his trip to Mexico, *Mexico: A Study of Two Americas* (1937), included praise for the native handicrafts of Central America, and thereafter, Chase pressed for an explicit place within the American economic structure for creative, purely individual production. The efforts of Ruskin and Kropotkin to nurture such esthetic achievement in the midst of mass industrial society similarly held Chase's admiration and were frequently cited by him.

George Soule's work was more soberly confined to the technical side of economic discussion; but on occasion a glimmer of esthetic sensibility would shine through. He was always grateful that he had thought to choose a dual major at Yale—economics and literature—and was pleased to recall the praise he had earned for his work in a graduate seminar on theories of English poetry.

b. Stuart Chase: A Redoubled Search for Reason

Stuart Chase, the most dauntless of critics, showed signs of discouragement with social engineering in the keen interest he took in the semantic
teachings of the Polish mathematician Count Alfred Korzybski and the
English literary critics C. K. Ogden and I. A. Richards.[13] A series of
articles by Chase in 1936 and 1937 preceded his full-length study of the
new and intriguing science of semantics, *The Tyranny of Words* (1938).[14]
At the outset of his book Chase confessed: "I have written several books
and many articles, but only lately have I begun to inquire into the nature
of the tools I use. . . . Carpenters, masons, and engineers who give no
thought to their tools and instruments are not likely to erect very durable
structures. Yet I follow a procedure common to most writers, for few of
us look to our tools.[15] He reflected upon the disappointments in communication he had suffered that had made him begin to consider his use
of language: "As a young reformer I had organized meetings, written
pamphlets, prepared lectures, concocted programs, spread publicity with
enthusiasm. Those already inclined to my point of view attended the
meetings, read the pamphlets, listened to the lectures, adopted the
programs, but the apathy of the unconverted was as colossal as it was
baffling."[16]
Chase's bafflement did not represent rejection of the program of
reform through scientific reason that he had advocated throughout the
decade. Rather, he felt that setbacks to that point had been largely the
result of tactical flaws. His assessment of people as fundamentally flexible
and susceptible to reason remained intact. "If original sin is an assumption without meaning . . . ," he posited; "if people as one meets them . . .
are, in overwhelming proportions, kindly and peaceful folk, and so I
find them; and if the human brain is an instrument of remarkable power
and capacity—as the physiologists assure us—there must be some reason,
some untoward crossing of wires, at the bottom of our inability to order
our lives more happily and to adapt ourselves and actions to our environment."[17]
With his customary deftness, Chase reduced the complex analyses of
Korzybski and Ogden and Richards to a clear and brief set of dicta for
eliminating various barriers to understanding. Chase's interpretation
profited, as well, from the writings of Thurman Arnold, whose sardonic
dissection of political irrationality, *The Symbols of Government* (1935),

Chase mightily admired, and of the mathematician Lancelot Hogben and the physicist P. W. Bridgman. [18] Two basic language faults emerged from the study: (1) the false identification of words with things, and (2) the misuse of abstract words by failure to tie them to concrete phenomena that can be tested and measured. Thus, Chase found people deplorably given to shouting at semantic scarecrows. Like the little girl who thought pigs well-named because they were so dirty, many people botched their dealings with life by failing to see that *things* gave meaning to *words* rather than the reverse. Turning to his special area of interest, Chase noted that economics should be defined in terms of concrete matters— the flow of goods, the material well-being of the citizenry, the mode of monetary exchange, and the like—not by certain abstract concepts of "economic law."

In many other areas the tendency to believe that words determine meaning brought grief. Dr. Goebbels and his company of word-mongers were able to mesmerize the German people by waving such terms as "Aryan," "Fatherland," and "Jew" in front of their upturned faces. Elsewhere, talk of "the masses," "due process," "bureaucracy," and "lawlessness" was driving people into various emotional states, most of them gloomy or belligerent.

Of all those given to committing the second sin—misuse of abstract terms—philosophers bore the heaviest guilt, in Chase's mind. He felt a special bitterness toward them, complaining of the many wasted hours he had spent trying to tie the lofty arguments of revered philosophic thinkers to the world of measurable reality. Philosophers habitually violate a pragmatic rationalist canon: *"They are not governed by the facts;* they are not humble before the facts; facts are not central in their concepts, but come in on tiptoe through the side door." [19] The dangers of such a cavalier attitude seemed to Chase clearly demonstrated in the modern world. "Bergson," Chase noted by way of example, "begins with the perceptions and then yanks in the facts. This gives a superior brand of truth. Hitler and his propaganda generals follow a similar technique to less gentle ends." [20]

Chase coupled his warnings about misused language with an endorsement of the description Ogden and Richards gave in *The Meaning of Meaning* of how words—or symbols—relate to concrete reality. The process was a triangular one: from the observation of some phenomenon, which Ogden and Richards called the "referent," the observer proceeds through reflection to fashion words or phrases to describe the phenomenon. There can be no direct tie between referent and symbol, the authors emphasize. Thus, a flawed triangle represents the process:

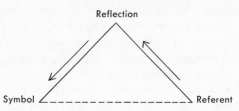

Reflection

Symbol   Referent

The indirectness of the contact between referent and symbol reinforced Chase's insistence on close attention to facts and measurable processes. Every situation contains its own set of facts and processes; and only a grasp of that particular set can impart accurate meaning to the observer. Such an attitude left little place for the idea of permanent principles— those noncorporeal imperatives that override the constant changes the world of fact undergoes.

Chase's indictment of attempts to operate by principle was broad and final. He felt such a procedure ignored the proven worth of the scientific method. "Principles are not tools by which discoveries are made," he declared, "for they tend to close the mind against free inquiry." [21] In the organization and study of society the unfortunate effects of following principles were especially vivid. "A major reason why the social studies are so backward compared to the physical sciences," Chase asserted, drawing heavily from Arnold's *Symbols of Government*, "is that the former are largely concerned with principles, the latter with experiments." [22] Carrying the invidious comparison further, Chase declared that "the struggle to formulate principles which are sound, systematic, and consistent often leads to the building of utopias by reformers and to the defense of abuses by conservatives. An engineer, on the other hand, is able to give an adequate explanation of what is wrong with a bridge which falls without blaming the girders that collapsed because they did not have the moral stamina to stand the strain." [23] Warming to his argument, Chase applied his semantic yardstick to the troubles facing Depression America: "If Americans were devoid of rigid principles, it is conceivable that poverty would have been virtually liquidated about 1925, when mass production became a dominating element in the manufacture of goods; that the great depression would not have taken place;

that the so-called Supreme crisis would not have arisen; that the labor situation would not have become acute; that the prospects of a war involving this country would be extinct; and that we could go peaceably about our business of improving our relations to the environment about us."[24]

Chase's semantic flight, underlining his prescription for scientific clarity, gave insight into the general pragmatic rationalist viewpoint. He noted that "'Fascism' today calls up more emotional associations than 'Divine.'"[25] But he did not share the alarm of many, including the liberal traditionalists, who found Fascism an implacable threat to civilization that must be confronted in mortal combat by non-Fascist nations. Chase took comfort in Bridgman's judgment that "society will not be able to demand permanently from the individual the acceptance of any conviction or creed which is not true, no matter what the gain in other ways to society." "Reading this," Chase sighed, "I suddenly feel relieved about the fraudulent concepts—racial and national—which Hitler is trying to foist upon the people of Germany. Sooner or later their falsity will destroy them."[26] He opposed America's joining in a bellicose United Front with other anti-Fascist nations, including Communist Russia. The force of reason, intelligently applied, would, he felt, steer the world clear of war. But in the event other nations should throw reason to the winds, America should remain aloof from the futile, negative exercise of war that would follow. In any case, Chase contended, the present quarrels in the world threatening war stemmed basically from sordid economic ambitions. So-called matters of principle that degenerated into violence would be either hopelessly muddled or covers for more sinister and selfish interests.

To his long-standing suspicion of philosophic logic Chase added apprehension about the state of confusion over reform goals into which liberals and intellectuals seemed to be plunging. Chase's fears on that account matched a widespread concern over the failure of rational reform enthusiasm and education to find answers for world problems. Education seemed less the golden door to progress than it had formerly appeared. Indeed, Chase remarked, "one wonders if modern methods of mass education promote as much knowledge in children's minds as they do confusion. Certainly in Germany, Italy, and Russia today the attempt is being made to bind the minds of children as once the feet of Chinese gentlewomen were bound."[27] Beyond the range of deliberate propaganda lay a wide field of sheer misinformation. The increasing complexity of modern life seemed to Chase to be making it more and more difficult for those who operate largely in the realm of thought to gain a thorough—and thereby intelligent—grasp of what was happening around them. Under the circumstances, Chase concluded, "the plain man by reason of richer firsthand experience may be a wiser human being than the intellectual, and has thus a genuine grievance against those who work sorceries with words."[28] Liberals, especially, with their obsession for having "sound opinions" on all subjects, were being driven unhappily into confusion and ignorance by the overwhelming range of modern social issues. Their sound opinions have, in the press of a bewildering array of questions, been reduced to mere foot rules. And in Chase's view, "the liberal type is too valuable to waste time befuddling himself with foot rules. I prefer to see it, as it sometimes does, modernize its approach to social problems, listen more to experts, reserve judgment, get full of referents rather than of principles and moral indignation. Intelligent individuals generally should stop feeling obliged to have 'sound opinions' on every issue. It is humanly impossible."[29]

Having disavowed the human tendency to cling to principle, and the particularly conspicuous failure of philosophers and liberals in that respect, Chase went on to deal with crucial problem areas in a highly relativist way. The great debate over whether to centralize or decentralize American society he dismissed as a virtually meaningless abstraction. Usually, he noted, such men as Walter Lippmann, Justice Brandeis, and Felix Frankfurter were classified as favoring decentralization—that is, moving local affairs away from the jurisdiction and planning of the central government. On the other side, Chase and others who had spoken in favor of economic planning were usually considered advocates of centralization. But Chase discounted the label for himself. He did not tie his criteria for action to a belief in central power. Rather, the test for proposed solutions for any social problem would be their appropriateness: Do they fit the operating facts of the situation, and will they produce what the people involved want or need? Arguments over the doctrinaire programs that had been thrust before the world in recent years lacked bite because those programs had not been adequately tested. They were "in the class of logical exercises rather than demonstrable projects: 'social credit,' 'single tax' (as a cure-all), 'consumers' cooperation for everything, 'public ownership of the means of production,' 'technocracy,' 'the Townsend Plan,' and the rest. One or another *might* work, but to date no one has established the proof of workability for impartial men to check."[30] Such inconclusiveness must lay a heavy burden of humility upon reformers who had been tempted in such troublous times to suggest sweeping panaceas. "I modestly suggest," Chase concluded, "that we divest our minds of immutable principles and march after tangible results. Use the ballot, social legislation, collective bargaining, co-operative associations, the TVA structure, conservative programs, holding-company regulations, stock-market control, central banking, public ownership—if, as, and when the context of situation, after study, gives promise for an advance. An advance to what? To making Adam and his family more comfortable and more secure."[31]

Chase's subsequent writings, mostly concerned with semantics, economics, and the darkening cloud of war, reiterated that subdued rationalism. The aura of collectivism that had been present in his work during the first years of the thirties had diminished to a mere glimmer. The selections he made from his previously published articles to reprint in *Idle Men, Idle Money* (1938) reflected his growing moderation. Veblen's ideal of an engineered society, so conspicuous in *The Economy of Abundance* (1934) and *Government in Business* (1935), had left the stage in favor of a Keynesian approach that would have the government come to the fore with planning and spending in hard times and recede to a mere regulating role when conditions improved. In either case, the emphasis must be on men, Chase insisted, not on theories of economics or on property holdings or on social planning.

More and more, as the world moved into war, Chase concerned himself with America's international role and, in accord with his work on semantics, with the effects on the American public of the mounting tide of propaganda and emotionalism. Following the disapproval of American involvement in the upheavals afflicting Europe that he had outlined in *The Tyranny of Words*, Chase joined the Keep America Out of War Congress and allowed a pamphlet attacking war to be distributed by America First, though he declined to be a member of that organization, shot through as it was with conservative elements that Chase had always disliked. In addition, he wrote a series of articles urging isolationism and crowned those efforts with the book *The New Western Front* (1939).

Holding the view that any war would come from a clash of economic interests, Chase was able to pass off the moral arguments of the liberal traditionalists with a shrug. With bland impartiality he stated that "I cannot follow the people who like Lewis Mumford, see 'fascism' in the form of the Devil incarnate, as real as that Satan whom Luther observed crawling through his window. . . . I see loathsome practices in Germany and Italy. I see practices only a little less loathsome in other countries. I see other nations, for instance the Poles, persecuting minorities, especially Jews."[32] Chase epitomized his own approach to war in *A Message to the Teachers of America*, a pamphlet he prepared for the Keep America Out of War Congress. First, modern methods of fighting have made war an insupportably horrible affair. Second, international power politics are always dubious and would prohibit any clear view of what victory would actually bring. Third, the United States does not need foreign trade; she is self-sufficient and safely situated. And finally, Americans have too many pressing problems to attend to at home without dissipating their efforts in European quarrels.[33]

The New Western Front elaborated on Chase's antipathy toward American involvement in war and proposed a Western Hemisphere autarchy to make America both self-sufficient and, in concert with the other nations in the hemisphere, invulnerable to direct attack. "The United States is unique and alone," he declared. "It does not have to act the way less fortunate nations are forced to act."[34] America has no stake in the chaotic issues convulsing Europe, Chase insisted. As if dismissing the logic of European racial disputes would ease the suffering going on in their name, he bade his readers remember that the minorities of Europe were not really racial and that self-determination had never been practiced consistently, anyway. Nor, he added, without assessing differences in degree, were all the abuses of self-determination and racial tolerance on the side of the Fascists.

Considering the background of America, the irrational racial problems of Europe were especially repugnant and irrelevant. America had rid itself for the most part of minority problems by means of the melting pot. "No group, even when living in a foreign 'quarter' and speaking no English, dreams of demanding self-determination," Chase maintained. "That's what they came to get away from."[35]

In America "the chief ideological battle . . . has been between Republicans and Democrats," Chase added. "It has been going on so long that the Democrats have mislaid some of their eternal principles—like States' Rights—for the Republicans to pick up; and vice versa."[36] But the truly crucial issue at that time, Chase felt, was unemployment. A chronic problem all during the decade, unemployment showed the inefficacy of New Deal economic practice—hindered as it was by compromise with the shoddy old shibboleths of "rugged individualism"—and provided a frustrated hard core of discarded workers for violent strains of thought to attract. Followers of the slain Huey Long, Father Coughlin, and Francis Townsend had been defeated in 1936, but their kind always had a chance to gain strength so long as unemployment provided them with an audience.

Chase's concern over unemployment increased his fear of war. War would draw attention away from critical domestic problems, even as it was creating a dangerous crisis mentality. Under the circumstances "we must be prepared to surrender our political and economic liberties [and] bind our lives over to a dictatorial war government. . . ."[37]

Although his mood was gloomy as the country edged toward war, once America had made the dreaded cold, deep plunge, Chase showed the optimism and flexibility that were more characteristic of him. In 1940 he anxiously speculated on the drift toward war and the disasters threatened by the New Deal's failure to proceed quickly enough with social planning. The nation seemed maddeningly willing just to stand still and await disaster.[38] After America was attacked in 1941, however, Chase began dwelling upon ways of making the experience of war produce some salutary results. From his often repeated attacks on the futility of warfare, harking back to the disappointments of World War I, Chase moved toward stressing the example wartime mobilization gave to social planners.[39] The War Industries Board in World War I, though quickly abandoned after the fighting stopped, indicated the possibility of efficiently galvanizing America's vast resources under public supervision. Perhaps World War II would revive, and improve upon, the work of that body and be forceful enough to impress upon the American mind the wisdom of planning wherever private industry has proven ineffective.

In any case, Chase concluded, the New Deal was gone, blown away by the blast of war; likewise, the old free-enterprise world was gone. Chase, like many other pragmatic rationalists, viewed the war as a great divide and looked forward to the postwar world with an unresolved blend of hopefulness and, in the midst of violence and unreason, apprehension about the future of liberalism and reform.[40]

c. George Soule: Democracy, Not War

George Soule, without venturing into the thickets of semantics, matched Chase in his dwindling enthusiasm for broad collectivist theories and solutions. Although his visit to the Soviet Union in 1936 impressed him with the progress of the Russian experiment, Soule continued in his opinion that Russia socialism would not be transplantable to American soil.[41] The next year he concluded that America had recovered to the point where any plans for major overhaul would be wasted on an indifferent public. "The strategy for attack on the major problems during the next four years would seem to be, therefore, not so much to attempt fundamental reform itself as to prepare the social forces and the means that will make possible fundamental reform when the appropriate time arrives."[42]

In his Weil Foundation Lecture on American citizenship at the University of North Carolina in 1935—later enlarged and reprinted in *The Future of Liberty* (1936)—Soule noted a disparity between the level of technological competence in America and the tenets of American tradition. The latter had simply not been expanded enough beyond their eighteenth-century origins to apply adequately to the complex industrialized nation America had since become. "Liberty, democracy, equality and reason are not ends in themselves; if they are to work in harness, they must be means to some other end, and must be defined in terms of that end. Where the American tradition has stopped short is in defining a national purpose suitable to our new technical environment." [43]

Soule's description of a blank spot in the American consciousness squared with his discouragement over the slow pace of reform. How could the New Deal, or any of its significant rivals, hope to revolutionize America when the tools they would have to use were not closely geared to controlling national traditions and aims? Both the programs of the reformers and the corpus of American tradition would have to shift somewhat, to meet at some point on the political scale moderately left of center.

Soule's concern over the lack of a suitable traditional backbone in American society carried him in the direction of the liberal traditionalists and away from Chase and others who banked on sheer rationality. But Soule's basic allegiance remained with rational planning. In 1939 he published *An Economic Constitution for Democracy* to summarize his

economic writings during the decade. "A well-ordered economic constitution is not the enemy of freedom in the modern world," he avowed,
"but its inevitable accompaniment."[44] Soule would have the government
greatly increase its intrusion into areas controlled by private business
and establish more projects on the order of the TVA. He stressed the
favorable effect public works and community-owned enterprises would
have on developing the spirit of cooperation which underlies successful
democracy.

War seemed to Soule a great threat to any plans for enhancing democracy in America. Europe's descent into the pit of violence and hate
made him look more anxiously to the flaws of American society. He
looked back upon cruelties Americans had been perpetrating throughout the decade and drew a sober connection with Fascism:

> We also have been struggling with lack of opportunity to work and
> play, with a general frustration. . . . Our rulers were not only extrava-
> gantly loved but extravagantly hated. There was a growing prejudice
> against outsiders—Jews, Communists, foreign immigrants of all
> kinds. . . . There was a well-established longing to externalize our
> aggression. At length Hitler was kind enough to provide a focus for
> these feelings. In the outburst of anger which we enjoyed after Munich,
> we felt a sudden relief in unity, a sense that after all we belonged to the
> same family. . . .
> But it was significant that at the very moment when we became most
> angry at the Nazis for their brutalities toward the Jews, there developed
> an opposition to relaxing the immigration laws for the benefit of the
> refugees. Anti-Semitism was felt to be actually on the increase in this
> country. We wanted to punish Hitler much more than we wanted to
> succor his victims.[45]

Soule used his post as an editor of the *New Republic* to express opposition to American entry into the war. His view of the conflict contained stronger moral censure of Fascism than did Chase's. But he did
not feel the situation required active American intervention such as the
liberal traditionalists urged. America's mission, as the emerging great
power in the world, was to provide a shining example that would bring
troubled areas of the world to their senses and eliminate Fascist unreason. "If we can prove to the world and ourselves that we mean business about democracy," he proclaimed, "we need have no fear that we

cannot defend it against external enemies. The chances are that in that case we shall not need to."[46]

In August, 1940, Soule felt impelled to clarify the viewpoint of the *New Republic* in the wake of Lewis Mumford's defection from the editorial board and the attacks on neutrality emanating from various interventionists.[47] Reviewing past *New Republic* policy, Soule commented that the editors had consistently favored sound action to insure peace. Unfortunately, when the British and French allowed the League of Nations to fall into desuetude during the first years of the 1930's, United States support of that body no longer made sense. Rather, the United States had then to stress the only stable alternative remaining—retreat from the turmoil of Europe into a position of noninvolvement, buttressed by the Neutrality Laws. That isolation would give the United States the chance to prepare for a truly beneficial world role: On the one hand, she could provide an example of how a nation at peace could advance humane values and material prosperity—providing that the New Deal and whatever administration succeeded it would continue and expand the social reforms begun during the Depression. On the other hand, America would be in a position to build an armed force that would protect her from any conceivable aggression. In talking of that prospective military toughness, Soule played down the issue of whether America should become an international policeman, imposing sanctions upon aggressor nations. He noted that America, through determined mobilization, could surely overwhelm Italy and Germany. But he chose to stress the alternative of reason, using the example of America's successful democracy as the prime lever to turn Europeans against the totalitarian schemes that had bewitched them.

Soule departed from Chase in favoring Britain's cause strongly and suggesting that aid be granted her up to a point well short of threatening America with direct confrontation by the Axis.[48] That aid, however, would be dependent upon Britain's assurance that she would use victory in the interests of democracy, not her own empire. Likewise, Soule would have America exercise extreme caution about joining any international organization arising from the ashes of war and promising to supply the world with international regulation. America must exact guarantees that the proposed world order would be democratic and would not be scuttled by another peace treaty like that conceived at Versailles after World War I. Soule's bland listing of conditions implied confidence on his part that such a rational peace could be achieved. In any case, reaction back to the old ways was impossible. Soule shared the pragmatic rationalist faith that "this war cannot restore the kind of Western world, or the kind of societies within it, which existed at its beginning." [49] Faced with the inevitable emergence of a new world after the war, America should "stop speculating which foreign creed we shall have to accept. It is time to be bold in our own right—to be bold without failing to be calm and shrewd." [50] Whatever values America was to fashion for herself, Soule felt sure that planning would be necessary. Without it, intelligent democracy and the maintenance of peace would be impossible. [51] In behalf of that linkage of democracy and planning—the identification pragmatic rationalists had sought to make throughout the decade, with waning success after 1936 —Soule urged that democracy recapture the revolutionary slogans the Fascists had stolen from it and reaffirm the value of collectivism as a precursor to a fuller individual life. [52]

d. Alfred Bingham: The End of a Career

The specter of Fascism aroused other pragmatic rationalists to action. *Common Sense* emerged from the shadows as war became imminent to make appeals against American involvement in the European crises. Its editor, Alfred Bingham, who had been relatively silent since the hopeful year of 1935 when he published *Insurgent America*, led a complementary assault on critical domestic problems.

More fully than the other pragmatic rationalists, Bingham showed a disposition to make a truce with the New Deal and accept fully the Keynesian notion of constant moderate adjustment rather than comprehensive planning. "The New Deal," Bingham declared in 1939, "is now, after six long years of often floundering experimentation, on the verge of finding itself." [53] Unlike Chase and Soule, who worried that the continuing curse of unemployment provided domestic Fascism with a great opportunity, Bingham contended cheerily that "the New Dealers seem at last to know how to end unemployment. After talking to most of those 'brain trusters' who have been responsible for New Deal policy I am convinced that there is more understanding and more unanimity than any previous time." [54]

Bingham did not see his new accord with the New Deal as a capitulation but as the result of the administration's at last adopting important pragmatic rationalist policies. "There is undoubtedly more diligent use of strict scientific method under the New Deal than under any other government or administration of modern times." And although "their devotion to facts, the collection, collation and scientific elucidation of facts has delayed the achievement of an over-all integrated program . . . , it is an error far less serious than that of most European social reformers—Marxian Socialists in particular—whose theorizing has been so far removed from the world of fact that in action they have often seemed mere hack politicians."[55]

One of the major factors in the New Deal's enlightenment, Bingham felt, was the alarming recession of 1937. Still hoping that government planning was an unhappy, temporary necessity, Roosevelt abandoned it when recovery seemed to be under way only to discover with a jolt that the hand of government must stay on the controls if the economy is to remain stable. Bingham joined Chase and Soule in praise of the report of seven Harvard and Tufts economists, *An Economic Program for American Democracy* (1938), which pointed out the error of Roosevelt's attempt to revert to free-enterprise capitalism.[56] Fortunately, the attempt was not disastrous, the report concluded. Given the administration's basic willingness to use Keynesian pump-priming, "the New Deal has not failed. Rather its great weakness has been a wavering adherence to its own principles."[57] At the close of their analysis the economists echoed pragmatic rationalist fears of chronic unemployment and of the chance that America might slide into war. With overtones of the "merchants of death" theory that convinced many after World War I of the tie between business interests and war fever, they stated that "here in America we can save our free democratic institutions only by using them to expand our national income. For private enterprise, left to its own devices, is no longer capable of achieving anything. . . . The need for immediate action to achieve this end cannot be over-emphasized. For the danger exists that businessmen, obsessed with a devil theory of government, will attempt to use their economic power to suppress democracy and place in its stead a dictatorship supposedly dedicated to the fulfillment of their desires. Should they succeed, it would then be too late to correct a grievous error. . . . Such a dictatorship would revive economic activity, but it would be activity devoted increasingly to producing weapons of death and destruction which must sooner or later be used to plunge the country into a holocaust of slaughter and bloodshed."[58]

Bingham, likewise, saw a need for more concerted action on the part of the New Deal toward greater economic democracy. Granted that "the economists in Washington are virtually all agreed that the restoration of full employment is dependent, following the Keynesian analysis, on the 'socialization' of 'investment' rather than of the 'means of production,' and that it is unnecessary to replace the market mechanism or price system with central planning of production, still they have reached no agreement on how to keep a price system running at full employment, while it is half 'monopolistic,' and rendered lop-sided by inequalities of income." [59]

After America entered the war, Bingham joined other pragmatic rationalists in speculating about the new America that would surely emerge from the ordeal. In *The Techniques of Democracy* (1942) he envisaged an industrialized society run by expert managers. Bingham felt anxious about a possible loss of human values. Though he believed in strong executive leadership, such as Roosevelt had shown on occasion, in order to coordinate the network of managerial function and to undercut self-seeking pressure groups, he stressed the need to involve the average citizen directly in public affairs. For that purpose the ballot was ineffectually remote, an inadequate check upon central bureaucracy. Bingham felt that the principle of federalism was the solution. He agreed with Soule that the TVA was the prime example of federalism in operation, providing decentralized management for an enormous national project. The same benefits of direct participation accrued to consumer cooperation, which had shown its worth many times in various locales. Even the liberal traditionalist idea of Distributism, which had faded from public view, impressed Bingham with its appeal for decentralization. Though he disagreed with the Distributist premise that man cannot live humanely in a large collectivist society, Bingham praised the Distributist emphasis on the individual as a needed counterweight to the trend of the time toward mass impersonality. But the key to a revived democracy lay in the improved techniques of management. Here Bingham joined Stuart Chase in extolling the advances made by industrial management and psychology. Bingham touched on James Burnham's incisive study, *The Managerial Revolution* (1941), but held back from the harsh lesson Burnham drew of a managerial elite in effective control of the nation's economic sinews. Bingham concluded instead that a new era of industrial democracy was beginning. He contended that proponents of enlightened leadership, most notably Ordway Tead and H. S. Person, had impressed business management with the value of cooperation and that rising unions had driven the lesson home with their refusal to accept arbitrary managerial tactics. In a happy coincidence, while industry was adopting more of the techniques of democracy, government was becoming more effectively managerial. The Brownlow study commission of 1935–37 had outlined important ways to streamline the ways of government; and the National Resources Planning Board contributed plans for coordinating national policies. The result of these converging trends, Bingham held, was a bringing together of the major private and public enterprises. He cited *Fortune*'s widely circulated ideas on "The Permanent Revolution" as an example of business' decision to abandon laissez-faire in exchange for partnership in the "mixed economy" promoted by the New Deal. In return for greater consideration of consumer welfare and acceptance of moderate regulation, business would receive assistance against the perils of recurrent depressions. Looking beyond the domestic equilibrium, Bingham saw no rational reason why the same concept of partnership should not be applied to the world at large. He did, however, recognize the obstacle of fear. The ever-expanding rings of involvement, from the lone person on through all his associations to the farthest global reaches, could not help but produce anxiety. It was already showing in the defensive character of Roosevelt's Four Freedoms—including freedom from want and freedom from fear—and in the general malaise as war unfolded. Bingham declared in an elegiac backward glance:

> Never was there a time in human history when there was so much that men could achieve together, in the building of a good society, as in the 1930's. Yet everything seemed to conspire to leave man in a frightened, meaningless isolation. The citizen was confounded by events.
>
> He had at last achieved freedom, and it was dust in his mouth. It was an emptiness rather than a fulfillment. Freedom *from* restraint, freedom *from* responsibility, freedom *from* his fellow men, rather than freedom *for* creative participation in a common task.[60]

Erich Fromm's *Escape From Freedom* (1941), with its gloomy analysis of the increasing frustration of men as they progressively lost contact with the social forces governing their lives, made a considerable impact upon Bingham. The compensatory search of many frightened persons for an ideal, a symbol, or a great leader—and the consequent abandonment of reason—disturbed Bingham's pragmatic rationalist sensibilities. He closed his book with a plea that Americans look to their own great philosophic guide, John Dewey, for an explanation of how education in scientific reason can prepare man to use wisely collectivist management of industry and politics.

Bingham amplified his discussion of postwar prospects in *The Practice of Idealism* (1944) and then stopped writing. Possibly the disparity between his view of future needs and the actual outcome of the successful war effort discouraged him. Fearful at signs that Americans were yearning to return to the old laissez-faire ways, Bingham intensified his support for a collectivist economy and called for "an economic general staff for peacetime." "We might call it an Office of Peace Mobilization," he continued. "It would issue very few orders. It would merely determine how much money, private and public, should be spent each year to assure that everybody who wanted a job could get it. And it would issue certain instructions to other government agencies to see that this volume of spending was maintained."[61] Without such planning, the economy as it lost the inflated cushion of wartime spending would crash more devastatingly than it did in 1929. Then hordes of goblins might leap out upon the country. Perhaps a brand of Fascism—the classic scavenger of distressed situations—would emerge. Or perhaps, with the formerly dominant Western nations prostrate, the nonwhite peoples would rise up to try to take control of the world. For Bingham, as for other surviving pragmatic rationalists who had once leaned toward isolationism, some form of world government seemed the necessary conservator of peace. The principle of cooperation, superseding more nationalist concepts of central planning, had come to be the guiding ideal.

e. John Dewey: "No Matter What Happens— Stay Out"

John Dewey, after his ill-fated efforts to help the League for Independent Political Action form a third party around a program of economic reconstruction, moved away from the economic reform concerns that continued to lie close to the heart of Chase, Soule, and other pragmatic rationalists. Dewey became a central figure in the growing American preoccupation with individual liberties and civil rights. Two articles in

Social Frontier in 1936 foreshadowed Dewey's growing involvement in those questions. In "Liberalism and Equality," the first of the articles, Dewey urged Americans to make a clean break from confused laissez-faire thought about the meaning of liberty. "The tragic breakdown of democracy," he contended, "is due to the fact that the identification of liberty with the maximum of unrestrained individualistic action in the economic sphere, under the institutions of capitalistic finance, is as fatal to the realization of liberty for all as it is fatal to the realization of equality. It is destructive of liberty for the many precisely because it is destructive of genuine equality of opportunity."[62] In the succeeding article, "Liberalism and Civil Liberties," Dewey gave a clear explanation of his concept of liberty as it operates in organized society. Civil liberties, he asserted, "are directly connected with the idea of citizenship. On this basis, civil liberties are those which belong to citizens as such and are different both from those which individuals are supposed to possess in a state of nature and from political rights such as the franchise and the right to hold office. Upon this basis, the justification for the various civil liberties is the contribution they make to the welfare of the community."[63] For that reason "the only hope for liberalism is to surrender, in theory and practice, the doctrine that liberty is a full-fledged ready-made possession of individuals independent of social institutions and arrangements, and to realize that social control, especially of economic forces, is necessary in order to render secure the liberties of the individual, including civil liberties."[64] Dewey thus matched the pragmatic rationalist suggestion that social engineers be the stewards of the general economic welfare with a plea for social control in the less tangible area of rights and liberties. Such a system of control would curb the outer limits of freedom while assuring most people greater and more secure liberty. The "liberty" to make money and gain power would give way when it came into conflict with the ideal of equal opportunity. Similarly, state and local liberties could not prevail against the will of the federal government to protect liberties guaranteed in the Bill of Rights and to insure effective use of the nation's resources.

Dewey accepted a difficult opportunity in 1937 to seek justice when he volunteered to head a commission that was to go to Mexico to examine the charges leveled against Leon Trotsky in the Moscow Treason Trials of 1936. Aside from the onerous burden of work that task placed upon

Dewey, then seventy-eight, and the interruption it forced in his work on the complex study *Logic: The Theory of Inquiry*, it subjected Dewey to a mighty barrage of criticism. The Communists, naturally, attacked the commission as an odious capitalist attempt to vindicate Trotsky. The Trotskyites, on the other hand, grumbled because the commission professed to be impartial. Liberals in general were nervous about opening such a bag of worms, and some among them declined invitations to join the commission.[65]

As finally assembled, the commission was a curious combination of lawyers and social critics of various hues, ranging from the near-Trotskyite Benjamin Stolberg to the far more moderate John Chamberlain.[66] The final report, refuting the charges brought against Trotsky but by no means endorsing his political views, was compiled by Suzanne La Follette, niece of Senator Robert La Follette and an accomplished journalist in her own right, under Dewey's painstaking supervision.[67] Describing the case against Trotsky as a "frame-up," the report concluded portentously that "the issue, even more than those involved in such historic cases as that of Dreyfus, Sacco-Vanzetti, or Dimitrov-Torgler, must therefore be regarded as international. It imperils countless human lives and compromises those standards of justice which mankind has painfully established to safeguard the individual against governmental oppression."[68]

In breasting the tide of response from friends and enemies of the commission, Dewey had hard things to say both about the Communists, who engineered the trials and thereby further demonstrated their callousness toward human liberties, and about Trotsky himself, an inflexible man of dogma. In the *New International* in August, 1938, Dewey brought his long-standing philosophic insistence on the indivisibility of means and ends to bear upon Trotsky's revolutionary doctrine.[69] Trotsky failed to realize that any class struggle that might exist was a means, not an end; thus he had the dangerous capacity of justifying actions without studying their exact consequences, assuming that if those actions accelerated class conflict, they must be in harmony with the beneficial flow of history.

Dewey's misgivings about the man he had exonerated matched his general concern about the growing force of unreason he observed around him as the thirties came to a close. That concern revealed itself in his commentaries on the issues of war and economic reconstruction and coincided with the outlooks of other pragmatic rationalists.

Reversing the position he had taken during World War I, Dewey declared himself at all costs against American involvement in war. "No Matter What Happens—Stay Out" Dewey titled his contribution to a symposium in *Common Sense* on the question of America's proper attitude toward war in Europe. He warned:

> . . . if the United States is drawn into the next war we shall have in effect if not in name a fascist government in this country. . . . The dire reaction that took place in the early twenties after the World War was mild in comparison with what would occur another time. . . . We are forgetting that the years before the last war were a time of growth for a strong and genuine progressivism in this country, and that if its career had not been interrupted we should have made whatever gains have been accomplished by the New Deal much earlier and in a much less costly way.
>
> It is quite conceivable that after the next war we should have in this country a semi-military, semi-financial autocracy, which would fasten class-divisions on this country for untold years. In any case we should have the suppression of all the democratic values for the sake of which we professedly went to war.[70]

By the end of the year, after Hitler's invasion of Poland had actually brought on the war he so much dreaded, Dewey had tempered his views. No doubt the actual confrontation of Fascism with the nations that at least professed to be the champions of democracy made him more hesitant to describe war as an unmitigated catastrophe for all involved. What if the Allies should lose? Was that prospect not dismal enough to make Americans at least consider lending assistance that would help prevent it without drawing the United States directly into the war? Perplexedly, Dewey stated: "I hesitate to predict anything whatever about the outcome of the present war. . . . For I believe that both pessimistic and optimistic expectations are likely to be based upon old data while it is highly possible that the world is undergoing a crisis which makes precedents and old data irrelevant to forming an estimate of the future."[71]

But whatever the outcome, the war had provided the sad but salutary service of dampening the mistaken enthusiasm of the 1930's for sweeping formulas that promised to bring an end to troubles. "The hypnotic spell is now broken," Dewey announced, looking about him at the widespread shock attendant on the start of a new World War. "I am willing to make one prediction," he ventured, "namely, that trust in panaceas and wholesale devices has received a shock from which it will not easily recover. . . . As we appreciate the inherent connection existing between attempts at wholesale social change and the methods of dictatorship, we shall be made ready to employ genuinely democratic methods more systematically and more intelligently than we have in the past." [72]

Dewey's softening on the war issue did not extend to advocacy of intervention. Rather, he joined with Oswald Garrison Villard, John Haynes Holmes, and others of like mind to attack the idea of American involvement. Willful risking of American lives through concerted aid to the Allies seemed immoral; and the notion that America's involvement in war, which would surely weaken her materially and spiritually, would increase her ability to help reconstruct the postwar world on a just basis seemed to Dewey mistaken. [73]

Dewey's economic outlook at the end of the decade coincided with that of other pragmatic rationalists in its judgment that unemployment was the great unsolved problem of the time. He criticized the New Deal for its policy of aiding agriculture and business by helping to maintain artificial scarcities and thus not meeting the needs of the consumers. Sound social planning, he reiterated, would save business from decline while distributing wealth and goods abundantly. A system of social planning that would replace the profit system with cooperation and provide work for all citizens would insure the nation's ability to absorb the high volume of goods industry was capable of producing. Unfortunately, however, Dewey conceded, the social planners' power to sell their case, always precarious in the most auspicious times, had been seriously damaged by misuse of the collectivist principle.

> What claims to be social planning is now found in Communist and Fascist countries. The *social* consequence is complete suppression of freedom of inquiry, communication and voluntary association, by means of a combination of personal violence, culminating in extirpation, and systematic partisan propaganda. The results are such that in the minds of many persons the very idea of social planning and violation of the integrity of the individual are becoming intimately bound together. But an immense difference divides the *planned* society from a *continuously planning* society. The former requires fixed blueprints imposed from above and therefore involving reliance upon

physical and psychological force to secure conformity to them. The
latter means the release of intelligence through the widest form of
cooperative give-and-take.[74]

Dewey himself came to have serious misgivings about the use of
collectivism to promote human welfare. Outlining his basic view of
life in the *Forum* series *What I Believe* (1938), Dewey announced "a
change in emphasis." "I should now wish to emphasize more than I
formerly did that individuals are the finally decisive factors of the nature
and movement of associated life," he declared. "The cause of this shift
of emphasis is the events of the intervening years. The rise of dictatorships and totalitarian states and the decline of democracy have been
accompanied with loud proclamation of the idea that only the state, the
political organization of society, can give security to individuals."[75]

The following year his book *Freedom and Culture* presented a far more
subdued defense of social planning than had been the case in his preced-
ing book on social conditions four years earlier, *Liberalism and Social
Action*. Dewey's cautious observations in the former book reflected a
foreboding about the degree of man's rationality. He observed that "the
view that love of freedom is so inherent in man that, if it only has a chance
given it by abolition of oppression exercised by church and state, it will
produce and maintain free institutions is no longer adequate. . . . Ad-
mission that men may be brought by long habit to hug their chains
implies a belief that second or acquired nature is stronger than original
nature."[76]

The example of Fascism conditioned much of the prevailing doubt
about man's rationality. But beyond that, the prevalence of Freudian
psychology and the cultural relativism advanced by such anthropologists as Franz Boas, Melville Herskovitz, and Ruth Benedict had a
marked impact. Dewey, long a foe of Freudianism, which he considered
unscientifically subjective in its premises, paid heed to the anthropologists. He felt that "the idea of culture that has been made familiar by
the work of anthropological students points to the conclusion that whatever are the native constituents of human nature, the culture of a period
and group is the determining influence in their arrangement. . . ."[77]
Thus, Dewey felt, the complacent view of liberals, which to a considerable extent had underlain pragmatic rationalism, that man was naturally
good and needed merely to have his potential for good released from the

bondage of ignorance, disease, and overwork in order to attain admirable ends, must be drastically amended. Man was not naturally anything but a bundle of possibilities. Whether he would be "good," indeed, even his opinions on goodness depended on his conditioning at the hands of his surroundings. His freedom must be preceded by education in whatever the scientific method of inquiry had demonstrated to be "good"—that is, in the best interests of the human beings involved. Otherwise he could not be trusted to use freedom wisely.

Life's suppleness requires Americans "to beware of supposing that totalitarian states are brought about by factors so foreign to us that 'It can't happen here'—to beware especially of the belief that these states rest only upon unmitigated coercion and intimidation. For in spite of the wide use of purges, executions, concentration camps, deprivation of property and of means of livelihood, no regime can endure long in a country where a scientific spirit has once existed unless it has the support of so-called idealistic elements in the human constitution."[78] Thus, as Dewey remarked toward the close of the book, "for practically the first time in human history, totalitarian states exist claiming to rest upon the active consent of the governed."[79]

The democratic progenitors of America had not adequately recognized this dark side of man's free will, Dewey lamented. In setting ideal standards they stressed freedom from political oppression and "did not foresee the non-political causes that might restrict its freedom, nor the economic factors that would put a heavy premium on centralization. And they failed to see how education in literacy could become a weapon in the hands of an oppressive government, not that the chief cause for promotion of elementary education in Europe would be increase of military power."[80]

The skill of the collectivists in sabotaging reason through perverse education, emotionalism, and propaganda caused Dewey to consider the wisdom of man having more to rely on than sheer rationality. He confessed his own excessive zeal in having been willing to jettison social customs that did not square with his ideal of reason working strictly through the scientific method. He concluded that cultural ties that were not the product of pure reason, but that held people to standards of justice and decency, were valuable and, insofar as they existed already in American life, should be retained. "In common with many others," Dewey acknowledged, "I have from time to time pointed out the harmful consequences the present regime of industry and finance has upon the reality of democratic ends and methods. I have nothing to retract. But conditions in totalitarian countries have brought home the fact, not sufficiently realized by critics, myself included, that the forms which still exist encourage freedom of discussion, criticism and voluntary associations, and thereby set a gulf between a country having suffrage and popular representation and a country having dictatorships, whether of the right or left—the differences between the two latter growing continually less as they borrow each other's techniques."[81]

Having sketched his own progress to a deeper understanding of the limitations of reason, Dewey felt moved to warn against the all too common fault of worshiping reason in the garb of science. Awed by the very real technological accomplishments of science, many had concluded that science could produce values. From that false vision, Dewey warned, it is a short step to the indiscriminate ascription of scientific warrant to social dogma.

The nonscientists, in Dewey's eyes, had been particularly culpable. Noting the intolerance of the British social critic John Strachey toward any criticism of the supposed "scientific" basis of Marxism, Dewey stated that "it helps explain why literary persons have been chiefly the ones in this country who have fallen for Marxist theory, since they are the ones who, having the least amount of scientific attitude, swallow most readily the notion that 'science' is a new kind of infallibility."[82]

In the same spirit, Dewey found, the defenders of laissez-faire economic doctrine had grandly assumed that science operated within and in behalf of the free-enterprise system.

Clearly, then "the wholesale mental attitude . . . persists [and] . . . leads to formation of ambitious and sweeping beliefs and policies." To be sure, Dewey conceded, "the human *ideal* is indeed comprehensive. . . . But the problem of production of change is one of infinite attention to means; and means can be determined only by definite analysis of the conditions of each problem as it presents itself." Dewey showed how his empirical approach confounded dogma by drawing an analogy between medical science and social reform. "Health," he noted, "is a comprehensive, a 'sweeping' ideal. But progress toward it has been made in the degree in which recourse to panaceas has been abandoned and inquiry has been directed to determinate disturbances and means for dealing with them."[83]

Dewey concluded his cautionary words about the place of science in society by insisting on the need to let desired social goals determine the uses of science and to hold those desires to strict moral accounting. Any other course would undermine the responsibilities of scientists and their patrons and thus "help create the attitudes that welcome and support the totalitarian state."[84] An appeal for patience in the face of great discouragements followed, illuminating the rather elegiac mood of pragmatic rationalists as the decade closed. "We have every right to appeal to the long and slow process of time to protect ourselves from the pessimism that comes from taking a short-span temporal view of events . . ." Dewey assured his readers.[85] And soon enough liberals were to test that patience in war discovering whether the long view could be maintained amid the immediate passions of struggle.

Aftermath: War and Renewal

The acrimonious debate over intervention came to an end with the bombing of Pearl Harbor. Both factions within independent liberalism moved to an accord on the moral rightness of the Allied cause and on the possibilities of bending the war to good purposes. Farther to the left, matters were far more chaotic and dismaying. Communists and their sympathizers had to switch from condemnation of interventionism, so long as Hitler and Stalin were in partnership, to fierce advocacy of war against the Axis when the Nazis invaded Russia in June, 1941. Many could not accept the volte-face and broke painfully from the Stalinists. They were disillusioned and uncertain as the United States moved into war. Supporters of the effort against Fascism, yet they were tired of militance and depressed about moving into alliance with their old Stalinist enemies. The *Partisan Review* expressed especially well their outlook. Begun as a literary house organ for the Communist John Reed Clubs in 1934, the *Partisan Review* soon drifted away from a proletarian outlook toward pure esthetics and undogmatic socialist politics. Key contributors and editors, such as Philip Rahv, Newton Arvin, Wallace Phelps, Edwin Seaver, and Kenneth Burke, led the fight against the "leftism" of the *New Masses* and its allies.

The outbreak of war in 1939 saw the *Partisan Review* very far removed from the social activism that first characterized it. It opposed both sides in the war, reserving special venom for Mumford and other interventionists, and became more intent than ever on helping art and the individual break free of mass pressures.[1] The editorial page attacked the apologies for Russia issued by Washington and by Hollywood and by such books as Joseph Davies' *Mission to Moscow*.[2] James Agee contributed painfully sensitive criticism of a mass production system that sent dehumanized books, movies, and music out in search of a fast dollar.[3] And, predictably, Saul Bellow's first book *The Dangling Man*

(1944) received special praise. The story dealt with a former Communist agonizing over whether to volunteer for the draft, which would bring him back into accord with America after a long spiritual exile, or to remain alienated by holding fast to his moral abhorrence of war. To the editors of the *Partisan Review*, Bellow's story seemed a parable of the dilemma radicals faced at the end of the thirties.[4]

Independent liberals, however, while opposed to the idea of war, agreed on the evil of Fascism and were not racked by inner turmoil when war struck. They agreed generally with the goals of the Allied war leaders for a United Nations, worldwide democratic freedoms, and guaranteed economic stability. For independent liberals the war against Fascism was grim business, but it entailed no painful shifts of allegiance or policy. Practical Stuart Chase and other anti-interventionists of similar mind had little difficulty in supporting armed struggle once it had been forced upon the nation. For others the move to war was even less complicated. It extended their long resistance to oppressive collectivism and their campaign for American unity on behalf of a civilized tradition. The central fact was the steadiness with which independent liberals moved into war and then on into the new era of reconstruction. They had prepared themselves with concepts that applied to the exigencies of the time. And their aloofness from the New Deal insulated them from overblown expectations of what Roosevelt would deliver and from too much enthusiasm for a worldwide cataclysm that many persons allowed themselves to view as a glorious struggle of heroes, wrapped in the armor of Churchillian prose, against the Axis villains.[5] Independent liberal programs and responses, remaining essentially consistent, served as a barometer of the social weather and of the way Americans approached issues of reform that had been tempered but never eliminated.

War fitted into the persistent concerns of pragmatic rationalists by reviving national mobilization and memories of promising experiments in planning that the War Industries Board had conducted in World War I. Agencies like the Twentieth Century Fund, the National Planning Association, and the League for Industrial Democracy assisted Roosevelt's organizers and pondered postwar reconstruction. The declaration of the New York *Times* in 1942 that the problem of full employment and production "overrides all other political and social ideas" emanating from the war fitted precisely the planning tendencies of the pragmatic reformers.[6] Stuart Chase in "Guide Line to America's Future" (1943) provided one of the key discussions of the practical problems of war and the future reconversion to peace. His analysis carried on the general conviction that overproduction and underconsumption caused the Crash of 1929. Chase agreed with most economists that the end of war would be followed by a drastic decline in consumption and, thus, the danger of a new depression. Chase could not believe that long-repressed consumer desires would burst forth into the peacetime market. He contended that people had become accustomed to scarcity during the Depression and would need prodding in order to consume enough to keep the economy going. Compounding the problem was the wide public demand for full employment revealed by Roper public opinion polls. If a sound production and consumption equilibrium were not maintained, industry could not obviously offer the desired jobs. But the workers' disillusionment over such an outcome would be insupportable, and, Chase warned cryptically, "If full employment is denied them, their opposition to more radical proposals is likely to wither rapidly."[7] Chase committed much of his energy to finding a moderate solution to the dilemma and was a highly useful source of information and encouragment to the drafters of the Employment Act of 1946. The act provided a Joint Economic Committee of Congress and a Council of Economic Advisers for the President and announced that reasonable economic security was to be guaranteed to the nation by private enterprise, if possible, or by the federal government in the last resort. No specific devices for carrying out the resolution were contained in the act; but it provided means for gathering the pertinent data, and the mere fact of its passage exerted a moral claim on Congress and industry.

Chase's concern for stability extended to the world scene. Long-range aircraft and the atomic bomb, whose use on Japan Chase opposed, made it plain that the protection offered by flanking oceans was gone. With isolationism now impossible an unstable world had become intolerable. Chase thus acclaimed the Atlantic Charter's provision for the United Nations. As time went on he noted a discouraging trend back toward the toothlessness of the League of Nations because of fear about relinquishing any national sovereignty. Still, Chase hoped that the world's need for peace in the face of nuclear power would herd nations, reluctant or not, into an international organization able to enforce the federal will of its members.

George Soule showed somewhat greater concern for the social aims that a reconstructed nation and world would hold. He was not as convinced as Chase that these would benignly and valuably flow from the attainment of security. We need, Soule insisted in 1942, a "daring reexamination of first principles," in the light of social and natural science. The war might in its vast and painful dislocations give the impetus for the development of new economic concepts "every bit as consistent and intellectually satisfying" as the old classical laws had been in earlier more self-confident days. He endorsed the prescription in Robert Lynd's *Knowledge for What?* (1939) for allowing immediate social problems to guide the development of the sciences. And enlightened Keynesianism seemed to Soule a good place to start, providing a flexible policy that could both guard society against hardship and allot resources for support of noble and artistic ventures.[8]

Liberal traditionalists approached the war with other concerns uppermost. The desire of the cultural pluralists for the assimilation of minorities intensified as the racist character of Fascism became ever more horrifyingly an instrument of policy. Horace Kallen turned once again to the Zionism he had left behind in the twenties as he watched largely unsuccessful efforts of persecuted Jews to find asylum.[9] Louis Adamic was also drawn toward Europe, even as he intensified his efforts at justifying the ways of recent immigrants in America to the better established WASP's. Adamic was earnestly set upon by Yugoslav representatives of the rival Mihailovic and Tito factions seeking support. He concluded finally that, unsympathetic as he was toward Communism, support for Tito was preferable to backing the coterie of sleazy aristocrats, rentiers, and reactionary churchmen who clung to Mihailovic.[10] While he was making that troubled choice, Adamic edited the cultural pluralist journal *Common Ground* (1940–47) and hurried along with the books in his series, *From Plymouth Rock to Ellis Island*.[11] By war's end Adamic had reached the peak of his contribution to the cultural pluralist movement and had developed a concern for world unity that was to make him a tragic foe of the cold war policy in ensuing years.

His book *Two Way Passage* (1941) marked his entry into internationalist planning. He proposed sending a special cadre of Americans of foreign descent back to the countries of their origins to assist in the reconstruction of those countries. The idea was abruptly rejected by the Allies, and Adamic, goaded by his emotional and impulsive nature, concluded that the men running the war were aiming at a restoration of the old status quo. His account of a *Dinner at the White House* (1946) painted a bitter picture of Churchill as the lion of British imperialism; and, in his rejection of Harry Truman as a small-minded man, appointed by a failing FDR, Adamic stood ready for a radical political alternative.

Archibald MacLeish, serving as Undersecretary of State in charge of public information, was the most firmly optimistic of the liberal advocates of a revived American tradition. He envisioned a great era after the war was over of artistic creativity, building on the aroused self-consciousness of the thirties.[12] Like MacLeish, Howard Odum also felt that the war would only distract temporarily from the task of explaining and deepening America's regional consciousness.[13]

Traditionalists who had a more universal scope than MacLeish and Odum were not so cheerful. The war was indeed an uplifting crusade for them, but its outcome was uncertain, even though they felt sure the Axis would lose. The sense of man's flagging spirit—his mechanized complacency—had long disturbed the advocates of a Great Tradition. Mumford began as early as 1938 to exhort Americans to mobilize against Hitler and by the time of American entry three years later had nurtured a powerful bitterness about the inadequacies of the American moral character. Too many Americans, he claimed in 1940, were "passive barbarians," who were allowing the world to sink into night. That indictment he was to continue with hardly a pause, while allowing for the possibility that men might, somehow, reach their true moral stature. In the midst of war Mumford worried that the lack of fiber might give way to the easy backward step of restoration. What struck him as the simple, practical necessity of "replacing an outworn civilization" with a new one might, he feared, be viewed as Utopian by people who wished merely to end the war and then rest. So, he urged them to adopt what they regarded as visionary and consider that "Utopia can no longer be an unknown land on the other side of the globe; it is, rather, the land one knows best, reapportioned, reshaped, and recultivated for permanent human occupation."[14]

Mumford's nationalist call to arms, echoed by Frank, MacLeish, Bernard De Voto, and other standard-bearers, aroused concern that the war effort might be preparing an authoritarian harvest. The ex-Marxist Granville Hicks, well versed in the ways of authoritarianism, gave a typical forecast of conservative reaction. It would feed upon mysticism and nationalism and a revival of laissez-faire, arguing a need to fend off the totalitarian horrors supposedly revealed at the core of collectivism.[15] Even Max Lerner, a critic early in favor of massive resistance to Fascism, allowed that the war effort could fasten authoritarian ways upon the country. Replying in 1941 to Hadley Cantrill, the public opinion specialist who was then polling commentators on their views of the future, Lerner speculated that war would accelerate planning to the point where economic processes were highly regimented. Militarism would advance, with young men finding it a choice career. Mass media would become government monopolies; there would be strict supervision over movies and the press, and threading their way through it all to keep everything under control would be a highly developed secret police. Remarkably, Lerner did not despair, judging that the gist of free religion and discussion would be retained and that a renaissance of art and literature would occur, inspired by the primary themes of the death of an old world and the birth of a new one. Lerner mingled with his prediction characteristic liberal optimism that America's free traditions were supreme. They would somehow survive all measures against Fascism—measures that were hardly debatable, considering the great evil being attacked.[16]

Thus, in a mood of fear and hope independent liberalism moved toward a dimly perceived peace. When peace finally came, two transcendent problems, the cold war and a widespread resignation to fate, gravely hindered action on overhaul of the world's social structure.

Still, some pragmatic rationalists found compensation during the cold war. By reviving a massive military budget in 1950, after temporarily letting the armed forces disband, the government greatly reduced any chance of a return to depressed economic conditions. A voracious consumer appetite in the immediate postwar years further checked repression. Stuart Chase confessed that he had been wrong about the public's having learned to do without during hard times. Apparently the desire for wordly goods was a constant, even if long subdued. Apparently, there also were vast consumption possibilities waiting to be tapped.[17] The idea of the American as essentially a creature of consumption—in contrast to the economic man, whose main drive was for production and profits—stirred the imagination of social critics. To David Potter, Americans were "people of plenty," distinguished from members of other societies and from their own ancestors by their unique abundance. David Riesman portrayed the growing sophistication with which members of America's "lonely crowd" were making consumer choice the chief national preoccupation.[18] The new emphasis recalled the efforts of the thirties to exalt consumerism; but in the Depression the New Deal Consumers' Advisory Board and reformers like Stuart Chase and his partner, F. J. Schlink of Consumers' Research, were concerned about efficient purchasing and honesty in selling. The problem in those lean years was to stretch the consumer's straitened budget. In the late forties and fifties it was to find imaginative uses of the cornucopia—a problem much more reminiscent of Veblen's description of conspicuous consumption than of the frugal aims of consumers' cooperation, EPIC, and kindred reform movements.

If the cold war struck the pragmatic rationalist planners with an embarrassment of riches, along with the disappointment of seeing chances for a cooperative world order fade, it had a more unrelievedly gloomy effect on liberal traditionalists who did not find material prosperity a good measure of human success. Indeed they feared that prosperity carried beyond strict bounds would invite decadence. Mumford tied excess affluence to excess power. He reacted violently against the use of atomic weapons, far more so than Chase who merely registered disapproval. The use of that fiendish scourge, along with strategic bombing, gave rise to one of Mumford's chief postwar theories: America's power had deranged her ruling group. Unable to imagine what destruction and misery they were able to wreak, the rulers had lapsed into self-defensive fantasy in which their victims, or potential victims, ceased to be real persons and became merely figures in a primitive myth that made everything opposed to American interests expendable. As his rage and despair mounted, Mumford turned, himself, to figurative renderings. He attacked the architecture of the Pentagon as "an effete and worthless baroque conceit"—a paradigm of paranoia with walls that enclosed its inmates and faced out every which way, as if looking around for trouble.[19] In 1962 Mumford issued an "Apology to Henry Adams" on behalf of himself and others who had not recognized the truth of Adams' prediction that the science of nuclear energy required a powerful moral ideology to guide it rather than the old-fashioned optimistic faith in automatic progress—or in "might makes right."[20] Finally, Mumford added his concept of the megamachine to his postwar appraisal of man and his prospects. Before the invention of massive mechanical apparatus, man had devised the greatest of machines —the flesh and blood megamachine constructed out of masses of people herded together to pool their muscle power. The great pyramids of Egypt illustrated the power of the megamachine. Gangs of men, perfectly drilled—and inhumanly exploited—performed prodigies of work in their construction. And to what end? The glorification of absolute power that expressed itself in gigantism and destruction— imperial cities to exalt the rulers and armies to devastate their enemies. Mumford found the link between the crude pretensions of the pharaohs and the present all too obvious. What are the Egyptian pyramids, he asked, "but the precise static equivalents of our own space rockets? Both devices for securing, at an extravagant cost, a passage to heaven for the favored few." [21] And what has the cancerous growth of technological and political power meant for those left behind as the rockets ascend? "So far has Western society departed from the ancient taboos against murder, theft, and rape that we are now faced with juvenile delinquents who have no inner check against wantonly assaulting other human beings at random 'for kicks' while we have adult delinquents capable of deliberately planning the extermination of tens of millions of human beings, in carrying out, also doubtless for kicks, a mathematical theory of games. Today our civilization is elapsing into a state far more primitive, far more irrational, than any taboo-ridden society now known—for lack of any effective taboos." [22] Powerful forces in society, he concluded, had proffered the gift of death to the postwar generation. "If man had originally inhabited a world as blankly uniform as a 'highrise' housing development, as featureless as a parking lot, as destitute of life as an automated factory, it is doubtful if he would have had a sufficiently varied sensory experience to retain images, mold language, or acquire ideas." [23]

Waldo Frank concentrated more than Mumford on exchanges between cultures—especially those of Hispania and North America—and so was more intently focused on international relations. In that Frank exhibited the aptness of his liberal traditionalist position to unfolding world events. His *Chart for Rough Waters* warned against belligerent isolationists. In their efforts to protect themselves from foreign threats they seek to control other countries which they have chosen not to learn enough about to be able to approach rationally and justly. The world is in a revolution, Frank insisted, from which there is no turning aside. In the same spirit with which he had always opposed insular narrowness Frank urged international unity and did so with a perception of gathering trends that was remarkable for 1947:

> Our army and navy diplomats are at present trying by the acquisition of bases to make the Pacific "an American lake," a *mare nostrum* of our Rome. It won't work; if we try to make it work, we shall be writing our own swift "decline and fall." The idea of these simpleminded diplomats is really a squeeze play over three oceans, the Atlantic, the Pacific, the Arctic, against the continental mass of Asia, Africa, and Europe. On this continental mass, by comparison with which the Americas are a *minority hemisphere*, lives the overwhelming majority of mankind. A generation will make a huge difference in their industrial power. If we proceed with the plans of our business and army strategists, we shall find ourselves, in the new alignment of world might, as isolated—not as Hitler was, but as Mussolini with his pipe dream of the Mediterranean as an Italian *mare nostrum*. . . .
>
> East and west have met already; already the two terms have lost their meaning. . . . India, China, Latin America, and Russia today are culturally more conscious than the United States. Consciousness *is* culture. If we direct our energies to bases and trade in the Pacific, we will be drowned there; and what will overwhelm us will not be air armadas but a wisdom that we have failed to assimilate and absorb. We are right to fear our atom bomb: our Maginot line. But what we should fear most is our victorious generals and captains of industry who, if they consolidate their power at home, will prove more lethal to us than they were to the Japanese whose acceptance of defeat has made them at last a nation with a future.[24]

If Frank saw imperial pretensions rising out of victory, he also recognized that these would stem more from fear than from confidence. All the experiences of war, capped by the atomic bomb and full disclosure of Hitler's "final solution," left Americans shaken, the old confidence in progress replaced by a desire for security and a sense of the deep sinfulness of human nature. The result was, as W. H. Auden put it in poetry and Leonard Bernstein in music, an "Age of Anxiety." The excesses of McCarthyism followed naturally, as did a return to religion —at least its outward forms. Reinhold Niebuhr expressed most powerfully the sober neo-Calvinism that took hold of a wide public. Given to paradoxes that argued the futility of seeking broad social reform or individual perfection, Niebuhr insisted that the Children of Darkness were, unfortunately, shrewder than the Children of Light. In a flawed society—created by flawed human beings—those who trafficked in evil were bound to be more realistic than those who turned from it. In *Signs of the Times* (1946) Niebuhr urged fortitude as Western society hung in the balance between two ages. He, as a member of the Socialist Party in the 1930's who had resigned in 1940, was one of many veterans of the Marxist and neo-Marxist left who looked upon World War II as a traumatic turning point in their lives. The tendency to see sin on every hand and to prescribe remorse and diminished hope was common, as was the turn to an anti-Communism that pitted an America that had turned out not to be not so bad after all against dire international perils. Niebuhr expressed the formula in a letter to a friend during the fifties: "Our domestic problems appear to be tolerably solved and our foreign problems appear to be insoluble."[25] Niebuhr's diagnosis received strong formal support in 1950 from the Federal Council of Churches in a six-volume study of the church's postwar role. Anti-perfectionist in its theological outlook, the report cast doubt on the social gospel and suggested that the emphasis of laissez-faire on individual responsibility for success or failure reflected the Protestant doctrine of personal salvation (and damnation).[26]

Misgivings about the capacity and reason of man and the concept that the postwar world was in transition between a blasted era and an unknown future also contributed greatly to an upsurge of existentialism. The doctrines of the nineteenth-century Danish churchman Soren Kierkegaard, who stressed the efficacy of faith in a world where nothing can be known for certain, complemented modern arguments of the nobility of trying to live as fully as possible with the realization that life has no demonstrable purpose.

The postwar mood solidified the political hold of the New Deal coalition after temporary challenges from the right and left had spent themselves. Conservatives sensed a great opportunity. Anti-Communism, the reaction against reform and ideology, and the sober revival of religion seemed exactly right for them. In 1946 the Republicans recaptured control of Congress and the rise of Joe McCarthy and his reactionary allies followed swiftly. But the surprising victory of Harry Truman in 1948 bore witness to the completeness with which the New

Deal welfare state had replaced the old Republican free-enterprise formula. Although Dwight Eisenhower restored the White House to the GOP, he was elected as a national hero, not a party representative. Even his immense popularity could not head off the steady run of the New Deal tide. In 1954 the Democrats took control of Congress and increased their margin while Eisenhower remained supreme. A lingering reformism, along with widespread desire for security and a drive toward the good life of consumer abundance, which seemed to signify both reform and security, proved more powerful than the neoconservative tendencies.

The left was likewise overborne by the New Deal legacy. Marxism—and ideological thinking in general—was in a shambles by the end of World War II. Yet, with a last gasp, dissenters on the left gathered in the Progressive Party of 1948, primarily to oppose the cold war and offer suggestions for accord with Soviet Russia. The new party's identification with the old La Follette farm-labor coalition was compromised by the large admixture of Communists; but Henry Wallace, calling for amity with the Russians, found the influx of domestic Reds hard to oppose. They brought money and tactical know-how. But, finally, they brought defeat. Wallace captured less than 3 percent of the vote, and his followers moved on under considerable handicap, vulnerable to the harsh anti-Communist crusade.[27]

One of those who suffered most was Louis Adamic. He had joined the Progressive Party because of his heart's desire to see accord among various peoples on a free and equal basis and his support of the Communist partisan, Tito, over Mihailovic. Adamic was affronted by the Truman administration for seeming to have hardened international policy into anti-Communism.[28] Yet he also alienated himself from the Communists by supporting Tito's defection from the Communist bloc. Adamic was a man of generous sympathy and loyalty, not one who could become an apparatchik, "counted on" to follow the party line. In the war of doctrines he became isolated. Anti-Communists vilified him as a fellow traveler. The Communists became enraged with his "deviations" and apparently used terror against him. He was beaten twice in unsuccessful efforts to steal his pro-Tito manuscript, *Eagle and the Roots*, before it could be published.[29] In September, 1951, he was found dead in his burning garage—either murdered or a suicide. His friend Carey McWilliams accepted the verdict of suicide, seeing in

Adamic's political entrapment the culmination of Adamic's long-standing fear that the tensions of American life would one day prove too much for him.[30]

The pressures on Adamic were of the sort that drove American politics toward the subdued middle and secured the New Deal venture against substantial further experiment. David Cushman Coyle, the eloquent engineer who had provided ideas for keeping New Deal planning down to "brass tacks" and had urged Truman to "give 'em hell" in the 1948 election, rejoiced that the demise of the Progressive Party eliminated the kooks on the flanks and left the centrist coalition intact.[31] And Arthur Schlesinger, Jr., heavily under the influence of Niebuhr, spoke in 1949 of New Deal liberalism as a "faith"—the "vital center"—whose avatars were "under attack from the far right and the far left." As Schlesinger saw it, reformist disagreement with the New Deal shaded quickly into mere sentimentality; for only political programs with clear chances to attain power were realistic, and the only possible loci of power were the Communist left, the reactionary big business right, and the New Deal center. His use of the term "progressive" illuminated both his conception of power and the New Dealers' growing sense of having become establishment. Traditionally the "progressive" label had been adopted by insurgent reformers who stood out against the status quo, as the New Deal had originally done. In *The Vital Center* Schlesinger reserved the term for foolish reformers of the sort enlisted by the Wallace movement. In his view "the defining characteristic of the progressive ... is the sentimentality of his approach to politics and culture. ... His sentimentality has softened up the progressive for Communist permeation and conquest. For the most chivalrous reasons, he cannot believe that ugly facts underlie fair words. However he looks at it, for example, the USSR keeps coming through as a kind of enlarged Brook Farm community, complete with folk dancing in native costumes, joyous work in the fields and progressive kindergartens. Nothing in his system has prepared him for Stalin."[32]

Yet the distinguishing feature of most independent liberals as they passed through the fires of war and into the postwar era was their steadiness in staying clear of both the Marxist left and the New Deal. The liberal traditionalists tended thus to feel isolated and gloomy, for "America was promises," as they saw it, and the promises of moral progress were not being well kept. The Red Scare of the forties and fifties blighted MacLeish's hopes for a flowering of American art and literature. He used the plight of Job as an example to stiffen the resolve of Americans against the fears and ignoble temptations of postwar life.[33] Those of Lewis Mumford's persuasion grew still more pessimistic and alienated. Jeremiah, not the long-suffering Job, was Mumford's preceptor as he thundered evenhandedly against all postwar political administrations with their atomic bombs, their ironical twisting of "security" into intimidation, and their refusal to face the need for fundamental reforms. "Our people are, as usual, far sounder than Congress or the newspapers would represent them as being," Mumford wrote to Van Wyck Brooks in 1951 by way of reaffirming his belief that a basic nonauthoritarian alternative was required to guide policy toward the nation's true character and purposes. "But as things go now, their voice is unheard; and those of us who would speak for them . . . are throttled by what is fast settling down into a universal censorship. . . . Looking at our leaders, their bad judgment, their coarse impudence, their inability to admit responsibility or accept blame, I am humiliated at being an American and ashamed of the country that bore them."[34]

Reaction against the technocratic state helped preserve enthusiasm for a return to the soil in what came to be known as the Green Revolution. More original was the dispersal of the Beats across the landscape beginning in the late 1950's. These were utter aliens from the affluent society—Dharma Bums for looking eastward for inspiration; Holy Barbarians for rejecting standard ways of the intellect. They supported themselves by singing and writing like ancient troubadours, if they were able, or by conning or any sort of odd job, if necessary. By the early 1960's some of them had begun to settle down on the basis of vaguely forming communal ethics. They remained radicals politically and socially. But their growing interest in the organic roots of life put them and allies in the Green Revolution in touch with a conservative tradition of attachment to the cyclical permanencies of nature. A revival of subsistence farming, folk art, and folk crafts followed hesitantly. And the more thoughtful worked to devise a counterculture in indirect answer to Van Wyck Brooks' call for a "usable past."[35]

Pragmatic rationalism also survived as a mode of reform. As in the 1930's a division existed between those who looked systematically to politics and others whose interest in politics was incidental. John Dewey made the steadiness of his independent appeal to politics clear during the 1948 election. In attacking the Progressive Party as the tool of the USSR—"the most reactionary imperialistic nation in the world today" —he reiterated his belief that a new liberal party was needed to tap the democratic radical spirit indigenous to America. His view that neither major political party offered a valid national purpose remained in force in his three criteria for the proposed new party: It must seek to extend the ideals of democracy; it must provide leadership that is morally responsible as well as adept at balancing interests and wielding power; and it must be rooted in the communal spirit of the labor movement that such men of principle as Sidney Hillman and Walter Reuther had advanced.[36]

Behind Dewey's political prescription lay the undiminished force of his commitment to the scientific method of intelligence. Indeed, when the war struck, he moved deliberately to invigorate the American cause with the pragmatic idealism he felt had been tragically ignored in World War I. In 1942 Dewey reissued his 1915 work on *German Philosophy and Politics* with a new introduction entitled "The One-World of Hitler's National Socialism." The German lapse into Naziism, Dewey contended, came partly from the lack of firm scientific opposition to Hitler's dream of tribal purity. The resultant chaos contained a lesson for Americans who sought to get along without a unifying conception of their condition. "As yet we have no adequately developed American philosophy," Dewey wrote, "because we have not as yet made articulate the methods and aims of the democratic way of life."[37] The dangers of that failure Dewey was to reiterate thereafter in defending science against attack and opposing the movement to build a Calvinist sense of man's innate depravity into the conduct of the nation's social and political affairs. Dewey criticized the conservative trend both because it blunted further an already inadequate reform impulse and because it worked against the sort of intellectual and social unity it claimed to favor. It was the conservatives, Dewey charged quite rightly, who most emphatically accepted C. P. Snow's notion of the two cultures, all the while accusing pragmatic rationalists of splitting man off from his spiritual nature by overemphasizing science. To Dewey there was no validity to the two-cultures critique. The method of intelligence was comprehensive, drawing the elements of "science" together with the emanations of the inner spirit to give man a full awareness of life and release his artistic imagination. As Dewey put it, in criticizing the educational plans of Robert

Hutchins for separating the essentials of the "natural moral order" from the dross of industrial society, "We do not have as yet an educational or any other social institution that is not a mixture of opposed elements. But the solution for that discord [lies] in integration, not further separation. Division between methods and conclusions in natural science and those prevailing in morals and religion is a serious matter, from whatever angle it be regarded. It means a society that is not unified in its most important concerns."[38]

Dewey saw a loss of nerve in the reaction against science and in the new wave of existentialism and neo-orthodox religion. That was the theme of his contribution to a *Partisan Review* series on "Religion and the Intellectuals" in 1950. The phenomenon of so many people losing their grips during those postwar years suggested to Dewey that they might not have had very tight holds in the first place. The preponderant failure to understand science—most poignant in the case of the workers whose jobs were increasingly governed by technology—had created an unstable pattern. As long as science delivered pleasurable goods the public endorsed it. When, however, science showed dangerous traits, its shaky allies pulled back. Similarly, in religion Dewey felt that the Calvinist revival revealed an infirm faith. In a letter to a young graduate student in 1947 Dewey concluded that "I have the impression that [Niebuhr] and Kierkegaard have both completely lost faith in traditional statements of Christianity, haven't got any modern substitute and so are making up, off the bat, something which supplies to them the gist of Christianity—what they find significant in it and what they approve of in modern thought—as when two newspapers are joined, the new organ always says 'retaining the best features of both.'" As for the notions of existentialists who abjured all faith, as well as confidence that the world might be made sense of: "I think they are the reactions of people who are scared and haven't got the guts to face life."[39]

Prosperity, as well as fear, fueled the new conservative mood. There were those who disparaged attempts at progressive reform as expressions of foolish optimism; others were inclined against reform because it interfered with a profitable status quo. With the revival of the economy during World War II the latter group was able to adopt a double attitude. Though they sought to slow substantial change, they presented their increasing productivity as evidence of progress. Some of the pragmatic rationalists accepted the proposition. Chase, Bingham, and others became increasingly enthusiastic over what appeared to be an enlightened business management contributing tangibly to the general welfare. Affluence, scientific management, and reform seemed to be advancing together.

John Dewey remained suspicious, however. In 1947, his sharp eye always out for criticisms of science, Dewey observed that a series of articles in *Commentary* on the social sciences all deplored the retreat of social scientists from close consideration of values. Especially discouraging was the inference that science, itself, dictated the retreat—another instance of the two-culture fallacy that sought to isolate science from social morality. Dewey noted that Daniel Bell's discussion of factory sociology came at the matter with especially subtle ambiguity. In describing the dehumanization of that branch of study Bell explained that the culprits, "being scientists . . . are concerned with 'what is' and are not inclined to involve themselves in questions of moral values or larger social issues." For Dewey, the quotation marks Bell wrapped around "what is" partially absolved him by indicating that Bell wanted to hold himself apart from the error of believing that science was value-free and limited to the facts at hand. But the social scientists employed in the factories were not so perceptive. They and the public were being misled by the shadow (not the substance) of science. In Dewey's view:

> That shrewd industrialists engage trained experts to study and report upon the conditions that create friction and lower efficiency and profits, proves only that they are shrewd in conducting their business. . . . But that inquiries are scientific which are carried on under conditions of an outlook, standpoint, and aim extraneous to scientific inquiry, is, to state the matter baldly, a delusion. And in the case of "social" inquiry it is a dangerous delusion.
>
> For instead of resulting in liberation from conditions previously fixed (which is the fruit of genuine scientific inquiry) it tends to give scientific warrant, barring minor changes, to the *status quo*—or the established order—a matter especially injurious in the case of economic inquiry.

From industrial sociology Dewey shifted his fire to formal economics:

> It is assumed in the first place that "economic" subject matter is so complete on its own account and of itself, inherently, and, as used to be said, "essentially," that it can be scientifically studied in independence of all other social (human) facts. In the second place, it is assumed that

what has "existed"—between whatever date is set between the beginning of the present state of industry, business, and finance and the year 1947 as limits—can be treated as a scientific sample or representative of the economic *order* without any reference to its antecedents or its consequences.[40]

The attractions of the industrial sociology trend for many pragmatic reformers were strong, however. Two major opportunities for organized planning research and experimentation existed after World War II: in government service, where the spirit of innovation was on the wane, and in private industry. The second area offered a more dramatic and extensive field for applied social science. Managers had far greater latitude for organizing people and activities than did politicians. Beyond that lay the promise of arranging economic security for the nation's workers in the midst of the heady, unexpected affluence that followed World War II. In an age of anxiety following long years of deprivation such economic security acquired value of a high order. In Stuart Chase's mind's eye the road from the horrid squalor of Rochester in 1914 to an era of abundance was a long one—and as it neared its final height, beautiful. Squabbling along the way over control of the road-building machinery seemed more an annoyance than noble democratic practice. Chase was eager to work toward a well-upholstered economic consensus in the private sector that would match the "vital center" consensus in politics. Always supporting his drive on results was an indomitable optimism. Chase did not fear Soviet Russia, which he felt had inadequate resources to maintain a far-flung empire, or the force of irrationality.[41] He welcomed the planning lessons of World War II, so much like those of World War I. The fearsome shaking America had undergone was compensated by the way more of the laissez-faire rust had been knocked out of the economic system.

Chase began his postwar contacts with enlightened management when he was invited in 1946 to visit the plants of Standard Oil of New Jersey in Bayonne and in Baton Rouge, Louisiana. The management of the company wanted him to observe a consensual system that had avoided major labor difficulties for thirty years. Chase was duly impressed, finding a spirit of industrial harmony that he had never seen duplicated. Workers in their own unaffiliated union consulted with management on all important matters and, in accord with Elton Mayo's findings, were never treated in a demeaning way. Chase drew an important distinction between the originator of the Standard plan, Clarence J. Hicks, a specialist in labor relations, and scientific management's founder, Frederick Taylor. Taylor, Chase noted, dealt primarily with materials, Hicks with men. In his summary of the reasons for Standard's success Chase included, along with rational planning, the good fortune of the oil business in maintaining a far steadier prosperity throughout the Depression than most industries. But the great key to their achievement, as Chase saw it, was intelligent cooperation which demonstrated how obsolete the notion of class struggle was in the interdependent power age. Two modes of cooperation could meet the needs: either programs advanced by workers, as had been the case with Sidney Hillman's Amalgamated Clothing Workers Union, or ideas provided by expert study of human relations under the auspices of management like Standard's. Perhaps it is better to have workers initiate the process, Chase concluded, than for management to provide. But either way the end is the same. "Whether we like it or not," Chase insisted, "the machine age has made us our brothers' keepers." [42]

In *Roads to Agreement* Chase extended the doctrine of industrial consensus. Though he had been able to describe oil refineries on the moors of New Jersey without making note of the stench and dreariness that usually has struck observers, Chase was, if anything, more inclined to stress the positive side of things in *Roads*. He was willing to take a cheerfully clinical view of all conflict. The threat of Communism from abroad would fall of its own weight, and at home the feasibility of economic abundance seemed equally assured. What tensions remained were largely matters of misunderstandings, unnecessary episodes of fear and ignorance. Chase admired the description of conflict a lawyer in Spokane once wrote to him: "Disputes are like cancer. If caught early enough, broadly speaking, they can be treated successfully, and the patient will enjoy complete recovery. But if allowed to go too long, they become incurable." Dickens' classic case of Jarndyce vs. Jarndyce occurred to Chase in the light of his friend's description. "We think, too," he added, "of a cold war that nobody caught in time." [43]

That outlook made Chase an enthusiastic admirer of the theories of group dynamics whose beginnings he had observed with interest in the 1920's when Eduard C. Lindemann, an industrial psychologist who admired Emerson's ideas of the transcendental bonds between persons, was beginning investigation in the field. [44] The climax of Chase's excursion into group dynamics came twenty-five years later during his visit to the National Training Laboratory in Group Development in Bethel, Maine. There he underwent group encounters that bore resemblance to the mechanized social mystique Kurt Vonnegut, Jr., depicts in his anti-Utopian novel, *Player Piano*, and to the encounter groups that were to appear in the sixties—sometimes far removed from, or in opposition to, the industrial establishment Lewin's associates served. The manipulative character of the groups Chase entered seems evident in retrospect; yet he considered them democratic. The problem was just as Dewey described; holding the right to make choices and experiment within a context may be taken as democratic and scientific when, in fact, careful arrangement of the context beforehand by privileged hands make the situation otherwise—"In T-groups we will bare our souls. In A-groups we will play our roles," Chase and his fellow visitors sang in the dining room. But the song was written elsewhere, in the planning room. The outcome was arranged—a feeling of fellowship within a society where achievement was oddly linked to mediocrity. Chase's summary judgment of the experience captured the mood. "It is encouraging," he announced, "to realize that people have much more ability and constructive energy inside them than normally comes out—a first principle in group dynamics. Great men are not so great as advertised, and little men are bigger than advertised—as well as being the kind the Lord must love because He makes so many of them. Greatness lies in the strength of the whole society and its capacity to adjust to changes, external and internal. Social science now makes plain the futility of struggling to beat society."[45] Chase had traveled far from the skepticism of the businessman's manipulative world that Veblen had early implanted in him. But he had always sought concrete results, and now that an affluent economy and a kindly business management seemed to be taking shape, he was anxious to tie the development in with the democratic cooperation he also cherished. Chase was more than willing to forgo the magnificent captains of industry in the leveling process, just as Veblen had been. He saw them being elbowed out by the new sociology of business in much the way that the great economist Joseph Schumpeter described in his monumental prediction of inevitable socialism, *Capitalism, Socialism and Democracy* (1942). But, unlike Chase, Schumpeter lamented the fact. He mourned the passing of the great entrepreneurs from fear that innovative genius would disappear.

Ironically, both Chase and Schumpeter, from their different perspectives, missed the same point. If harmoniously planned business eliminated the lordly tycoon, it yet was necessary to have the tycoon's more genial counterpart serve as coordinator of the intricate social web, or as invisible hand behind the scenes.

There was an element of sham in the situation that became increasingly clear as managers borrowed cooperative techniques yet resisted the democratic substance of cooperation. Neither stockholders nor workers nor consumers gained a significant voice in determining industrial goals. The cries from the left urging industrial democracy died down after the violent labor disputes of the thirties had ended, although the essential concepts industrial democrats had always fought for had not been realized. The contrast between political democracy, however flawed, and industrial autarchy remained in force. As realization of the discrepancy broadened, promoters of "industrial cooperation" lost enthusiasm. They turned from communal ethics to a stress on the good life of self-indulgence. And critics from outside industry moved swiftly toward the two major expressions of the sixties: sardonic laughter at fatuousness and hypocrisy and, on the part of those who were not amused, rage that extended to a Marxist revival and even nihilism.[46]

The consensus Chase and like-minded pragmatic reformers celebrated, then, was mythical and sliding toward a hard fate. It had been accepted with all its instability, not so much because its leadership principle was misconstrued but because the postwar sense of release from the troubles of the past and of the outside world was so powerful that many vital social factors were overlooked. Minority groups were not brought into the consensus. The strain on environment of a steadily growing population and industrial output was not given close thought. The aspirations of the Third World were underestimated in their intensity. And the sort of warning Frank gave of a military-industrial complex and the accompanying desire for world hegemony went largely unheeded. Finally, the mounting anticlimax of affluence was not adequately foreseen. After the possession of goods and security, what then? Surely not just a further effort to obtain more! Our society has become "a canonized life insurance company," lamented Edward Dahlberg as the sixties began.[47] And its urgent desire for insurance reflected apprehension of crises as the neglects of the fifties gave way to the explosive disaffections of minorities, youth, and other dissidents.

The great cultural shift of the sixties, reminiscent of the thirties in its mood of discontent, came when most independent liberal survivors from the thirties were dead or had retired from the social wars. One old soldier who did not merely fade away, John Dewey, had died in 1952, aged ninety-two. Of those left, only Lewis Mumford retained his crusading zeal, but far removed from the nation's managers whom he despised.

Yet the efforts of independent liberals to find principles for reconstructing the country, rooted as they were in fundamental thought patterns of the twentieth century and productive of memorable work, did not disappear. Criticism of vulgarity in the mass media, of botched city planning, of unreason in politics, and of meanness in social relations between different groups used the independent liberal critiques. The attacks of John Kenneth Galbraith on the conventional wisdom of professional economics served as an example of the pragmatic rationalist "method of intelligence" generally free of institutional pieties yet strongly concerned with the moral content of policies. C. Wright Mills, before his tragically premature death, drew heavily on John Dewey and Thorstein Veblen to depict a self-aggrandizing power elite. And Paul Goodman shortly afterward emerged as the most comprehensive heir of independent liberalism.

Goodman brought many elements of the pragmatic rationalism and liberal traditionalist critiques into an innovative coalition of ideas. As a young man in his twenties during the Depression, he entered the reformist ambiance of New York. He attended Columbia and began writing after the war for *Commentary* magazine in the company of Dewey, Niebuhr, Daniel Bell, and other significant critics. But Goodman did not grow into his critical positions through the standard Marxism or liberalism. Instead he developed an anarchist outlook that drew on Gestalt psychology and the distrust of collective power that was rising at the end of the thirties.

Goodman's anarchism was pacific and experimentally homegrown. It subsumed the theories of Kropotkin and Bakunin within appraisals of the American situation by Jefferson, Thoreau, and the pragmatists. Anarchism was for Goodman an incremental process not a total program. Any social movement that had succeeded in loosening the grip of authority had, in his view, advanced the anarchist cause. Victories for civil liberties, the ending of slavery, the broadening of academic freedom, and other extensions of personal autonomy all qualified as progress. Goodman gratefully noted his debt to Dewey's reformist approach, but he was not in close accord with all pragmatic nationalists. He advocated planning on a small communal basis but, with anarchic distrust of massed power, resisted the sort of central planning that Soule, Chase, and Lorwin urged.

The organic concerns of liberal traditionalism found a counterpart in the Gestalt psychology of Goodman. A blend of Oriental spirituality and Western psychology, Gestalt emphasized spontaneity and harmony with one's environment. Thus the doctrine bears practical resemblance to Waldo Frank's mystical conception of the whole and Lewis Mumford's insistence on the organic bases of life. It followed that Goodman, like Frank and Mumford, supported regionalism and acknowledged the great force of religious instincts. Summarily, he agreed that the inner spirit has more determining force than any form of external conditioning.

Goodman formed a working synthesis, then, between pragmatism as a way of using moral intelligence and liberal traditionalism as a way of conceiving the natures of men and society. His characteristic earnestness led him to extend his pragmatic inquiry all the way to a literal-minded—"dumb-bunny," as he called it—consideration of details that sought to plug loopholes and shatter defenses against unhappy realizations. He attacked "middle-class squeamishness" as the great American vice preventing people from understanding the full consequences of their lives, and was not embarrassed to press examination of ideas or systems to the point where awkward absurdities began to show through and the pious began to complain. Thus, he became a kind of sidewalk Socrates, asking impolitic questions and receiving the predictable mixture of reward and abuse.

In *Communitas* (1947), Goodman's first important work of social criticism, written with his architect-brother, Percival, he outlined three paradigms of social organization that applied his beliefs to emerging postwar society. In their first paradigm the Goodmans invented a society designed to bring the level of consumption up to meet unfettered production. With deadpan satire they sketched a city devolving upon a gigantic department store. Each year, gorged on consumer products, the citizens hold a festival of destruction to rid themselves of all surplus stock and make room for the next year's glut. The second paradigm, a society where town and country are in close contact and their cultural styles harmoniously intertwined, was the Goodmans' ideal. They reserved some sympathy for the more ascetic third paradigm of self-sufficient country living, but the blend of town and country seemed ultimately more valuable. Though the countryside may be the seat of virtue, cultivation of the highest human capacities to think and feel has always taken place mainly in the cities.

Communitas was greeted with some enthusiasm. Lewis Mumford, for example, described it as "a fresh and original theoretic contribution to the art of building cities . . . [that] deals with the underlying values and purposes, political and moral, on which planning of any sort must be based . . ." But it made little difference to the onrush of events and soon went out of print. That outcome helped to determine Goodman's subsequent emphasis on the absurdity of the American situation. At times he grew pessimistic—his love of humanity plagued by mental images of people as vermin. But his lingering hope for the use of the pragmatic method to obtain spiritual ends kept him at work dissecting social institutions with great energy. His books on education, *Growing Up Absurd* (1962), *A Community of Scholars* (1962), and *Compulsory Mis-Education* (1964) gained favor with students and reformist educators. And his subsequent forays against the Vietnam War and social repression carried him on in full association with young rebels and idealists into the social wars of the sixties. For a time it seemed that Goodman might figure heavily in a revival of independent liberalism. But the new left— or the New Reformation, as Goodman has chosen to call it—sought bitter release for their rage in a neo-Marxist ideology as the sixties came to a close. A strain set in between Goodman and those he had once been able to term fondly his "crazy allies." In 1970 Goodman felt himself sliding back into the isolation he had endured in the fifties. On his right stood the power blocs of society—the "absurdists" who ran the giant corporations in business and education and brandished their overkill at the outside world. On the left, slipping away, were the new social rebels. But it was not really quite so neatly a right and left problem. To Goodman it seemed more a total break in social consciousness between past and future. The new generation threatened to reject their culture wholesale. Like the young men of the Reformation—more than the young men of the American Revolution—they seemed in search of new institutions and a new way of perceiving reality. If that was truly their aim, then their expressions of Marxism did not signify a return to the thirties or fusion with the Third World but dramatized rejection—an intent to clear away one culture and prepare a space for another, as yet unknowable.[48]

Whether or not Goodman's anticipation of a new reformation was to be fulfilled, his perception of impasse was accurate. The expedient political ways inherited from the New Deal era had difficulty justifying their incompleteness, and, therefore, their lack of full rationality, except in response to crises. They provided immediate relief from the ills of depression and improvised victory in war. But afterward, when it came time to establish new social purposes, the orthodox mentality proved inadequate and even dangerous. In the name of realism and toughness it dealt gingerly with the great issues of race, control over science, economic imbalance, conservation, and the need of a nation to share viable ideals. Its preference for action over reflection led it to be hesitant about subtle domestic issues, but bold abroad. No greater irony could have followed than that the self-styled political realism of the sixties should draw the nation into a madly unrealistic war in Vietnam, while at home the sense of an equally mad disordering of priorities increased to the danger point. Some men of intelligence began turning once again to radical options. Marxism and anarchism found new champions, and the ideas of independent liberalism gained new life in cooperative experiments, concern about man's organic relationship with his environment, and a spreading desire for a morally planful approach to community life. Though all the revived concepts had suffered reverses in the past, independent liberalism perhaps enjoyed an advantage. Its attempts to enact programs of reconstruction had failed in the thirties. But, unlike radicalism farther to the left, it had not been caught up in disastrous contradictions or vehement public repudiation. With strong claims on goodwill it stood closer to the center of affairs, at hand for whoever would seize the day.

Notes

INTRODUCTION

[1] W. Scott Morgan, *History of the Wheel and Alliance and Impending Revolution* (Kansas, 1889), quoted in Norman Pollack, ed., *The Populist Mind* (Indianapolis: Bobbs-Merrill Co., 1967), p. 32.

[2] Theodore J. Lowi, *The End of Liberalism. Ideology, Policy, and the Crisis of Public Authority* (New York: W. W. Norton, 1969), p. 41.

[3] Arthur Bentley, *The Process of Government* (Chicago: U. of Chicago Press, 1908), Chapter 10, "Government." Lowi in *The End of Liberalism* cites Bentley to sustain his attack on pluralism.

[4] Quoted in a "Postcript" to Edward Bellamy, *Looking Backward* (New York: New American Library, 1960), pp. 221–22.

[5] Henry George, *Social Problems* (Garden City, New York: Country Life Press, 1883), p. 81.

[6] Upton Sinclair, *The Industrial Republic. A Study of the America of Ten Years Hence* (New York: Doubleday, 1907), x.

[7] H. G. Wells, *New Worlds for Old* (New York: Macmillan, 1909), p. 328.

[8] Graham Wallas, *Human Nature in Politics* (London: Constable and Co., 1908); *The Great Society* (New York: Macmillan, 1914); Walter Lippmann, *A Preface to Politics* (New York: Kennerley, 1913); *Drift and Mastery* (New York: Kennerley, 1914). A study by Paul Bourke of the relations between British Fabians and American reformers is due to appear in 1971.

[9] Wallas, *The Great Society*, pp. 368–69.

[10] Henry Adams, "A Dynamic Theory of History" (1904), quoted in Edward Saveth, ed., *Henry Adams. The Education of Henry Adams and Other Selected Writings* (New York: Washington Square Press, 1963), p. 187.

[11] Thorstein Veblen, *Absentee Ownership and Business Enterprise in Recent Times* (New York: B. W. Huebsch, 1923), p. 107.

[12] The sense of accumulating logical pressure toward unity permeated a great deal of Peirce's writings, as one can see by reading in his *Collected Papers*, Arthur W. Burke, Charles Hartshorne, and Paul Weiss, eds. See, especially, "The Order of Nature" (1908); "What Pragmaticism Is" (1905); and "Issues of Pragmatism" (1905). An illuminating discussion of Peirce's ideal of community is given by R. Jackson Wilson in *In Quest of Community* (New York: John Wiley, 1968), Chapter 2, "Charles Sanders Peirce: The Community of Inquiry."

[13] Royce's fullest statements of his communal ideals are contained in *The Philosophy of Loyalty* (New York: Macmillan, 1908); his Gifford lectures, *The World and the Individual* (New York: Macmillan, 1901); and *The Hope of the Great Community* (New York: Macmillan, 1916). For a useful secondary summary see R. J. Wilson, *In Quest of Community*, Chapter 6.

[14] John Jay Chapman, *Memories and Milestones* (New York: Moffat, Yard and Co., 1915), p. 106.

[15] Letter from Bourne to Brooks, quoted in *The World of Randolph Bourne*, Lillian Schlissel, ed. (New York: E. P. Dutton, 1965), pp. 316–17.

[16] Van Wyck Brooks, "Introduction" to the posthumous collection of Bourne's essays, *The History of a Literary Radical and Other Papers* (1919) (New York: S. A. Russell, 1956), pp. 13, 20.

[17] Herbert Croly, *The Promise of American Life* (Indianapolis and New York: Bobbs-Merrill, 1965), p. 343.

[18] *Ibid.*, p. 343.

[19] Letter from John Dewey, quoted in C. Wright Mills, *Sociology and Pragmatism* (New York: Oxford U. Press, 1966), p. 302.

[20] Dewey, "Matthew Arnold and Robert Browning," *Andover Review* (1891), reprinted in *Characters and Events* (New York: Henry Holt, 1929), Vol. I, p. 17.

[21] Dewey, "Does Reality Possess Practical Character?" in *Essays, Philosophical and Psychological*, in honor of William James (New York: Longmans, Green, 1908), p. 63.

[22] Dewey, *Studies in Logical Theory* (Chicago: University of Chicago Press, 1903), pp. 19–20.

[23] Dewey, "Force and Coercion," *The International Journal of Ethics* (1916), reprinted in *Characters and Events*, Vol. II, p. 788.

[24] Randolph Bourne, "Twilight of the Idols," *War and the Intellectuals* (New York: Harper & Row, 1964), p. 59.

[25] *Ibid.*, p. 64.

[26] Van Wyck Brooks, "On Creating a Usable Past," *Dial*, LXIV (April 11, 1918), 337–41. Claire Sprague. Harper & Row.

[27] Dewey, *Reconstruction in Philosophy* (Boston: Beacon Press, 1948), xxxix.

[28] Waldo Frank, *Virgin Spain* (New York: Boni and Liveright, 1926); *America Hispaña* (New York: Charles Scribner's, 1931); *South American Journey* (New York: Duell, Sloan and Pearce, 1943).

PART I: Chapter 1

[1] These sentiments of the League are well summarized, along with the reform program they envisaged, in "A Four Year Presidential Plan 1932–1936," editorial in *LIPA News Bulletin*, I (February–March, 1932), pp. 1–4.

[2] Paul Howard Douglas, *The Coming of a New Party* (New York: Whittlesey House, 1932).

[3] The tale of Populist relations with the outside world is a tangled one. The criticism of Populism as narrow-minded to the point of rejecting Jews, foreigners, and ideas emanating from the cities that enlivens Richard Hofstadter's account of *The Age of Reform* (New York: A. A. Knopf, 1955) has provided considerable controversy. The noted early study, John Hicks, *The Populist Revolt* (University of Minnesota Press, 1931), deals mainly with the Populists' politics. But Hicks did agree with Hofstadter that the Populists sternly set their faces against the cities, where the new historical and institutional schools of economics were being developed. Newer studies attempting to enhance the Populists' reputation, notably Norman Pollack, *The Populist Response to Industrial America* (Harvard University Press, 1962) and Walter T. K. Nugent, *The Tolerant Populists* (University of Chicago Press, 1963), have attributed considerable breadth of mind to the Populists. But both writers acknowledge that the Populists were estranged from the East and from the most advanced economic thought then being developed. Most likely both factions were at fault: progressive economists and social

engineers for fastening their attention on urban problems and their hopes on the Republican establishment and Populists for being mesmerized by the Free Silver issue.

4 Paul Douglas, *The Coming of a New Party*, p. 206.

5 Wesley Mitchell, *Business Cycles, The Problem and Its Setting* (New York: National Bureau of Economic Research, Inc., 1927).

6 Douglas expressed similar doubts in a pamphlet he wrote for LIPA, *Why a Political Realignment?* (New York: LIPA, 1930), pp. 16–17. Thorstein Veblen, to whom Dewey, Douglas, and others in the League deferred, vigorously discounted the scientific pretensions of Socialists and Marxists, just as he dismissed the efforts by classical economists to formulate immutable "laws." Some of his most trenchant attacks on the ideologies are contained in his essays collected by his student Leon Ardzrooni, in *The Place of Science in Modern Civilization and Other Essays* (New York: B. W. Huebsch, 1919).

7 For a concise summary of the League's political plans see: "A Four Year Presidential Plan 1932–1936" and, issued the previous year, "A Statement by the Executive Committee," *LIPA News Bulletin*, I (February, 1931), p. 1; the article in the same issue of 1931 by Nathan Fine, "Our Two Main Tasks," p. 2, sheds useful extra light.

8 "The League Challenges the Insurgents," *LIPA News Bulletin*, I (January, 1931), pp. 1–3. Dewey invited Norris, Borah, and Brookhart on Christmas Day, 1930 (New York *Times*, December 26, 1930). Norris declined immediately, and an exchange of letters between the Progressives and LIPA ensued (New York *Times*, December 27–28, 1930). One of the discouraging results was the resignation from LIPA of A. J. Musts on the grounds that a new party must be built up from an organization of workingmen, not downward from a few well-known "messiahs" (New York *Times*, December 30, 1930).

9 *Ibid.*, p. 3.

10 Howard Y. Williams, "Making Your Vote Count," *LIPA News Bulletin*, I (September–October, 1932), pp. 1–2.

11 "A Four Year Presidential Plan," *LIPA News Bulletin*, I (February–March, 1932), pp. 1–4.

12 Alfred Bingham, "The Farmer Labor Political Federation," *Common Sense*, II (October, 1933), pp. 18–20; letter from Morris Hillquit, chairman of the National Executive Committee of the Socialist Party to LIPA, *LIPA News Bulletin*, I (December 30, 1931), p. 1.

13 Norman Thomas, *The Choice Before Us* (New York: Macmillan, 1934), pp. 146–47. Thomas in *America's Way Out. A Program for Democracy* (New York: Macmillan, 1931) acknowledged the existence of LIPA in a note at the end because, after he had completed the text, word of LIPA's invitation to George Norris reached him. The incident, he claimed, "proved that a new party will not be built up by asking some progressive senator to be a Moses to lead us out of the House of Bondage" (p. 291). In *As I See It* (New York: Macmillan, 1932), issued in anticipation of the crucial fall elections, Thomas made no mention of LIPA.

14 Bingham, "The Farmer Labor Political Federation," p. 19.

15 *Audacity! More Audacity! Always Audacity!* Pamphlet of the United Action Committee (New York: League for Independent Political Action, 1933), p. 2.

16 John Dewey, Introduction to Harry Gunnison Brown, editor, "Significant Paragraphs from Henry George's *Progress and Poverty*" (New York: Robert Schalkenbach Foundation, 1929). The enthusiasm of the League members for Henry George and Edward Bellamy inhibited their chances of gaining desired

support from professional economists. Paul Samuelson recalled how Frank Taussig, the dean of American economists, was filled with despair upon learning of Dewey's endorsement of George, whom Taussig considered "a confused child." See: Paul A. Samuelson, "Economic Thought and the New Industrialism," in Arthur M. Schlesinger, Jr., and Morton White, eds., *Paths of American Thought* (Boston: Houghton Mifflin, 1963), p. 233.

[17] Edward Bellamy, *Equality* (New York: J. Appelton & Co., 1897), p. 61; cited in Dewey, "A Great American Prophet," *Common Sense*, III (April, 1934), p. 7.

[18] Thomas Amlie, "Thorstein Veblen Today," *Common Sense*, IV (April, 1935), pp. 14–16.

[19] *Ibid.*, p. 15.

[20] *Ibid.*, p. 14.

PART I: Chapter 2

[21] George Santayana, "The Genteel Tradition in American Philosophy," *The Genteel Tradition*, Douglas L. Wilson, ed. (Cambridge: Harvard University Press, 1967), p. 64.

[22] Quoted in Frederick J. Hoffman, *The Twenties* (New York: The Free Press, 1949), p. 276. Hoffman's book is a superb summary of thought during the twenties. I am especially indebted to Chapter 6, "Science and the 'Precious Object.'"

[23] Charles Beard, ed., *Whither Mankind. A Panorama of Modern Civilization* (New York: Longmans Green, 1928), "Introduction," p. 24.

[24] Charles Beard, ed., *Toward Civilization* (New York: Longmans, Green, 1930), "Preface," p. v.

[25] Charles Beard, "Introduction," to J. B. Bury, *The Idea of Progress* (New York: Macmillan, 1932), pp. xxii, xxv.

[26] Charles Beard, ed., *America Faces the Future* (Boston: Houghton Mifflin, 1932), p. 117.

[27] Carl Becker, *Progress and Power* (Palo Alto: Stanford University Press, 1936), p. 91.

[28] Quoted in George Soule, *Planning U.S.A.* (New York: Bantam, 1967), p. 88. Person went on to become a staunch advocate of national planning and urged government action on the planners' strongest ally in the Senate, Robert La Follette, Jr. Person made his view clearest in "The Approach of Scientific Management to the Problem of National Planning," which appeared in the edition of the *Annals of the American Academy of Political and Social Science* devoted to planning, CLXII (July, 1932), pp. 19–26.

[29] Morris S. Viteles, "The Role of Industrial Psychology in Defending the Future of America," *Annals of the American Academy of Political and Social Science*, CCXVI (July, 1941), pp. 156–62.

[30] Ordway Tead, *The Art of Leadership* (New York: McGraw-Hill, 1935), p. 91.

[31] Ordway Tead, interview, November 14, 1968.

[32] Realization that the 1930's was not so ardently ideological an era as has been commonly believed has recently been dawning. For a shrewd and detailed examination of the issue see: Warren Susman, "The Thirties," *The Development of an American Culture*, Stanley Coben and Lorman Ratner, eds. (Englewood Cliffs, New Jersey: Prentice-Hall, 1970), pp. 179–218.

[33] The doctrine of social credit, which C. H. Douglas promoted first during the twenties, rested on the proposition that in a free market there can never be enough purchasing power to absorb production. Douglas explained his con-

clusion in the famous $A + B$ theorem. A equals payments to individuals within the productive complex; B equals external costs of production. Prices, then, equal A plus B, which results in an automatic surplus of goods, tending toward depression. Douglas would have government cure the imbalance by issuing monetary credits to wholesalers and retailers so that they could charge the just price, the price at which the consumer supply of money could absorb production. Social credit took political shape in altered form in the Social Credit Party in Canada. In the United States it was debated for a time but never applied. It existed, however, in an interesting relationship with other reform thought and deserves study. Its journal, *New Democracy*, lasted from 1933 to 1936 and drew commentary from a wide array of speculative reformers, including Archibald MacLeish, William Carlos Williams, agrarians who had always concentrated on the reform of the money system, and, of course, Ezra Pound, whose unwelcome contributions were likened by one Social Credit leader to "an explosion in a rock quarry." For a full account of Social Credit see the book by *New Democracy*'s editor, Gorham Munson, entitled *Aladdin's Lamp* (New York: Creative Age Press, 1945).

34 Sinclair succinctly outlined the twelve points of his EPIC plan in "The EPIC Plan: Can Poverty Be Ended?" *Common Sense*, III (May, 1934), pp. 6–8.

35 A brief but detailed account of the EPIC campaign is included in William Leuchtenburg, *Franklin Delano Roosevelt and the New Deal* (New York: Harper, 1963), pp. 114–15. In addition to his book *How I Ran for Governor of California and Got Licked*, Sinclair gives an account in a more reflective vein, removed from the heat of battle, in his *Autobiography* (New York: Harcourt, Brace and World, 1962), pp. 268–77. Other accounts of EPIC, included as parts of larger works on California, are in Robert Glass Cleland, *California in Our Time* (New York: A. A. Knopf, 1947), pp. 222–24; Carey McWilliams, *California; The Great Exception* (New York: Current Books, 1949); Robert E. Burke, *Olson's New Deal for California* (Berkeley: University of California Press, 1953), pp. 1–5. Jerry Voorhis, long an advocate of cooperatist economics and for a time a U.S. Representative from California, included EPIC as a positive example of cooperatist principles translated into politics in *Confessions of a Congressman* (Garden City: Doubleday, 1947).

PART I: Chapter 3

36 Marquis Childs' most influential book was *Sweden: The Middle Way* (New Haven: Yale University Press, 1936). He amplified his praise for Sweden's economic mixture of capitalism, socialism, and cooperation in *This Is Democracy. Collective Bargaining in Scandinavia* (New Haven: Yale University Press, 1938).

37 James Peter Warbasse, "When Fascism Comes," *The Cooperative League Yearbook* (Minneapolis: Northern States Cooperative League, 1939), p. 9. The following year Warbasse warned that socialism was also dangerous and that the war could lead to statism whichever side won unless cooperation could check the drift to statism. Warbasse, *The Socialistic Trend as Affecting the Cooperative Movement* (New York: Cooperative League of the U.S.A., 1940).

PART I: Chapter 4

38 Lewis Lorwin, "The Problem of Economic Planning," *World Social Economic Planning* (The Hague, Netherlands: International Industrial Relations Institute, 1931), pp. 257–70.

[39] *Congressional Digest*, XI, No. 4 (April, 1932), "Congress Considers National Economic Planning." The hearings were followed by a flurry of writings about planning. One of the most important clusters of articles appeared in the issue of the *Annals* of the American Academy of Political and Social Science on planning (July, 1932).

[40] Rexford G. Tugwell, *The Trend of Economics* (New York: F. S. Crofts, 1924), p. 384.

[41] Rexford Tugwell, "The Principle of Planning and the Institution of Laissez Faire," *American Economic Review Supplement*, XXII (March, 1932), p. 75.

[42] *Ibid.*, p. 86.

[43] *Ibid.*, p. 94.

[44] Oscar Ameringer, *If You Don't Weaken* (New York: Henry Holt, 1940), p. 436. Arthur Schlesinger's *The Coming of the New Deal* (Boston: Houghton Mifflin, 1959) deals perceptively with Tugwell's role within the larger struggles of the New Deal for planning and agrarian renewal. See especially Part I, "The Fight for Agricultural Balance," and Section 21, "The Revival of Community."

[45] Rexford Tugwell, *The Brains Trust* (New York: Viking, 1968), xxi.

PART I: Chapter 5

[46] George Soule, *Recent Developments in Trade Unionism* (New York: Amalgamated Clothing Workers of America, 1921), p. 27.

[47] George Soule, *The Intellectual and the Labor Movement* (New York: League for Industrial Democracy, 1923), p. 9.

[48] *Ibid.*, p. 21.

[49] George Soule, *A Planned Society* (New York: Macmillan, 1934), p. 28.

[50] Interview between Soule and the author, September, 1964. Soule, during the thirties, indicated the hope that Roosevelt's genuine desire for reform and his economic naïveté would combine to make him receptive to new ideas. See: George Soule, "Roosevelt Confronts Capitalism," *New Republic*, 76 (October 18, 1933), pp. 267–71, and *A Planned Society*.

[51] Interview, September, 1964.

[52] Soule, *A Planned Society*, p. 2.

[53] *Ibid.*, p. 276.

[54] *Ibid.*, p. 134.

[55] *Ibid.*, p. 138.

[56] *Ibid.*, p. 216.

[57] Soule, *The Coming American Revolution* (New York: Macmillan, 1934), p. 260.

[58] *Ibid.*, p. 281.

[59] *Ibid.*, p. 295.

[60] *Ibid.*, p. 207.

[61] *Ibid.*, p. 209.

[62] *Ibid.*, pp. 303–4.

PART I: Chapter 6

[63] Stuart and Margaret Chase, *A Honeymoon Experiment* (Boston: Houghton Mifflin, 1916), p. 82.

[64] *Ibid.*, p. 84.

[65] Stuart Chase, *Technocracy: An Interpretation* (New York: John Day Co., 1933), pamphlet no. 19, p. 7.

66 Stuart Chase, "New Deal for America," *New Republic*, LXXI (June 29, 1932), p. 201.

67 Stuart Chase, "This Age of Plenty," *Harper's*, CLXVIII (March, 1934), p. 387.

68 Chase, "Harnessing the Wild Horses of Industry," *Atlantic Monthly*, 147 (June, 1931), p. 787.

69 Chase, *A New Deal* (New York: Macmillan, 1932), p. 252.

70 Without in the least wishing America to adopt the Soviet system, Chase repeatedly suggested that Americans had much to learn from Russia's Communist experiment and should not avert their eyes as if a single glimpse would turn them into pillars of salt. Chase, "Soviet Russia after Ten Years," 99th New York luncheon discussion of the Foreign Policy Association, November 19, 1927.

In many of his other writings that did not concern themselves directly with Russia Chase reiterated his belief in the lessons Russia had to teach the Western democracies. See, for example, in chronological sequence, *Prosperity: Fact or Myth* (New York: Charles Boni, 1929); "Harnessing the Wild Horses of Industry," *Atlantic Monthly*, 147 (June, 1931), pp. 776–87; *Poor Old Competition*, Pamphlet for LID (New York: 1931); "Mr. Chase Replies," *New Republic*, 69 (February 10, 1932), pp. 348–49; *A New Deal* (New York: Macmillan, 1932); "On the Paradox of Plenty," *New Republic* (January 18, 1933), pp. 258–60; "Prosperity in the Power Age," *Scribner's*, 95 (March, 1934), pp. 161–67. Chase's disinclination to copy the Russian approach is shown very clearly in the fact that his most militant plea for planning, *The Economy of Abundance* (New York: Macmillan, 1934) contains some of his most vehement criticism of planning in the Russian Communist state.

71 Stuart Chase, with Marian Tyler, *Mexico: A Study of Two Americas* (New York: Macmillan, 1931), p. 188.

72 *Ibid.*, p. 317.

73 *Ibid.*, p. 247.

74 Chase, *Prosperity: Fact or Myth* (New York: Charles Boni, 1929), p. 188.

75 Chase, *The Nemesis of American Business* (New York: Macmillan, 1931), p. 107.

76 Chase, "Declaration of Independence," *Harper's*, CLXIV (December, 1931), p. 35.

77 *Ibid.*, p. 34.

78 Chase, "Poor Old Competition" (New York: League for Industrial Democracy Pamphlet, 1931), p. 17.

79 *Ibid.*, p. 17.

80 Chase, *A New Deal*, p. 179.

81 *Ibid.*, p. 247.

82 *Ibid.*, p. 248.

83 Chase, "This Age of Plenty"; Chase drew most of his text on the failure of partial regulation in Germany from Robert A. Brady, *The Rationalization Movement in German Industry* (Berkeley: University of California Press, 1933). Chase remained opposed to regulation and an advocate of coordinated, comprehensive planning, largely on the grounds that regulatory agencies in the United States have traditionally become the tools of the enterprises they were designed to regulate. See: Chase, "How Can the State Do Business?" *Current History*, XLII (May, 1935), pp. 126–35; *Government in Business* (New York: Macmillan, 1935), Chapter 13, "Models for Regulation and Control."

84 Chase, *The Economy of Abundance* (New York: Macmillan, 1934), p. 313.

85 *Ibid.*, p. 315.

[86] Chase favored "revised and simplified political forms. The scrapping of outworn political boundaries and of constitutional checks and balances where the issues involved are technical." Point 16 of an 18-point program of reconstruction presented in "This Age of Plenty," p. 386.

[87] Chase, "If Roosevelt Fails," *Scribner's*, LXXXXVI (July, 1934), p. 10.

[88] *Ibid.*, p. 11.

PART I: Chapter 7

[89] Alfred Bingham summarized much of the reformist focus on the middle class present in the work of Chase, Soule, Dewey, and other pragmatic rationalists, both in and out of the League for Independent Political Action, in his book *Insurgent America* (New York: W. W. Norton, 1935). An influential study at the end of the decade that reiterated the key importance of the middle class to the era was Arthur N. Holcombe, *The Middle Classes in American Politics* (Cambridge: Harvard University Press, 1940).

[90] John Strachey, *The Menace of Fascism* (New York: Covici Friede, 1933), p. 148.

[91] Benjamin Stolberg and Warren Jay Vinton, *The Economic Consequences of the New Deal* (New York: Harcourt, Brace and Co., 1933), p. 48.

[92] Chase, "The Road of Revolution," *New Republic*, LXXI (July 6, 1932), p. 200. Cf. George Soule, "Are We Going to Have a Revolution?" *Harper's*, CLXV (August, 1932), pp. 277–86; Elmer Davis, "The Red Peril," *Saturday Review of Literature*, VIII (February 27, 1932), p. 661.

PART I: Chapter 8

[93] Arthur M. Schlesinger, Jr., *The Age of Roosevelt*, Vol. I: *The Crisis of the Old Order* (Boston: Houghton Mifflin, 1957), Chapter 23, "Agenda of Reform"; *The Vital Center* (Boston: Houghton Mifflin, 1949), esp. Chapter III, "The Failure of the Left."

[94] Elmer Davis, "Interregnum," *Saturday Review of Literature*, VII (May 16, 1931), p. 830.

[95] Louis Adamic, "What the Proletariat Reads," *Saturday Review of Literature*, XI (December 1, 1934), pp. 321–22.

[96] Adamic, "Voltaire from Kansas," *Outlook*, CLV (June 25, 1930), pp. 282–85.

[97] William Morris, "Looking Backward," *Commonweal*, V (June 22, 1889), p. 194. Cited in Arthur E. Morgan, *Edward Bellamy* (New York: Columbia University Press, 1944), p. 403.

[98] Archibald MacLeish, review of *The ABC of Technocracy*, by Frank Arkwright, *Saturday Review of Literature*, IX (January 14, 1933), p. 374. Two weeks later MacLeish wrote another critique of Technocracy in much the same vein: review of *Introduction to Technocracy*, by Howard Scott, *Saturday Review of Literature*, IX (January 28, 1933), p. 400.

[99] Walter Edwin Peck, review of *A Common Faith*, by John Dewey, *Common Sense*, III (December, 1934), 26. That review was more friendly than Huntington Cairns' dismissal of Dewey in a review written three years earlier: "By his abandonment of his own philosophy during the war, and because of his fundamental defects as a creative artist," Cairns wrote, "we can thus perhaps account for the [discredited] position he occupies today. . . ." Cairns concluded that when "the intellectual leader who has failed in the major crisis of his life [World War I] lacks that art upon which all appeal primarily depends there are few who would venture to prophesy he will be remembered." Huntington Cairns, review of *Character and Events*, by John Dewey, *Modern Quarterly*, V (1931), p. 376.

PART I: Chapter 9

[100] George Soule, "The New Deal in Practice," *New Republic*, LXXV (July 5, 1933), p. 199.

[101] Soule, "Roosevelt Confronts Capitalism," *New Republic*, LXXVI (October 18, 1933), p. 269.

[102] *Ibid.*, p. 270.

[103] Arthur Schlesinger, Jr., *The Crisis of the Old Order* (Boston: Houghton, 1957), p. 181.

[104] Alfred Bingham, *Insurgent America*, pp. 97–98.

[105] Robert S. and Helen Merrill Lynd, *Middletown in Transition* (New York: Harcourt Brace, 1937), p. 443.

[106] *Ibid.*, p. 387.

[107] Matthew Josephson, *Nazi Culture: The Brown Darkness over Germany*, John Day Pamphlet No. 33 (New York: John Day Co., 1933).

[108] "When America Goes to War," symposium, *Modern Monthly*, IX (June, 1935), pp. 199–204.

[109] Sinclair Lewis, *It Can't Happen Here* (New York: Doubleday & Doran, 1935), pp. 441–42.

[110] Editorial, "Perilous Days," *Common Sense*, V (August, 1936), p. 4.

[111] Editorial, "How Shall I Vote?" *Common Sense*, V (October, 1936), pp. 3–4 ff.

[112] In their postmortem of the election the pragmatic rationalist editors of *Common Sense* declared their surprise that a landslide had occurred: "Not a Labor Party," *Common Sense*, V (December, 1936), pp. 3–5.

[113] Editorial, "Perilous Days," *Common Sense*, V (August, 1936), p. 4.

PART II: Chapter 1

[1] Malcolm Cowley, "The 1930's Were an Age of Faith," New York *Times* Book Review Section (December 13, 1964), pp. 4 ff. In a sequel Cowley spoke with wry chagrin of how the Communistic involvement of writers during the thirties has been exaggerated through failure to understand that the Communist Party would never fully accept literary men from middle-class backgrounds as part of its own. See: Malcolm Cowley, "Remembrance of the Red Romance," *Esquire*, 61 (March, 1964), pp. 124 ff.; (April, 1964), pp. 78–79 ff. James Farrell, looking back on the thirties just after World War II, emphasized the extra vulnerability of writers to emotional political appeals and the futility of their succumbing to such appeals: "Literary men have the habit of rushing into the periphery of politics and they contribute to political struggles—not knowledge, not practical experience, not theoretical analysis, but rhetoric. Rhetoric is the one commodity in politics of which there has never been a scarcity." James Farrell, *The League of Frightened Philistines* (New York: Vanguard Press, 1946), p. 97. The shrewdest of commentaries on the intellectuals' involvement with Communism is given by William Phillips, "What Happened in the Thirties," *Commentary*, XXXIV (September, 1962), pp. 204–12. Phillips' essay contains a generally praiseful review of the standard work on the subject, Daniel Aaron, *Writers on the Left* (New York: Harcourt, Brace & World, 1961).

[2] Charles Frankel, "John Dewey's Legacy," *The American Scholar*, 29 (Summer 1960), p. 320.

[3] *Ibid.*, p. 321.

[4] John Dewey, *A Common Faith* (New Haven: Yale University Press, 1934), quoted in Joseph Ratner, ed., *Intelligence in the Modern World* (New York: Random House, 1939), pp. 1,021–22, 1,026.

[5] Sidney Hook, *John Dewey: An Intellectual Portrait* (New York: The John Day Co., 1939), p. 9. In a conversation about Dewey carried on by several of his closest and most noted colleagues and broadcast in 1958 on radio, Corliss Lamont mentioned that Dewey had a manuscript, summarizing his life work in philosophy, stolen from a taxi in New York. An interesting argument ensued between Lamont, who considered the loss a tragedy, and Horace Kallen, who saw it as a blessing in disguise. Kallen felt Dewey had been saved from the impossibility of trying to systematize a philosophy which had as one of its strengths a strong opposition to philosophic systems. Corliss Lamont, ed., *Dialogue on John Dewey* (New York: Horizon Press, 1959), pp. 50–52.

[6] Dewey, *Reconstruction in Philosophy* (New York: Henry Holt and Co., 1920), pp. 41–42.

[7] Dewey, *Experience and Nature* (Chicago: Open Court Publishing Co., 1925), p. 163.

[8] Dewey gives this version of the history of science in his most readable prose in *Reconstruction in Philosophy*, Chapters 1–3.

[9] Dewey, *The Public and Its Problems* (New York: Henry Holt, 1927), p. 164.

[10] John Stuart Mill, *Logic*, Book VI, Chapter 7, Sec. 1; quoted in Dewey, *The Public and Its Problems*, p. 195.

[11] *Ibid.*, p. 195.

[12] *Ibid.*, p. 126.

[13] Dewey, *The Quest for Certainty* (New York: Minton, Balch, 1929), p. 80.

[14] Dewey, *The Public and Its Problems*, p. 175. At the opposite end of the social scale the pecuniary values also work harm: "The evils thereby affecting the superior class are less material and less perceptible, but equally real. Their culture tends to become sterile, to be turned back to feed upon itself; their art becomes a showy display and artificial; their wealth luxurious; their knowledge overspecialized; their manners fastidious rather than humane." Dewey, *Democracy and Education* (New York: Macmillan, 1916), p. 98.

[15] Dewey, *Reconstruction in Philosophy*, p. 61. Dewey's concept of change was much affected by his study of Darwin's theories of evolution. See: Dewey, *The Influence of Darwin on Philosophy and Other Essays in Contemporary Thought* (New York: Henry Holt, 1910).

[16] Dewey, *Experience and Nature*, p. 146.

[17] Dewey, *Philosophy and Civilization*, pp. 293–94. Dewey's analogy between the individualistic phenomenon in a field of scientific investigation and an individual person in society is typical of his tendency to use the facts of one area to demonstrate a contention in another. Charles Frankel has written of Dewey's practice of calling on science to stamp sociological statements with authority that "Dewey repeatedly failed to distinguish between facts as they exist and those beliefs about the facts that have the warrant of science at some particular time": Frankel, "John Dewey's Legacy," p. 327. That faulty practice does, indeed, reduce some of Dewey's "proofs" to metaphors.

[18] Dewey's most vehement attackers on the issue of idealism were generally spokesmen for religious views. The Protestant theologian Reinhold Niebuhr carried on his own Thirty Years War against Dewey from the early twenties until Dewey's death in 1952. The Catholic Church was, if anything, more hostile toward Dewey

because of his denial of eternal, supernatural verities. Mortimer Adler, a Thomistic philosopher without formal attachment to any church body, has been conspicuous in his attacks upon Dewey for failing to support the idea of an immutable Western tradition. A useful general account of Dewey's idealist detractors is found in George R. Geiger, *John Dewey in Perspective* (New York: Oxford University Press, 1958). Similar discussion is offered in Sidney Hook, *John Dewey: An Intellectual Portrait*, and Jerome Nathanson, *John Dewey: The Reconstruction of the Democratic Life* (New York: Scribner's, 1951). Of the many critical pieces written about Dewey by his idealist opponents perhaps the most representative and informative are the selections from the writings of Lewis Mumford, Reinhold Niebuhr, and Mortimer Adler contained in Gail Kennedy, ed., *Pragmatism and American Culture*, Heath Series Pamphlet (Boston: D. C. Heath, 1950). A spirited, often indignant defense of Dewey is offered in the collection of essays by his friend the novelist James Farrell in *The League of Frightened Philistines* (New York: Vanguard Press, 1946). The Catholic Church's antagonism toward Dewey and pragmatism in general clearly illuminates the collection of essays about Dewey prepared by Church spokesmen in John Blewett, S. J., ed., *John Dewey: His Thought and Influence* (New York: Fordham University Press, 1960).

[19] George Santayana, "Dewey's Naturalistic Metaphysics," *Journal of Philosophy*, 22 (December 3, 1925), pp. 674–75.

[20] *Ibid.*, p. 675.

[21] Horace Kallen, "John Dewey and the Spirit of Pragmatism," in Sidney Hook, ed., *John Dewey: Philosopher of Science and Freedom* (New York: Dial Press, 1950), p. 39. In his response to Santayana's criticisms Dewey concentrated on disputing the charge that he believed only immediate experience is real. He did not see fit to answer Santayana's contention that he was the spokesman of American business materialism. See: Dewey, "Half-Hearted Naturalism," *Journal of Philosophy*, 24 (February 3, 1927), pp. 57–64. In *Experience and Nature*, the book that had most directly provoked Santayana's criticism, Dewey spoke out against the sort of emphasis on a purely personal "intuition of . . . essence" that pervaded Santayana's own philosophy. "Romanticism," Dewey contended, "has made the best and the worst of the discovery of the private and incommunicable. . . . In conceiving that this inexpugnable uniqueness, this ultimate singularity, exhausts the self, it has created a vast and somnambulic egotism out of the fact of subjectivity. For every existence in addition to its qualitative and intrinsic boundaries has affinities and active outreachings for connection and intimate union." *Experience and Nature*, pp. 242–43.

[22] William James, *Essays in Radical Empiricism* (London: Longmans, Green and Company, 1912). Cf. Dewey, *Experience and Nature*, Chapter 7, "Nature, Life and Body-mind," pp. 248–97.

[23] Dewey, "Authority and Resistance to Social Change," written in 1936 and reprinted in *Problems of Men* (New York: Philosophic Library, 1946), pp. 93–110, offers a particularly good statement of Dewey's linkage between science and collectivism.

[24] Dewey, *Problems of Men*, p. 106.

[25] Dewey, *Philosophy and Civilization*, p. 297.

[26] Dewey, *The Public and Its Problems*, p. 150.

[27] Dewey, *Intelligence in the Modern World*, p. 765.

[28] Dewey, *The Public and Its Problems*, p. 151. Cf. Dewey's comments on equality of opportunity as the keystone of the democratic state in "Democracy and Educational Administration," *School and Society*, 45 (April 3, 1937), pp. 457–62, and

"Individualism, Equality and Superiority," *New Republic*, 33 (December 13, 1922), pp. 61–63. Dewey emphasized that he was advocating equality of *opportunity*, as against a leveling equality of *condition*, which would deny innate differences of talent and ambition. That view of equality underlay the admiration of Jefferson he expressed in his Introduction to the excerpts from Jefferson's writings that he collected in *The Living Thoughts of Thomas Jefferson* (New York: Longmans, Green and Co., 1940).

29 Dewey, *Human Nature and Conduct* (New York: Henry Holt, 1922), pp. 246–47.

30 Dewey, *Philosophy and Civilization*, p. 285.

31 *Ibid.*, p. 287.

32 Dewey, *The Public and Its Problems*, p. 151.

33 *Ibid.*, p. 149.

34 Dewey, *The Quest for Certainty*, p. 81.

35 Dewey, "Philosophy as Education," quoted in Irwin Edman, ed., *John Dewey: His Contribution to the American Tradition* (New York: Bobbs-Merrill, 1955), p. 210.

36 The remark was made by the Columbia philosopher Herbert Schneider in Corliss Lamont, ed., *Dialogue on John Dewey*, p. 134.

PART II: Chapter 2

37 See the exchange between Dewey and William E. Hocking consisting of Hocking's article "Political Philosophy in Germany," *New Republic*, 4 (October 2, 1915), pp. 234–36, and Dewey's reply, p. 236; and Dewey, "Traffic in Absolutes," with a review by Francis Hackett and a footnote by Walter Lippmann, *New Republic*, 3 (July 27, 1915), pp. 281–85.

38 Hook, *John Dewey: An Intellectual Portrait*, pp. 149–76. Dewey's growing pessimism emerged interestingly in his change of estimate of William James's service to American thought. In 1910 he wrote that James, with Emerson, will "stand out as the prophetic forerunner of the attained creed of values." By 1926 he had concluded that a certain sadness had descended over the legacy of James. With vulgar businessmen distorting pragmatism to their own selfish ends, it was difficult to tell to what extent James would stand as the spokesman for a worthy American tradition. *Characters and Events*, Vol. I, pp. 117–20. In the years immediately after World War I Dewey's mood became depressed enough for him to ascribe to the ideas of one Harry Matthias Alexander, whose book *Man's Supreme Inheritance* outlined posture exercises designed to reduce mental tension. Corliss Lamont, ed., *Dialogue on John Dewey*, pp. 24–29.

39 *Reconstruction in Philosophy* (1920); *Human Nature and Conduct* (1922); *Experience and Nature* (1925); *The Public and Its Problems* (1927); *The Quest for Certainty* (1929).

40 A useful account of the founding of the New School is included in the autobiography of one of its founders, Alvin Johnson. *Pioneer's Progress* (New York: Viking Press, 1952), Chapter 27, "The New School," pp. 271–88.

41 Sidney Hook recalled Dewey remarking of his Vermont background that "where I was raised the Hoovers and the Mellons would have had a hard time passing for Americans." Sidney Hook, *John Dewey: An Intellectual Portrait*, p. 6. Nevertheless, Vermonters voted steadfastly for the Hoovers and the Mellons.

42 Sidney Ratner, ed., introduction to *John Dewey and Arthur F. Bentley: A Philosophic Correspondence, 1932–1951* (New Brunswick, N.J.: Rutgers University Press, 1964), pp. 1–45; Sidney Hook, *John Dewey: An Intellectual Portrait*.

43 New York *Times*, October 23, 1924.

44 John Stoner, *S. O. Levinson and the Pact of Paris: A Study in the Techniques of Influence* (Chicago: University of Chicago Press, 1942); Dewey contributed a foreword to the book, pp. vii–viii.

45 A detailed account of Dewey's activities in support of the Outlawry movement is given by Joseph Ratner in the book of Dewey's writings he edited, *Intelligence in the Modern World*, pp. 525–66. Some of Dewey's best writings on the subject are contained in *Characters and Events*, Vol. II. Cf. Sidney Hook's account of Dewey's conversion to pacifism after World War I: *John Dewey: An Intellectual Portrait*.

46 Murray Kempton gives a vivid account of the effect of the Sacco-Vanzetti case on liberal opinion in *Part of Our Time* (New York: Simon and Schuster, 1955), Chapter 2, "The Dry Bones," an account of Gardner Jackson and Lee Pressman, pp. 37–81. Cf. Edmund Wilson, *The Shores of Light* (New York: Farrar, Straus and Young, 1952).

47 John Dewey, "Psychology and Justice," *New Republic*, 53 (November 23, 1927), pp. 9–12.

48 Sidney Hook, *John Dewey: An Intellectual Portrait*, p. 24.

PART II: Chapter 3

49 Dewey, "The Irrepressible Conflict," *League for Independent Political Action Bulletin*, 1 (January, 1931), p. 4.

50 *Ibid.*, p. 4.

51 Dewey, "What Do Liberals Want?" *Outlook*, 153 (October 16, 1929), p. 261.

52 *Ibid.*, p. 261; cf. Dewey, "A Third Party Program," *New Republic*, 70 (February 24, 1932), pp. 48–49.

53 Editorial, *League for Independent Political Action News Bulletin*, 1 (February, 1931), p. 1. Dewey reiterated that view in the keynote address at the Cleveland League Convention in July, 1932, "Democracy Joins the Unemployed," reported in *League for Independent Political Action News Bulletin*, 1 (September–October, 1932), p. 1.

54 Dewey, "The Need for a New Party," *New Republic*, 68 (March 18, 1931), pp. 115–17; Dewey, "What Hope Is There for Politics?" *Scribner's*, 89 (May, 1931), pp. 483–87.

55 Dewey, "A Third Party Program," pp. 48–89.

56 Dewey, "The Need for a New Party," p. 117.

57 Dewey, "Who Might Make a New Party?" *New Republic*, 68 (April 1, 1931), p. 177.

58 Dewey, "What Hope Is There for Politics?" pp. 486–87.

59 Dewey, "Policies for a New Party," pp. 203–4.

60 Dewey, "After the Election—What?" *League for Independent Political Action News Bulletin*, 1 (November–December, 1932), p. 1.

61 *Ibid.*, p. 1.

62 Dewey, "Unity and Progress," *World Tomorrow*, 16 (March 8, 1933), p. 233.

PART II: Chapter 4

63 Dewey, *Individualism, Old and New* (New York: Minton, Balch and Co., 1929), p. 120.

64 *Ibid.*, p. 52.

65 Dewey, *Liberalism and Social Action* (New York: G. P. Putnam's Sons, 1935), p. 74.

[66] Dewey, "Intelligence and Power," *New Republic*, 78 (April 25, 1934), p. 306.

[67] *Ibid.*, p. 306.

[68] *Ibid.*, p. 307.

[69] Dewey, "The Future of Liberalism," *Journal of Philosophy*, 32 (April 25, 1935), p. 228.

[70] Dewey did not go as far in advocating indoctrination for social progress as did others among the pragmatic rationalists. Undoubtedly that reluctance was related to his belief in the necessity of free choice. Other, bolder reformers criticized him for this cautious view, *e.g.*, the critique by William E. Hocking of Dewey's address before the American Philosophical Association, later printed as "The Future of Liberalism" in the *Journal of Philosophy, supra.* Liberals must come to accept the fact that the state must gain greater coercive powers and "in spite of itself will have to deal with human motives." They will then be able to realize that "the Absolute of individual liberty is a liberty of *the inner man* and not of his external person."

[71] Dewey, "Who Might Make a New Party?"

[72] Dewey, "Prospects for a Third Party," *New Republic*, 71 (July 27, 1932), pp. 278–80.

[73] Dewey, "Is There Hope for Politics?" pp. 486–87.

[74] Stuart Chase, *Government in Business*, pp. 154 ff.

[75] Carmen Haider, *Do We Want Fascism?* (New York: The John Day Co., 1934).

[76] Alfred Bingham, "How Red Is America?" *Saturday Review of Literature*, 12 (August 10, 1935), p. 12.

[77] Dewey, *Liberalism and Social Action*, p. 52. One of Dewey's prime elaborations on that theme is included in "Democracy and Education in the World of Today," reprinted in *Problems of Men* (New York: Philosophical Library, 1946), pp. 34–45. See also: *Individualism, Old and New*, pp. 165–67; "The Future of Liberalism," p. 230.

[78] Dewey, "Social Change and Its Human Direction," *Modern Quarterly*, 5 (1931), pp. 422–25. "The economic philosophy of history," Dewey declared, "with its doctrine of inevitable final change of a specified sort which many Marxians derived from Marx, is a typical rationalization of a condition of immediate powerlessness." "Unity and Progress," p. 233.

[79] Dewey, "Why I Am Not a Communist," *Modern Monthly*, 8 (April, 1934), p. 137.

[80] Dewey, *Individualism, Old and New*, p. 105.

[81] Dewey, "American Ideals: The Theory of Liberty vs. the Fact of Regimentation," *Common Sense*, 3 (December, 1934), p. 11.

[82] Dewey, *Individualism, Old and New*, p. 18.

[83] Dewey, *Reconstruction in Philosophy*, p. 73.

[84] See Dewey, *Experience and Nature*, Chapter 4, "Nature, Means and Knowledge," pp. 121–65; *Ethics*, esp. Part II, "Ends, the Good and Wisdom," reissued as *Theory of the Moral Life* (New York: Holt, Rinehart, Winston, 1960).

[85] Dewey, *Philosophy and Civilization*, p. 120.

[86] Dewey, *Experience and Nature*, p. 358.

[87] Dewey, *Philosophy and Civilization*, p. 120. Dewey's devotion to art as an end was strong enough to lead one unsympathetic critic, writing from a conservative Protestant point of view, to brand Dewey a latent hedonist of the sort that signals the coming decline of a civilization into self-indulgence.

[88] Dewey, "Our Un-Free Press," *Common Sense*, IV (November, 1935), pp. 6–7.

Dewey's view of the incompatibility of a free press and the profit system dated back to his contact in Michigan in the 1890's with the volcanic reform journalists Franklin and Corydon Ford. See: Lewis Feuer, "John Dewey and the Back to the People Movement in American Thought," *Journal of the History of Ideas*, XX (October–December, 1959), pp. 545–68; and Earl James Weaver, *John Dewey: A Spokesman for Progressive Liberalism*, unpublished PhD dissertation, Brown University (1963).

[89] Dewey, "Our Un-Free Press," p. 7.

[90] Dewey, "Liberalism and Civil Liberties," *Social Frontier*, 2 (February, 1936), p. 137. Cf. Dewey, "Liberty and Equality," *Social Frontier*, 2 (January, 1936), pp. 105–6.

[91] Dewey, "Liberalism and Civil Liberties," p. 137.

[92] *Ibid.*, pp. 137–38.

[93] Dewey, "Can Education Share in Social Reconstruction?" *Social Frontier*, 1 (October, 1934), pp. 11–12.

[94] Dewey, "The Future of Liberalism," p. 229.

[95] "Orientation," editorial, *Social Frontier*, 1 (October, 1934), p. 3.

[96] Dewey, "Can Education Share in Social Reconstruction?" p. 12.

[97] Dewey, "Toward a National System of Education," *Social Frontier*, 1 (June, 1935), p. 10.

[98] Dewey, *Liberalism and Social Action*, p. 62.

[99] *Ibid.*, p. 71.

PART III: The Liberal Traditionalist Response

[1] F. Jay Taylor, *The United States and the Spanish Civil War* (New York: Bookman Associates, 1956); Allen Guttmann, *The Wound in the Heart* (New York: The Free Press of Glencoe, 1962).

[2] An analysis of books reviewed in the *Saturday Review of Literature* over the eleven-year period 1930–41 indicated a marked increase of interest after 1935 in the key issues of Fascism, propaganda and the persuasive power of the irrational, American involvement abroad, and cooperative economics. Writings on the first three issues showed enmity toward Fascism and stressed ways American resources might best be concerted to avoid or oppose its menace. Interest in cooperative economics at the same time suggests that many regarded cooperation as the logical alternative to Fascism, Communism, and apparently moribund capitalism.

PART III: Chapter 1

[3] Herbert Agar, "The Task for Conservatism," *American Review*, 3 (April, 1934) pp. 1–22.

[4] Agar, "A Plea to Mr. Charles A. Beard," *American Review*, 3 (January, 1935), pp. 297–309.

[5] Hayek later gathered his laissez-faire theories together in a widely discussed book, *The Road to Serfdom* (Chicago: University of Chicago Press, 1944).

[6] Agar, "Just Why Economics?" *North American Review*, 240 (September, 1935), p. 208.

[7] *Ibid.*, p. 210.

[8] Tate and Agar, eds., *Who Owns America?* (Boston: Houghton, Mifflin, 1936), p. 20.

[9] *Ibid.*, p. 20.

[10] This view echoes the opinions expressed in the extremely influential book, Adolph Berle and Gardiner C. Means, *The Modern Corporation and Private Property* (New York: Macmillan, 1933).

[11] Tate and Agar, eds., *Who Owns America?*, p. 90.

[12] *Ibid.*, p. 107.

[13] *Ibid.*, p. 107.

[14] *Ibid.*, p. 202.

[15] William Yandell Elliott, *The Need for Constitutional Reform* (New York: McGraw-Hill, 1935).

[16] Agar and Tate, *Who Owns America?*, pp. 94–113.

[17] Odum's earlier works on sociology were: *Sociology and Social Problems* (Chicago: American Library Association, 1925); *Southern Pioneers in Social Interpretation* (Chapel Hill: University of North Carolina Press, 1925); *Man's Quest for Social Guidance* (New York: Henry Holt, 1929); *An American Epoch* (New York: Henry Holt, 1930). In addition Odum wrote three novels, all dealing with Negro life: *Rainbow Round My Shoulder* (Indianapolis: Bobbs-Merrill, 1928); *Wings on My Feet* (Indianapolis: Bobbs-Merrill, 1929); *Cold Blue Moon* (Indianapolis: Bobbs-Merrill, 1931).

[18] Howard Odum, *Southern Regions of the United States* (Chapel Hill: University of North Carolina Press, 1936), pp. 212–13.

[19] *Ibid.*, p. 217.

[20] *Ibid.*, p. 217.

[21] *Ibid.*, p. 233.

[22] *Ibid.*, p. 259.

[23] An interesting plea for much the same sort of regional policy, with a special interest shown for the sorry plight of the Southwest during the Depression, was provided by the historian Walter Prescott Webb in *Divided We Stand* (New York: Farrar & Rinehart, 1937).

[24] Arthur M. Schlesinger, *The Politics of Upheaval* (Boston: Houghton, Mifflin, 1960), Chapter 23, "The Roosevelt Coalition," pp. 424–47. Particularly useful summaries of the Supreme Court's civil liberties activities in this period are given in Robert G. McCloskey, *The American Supreme Court* (Chicago: University of Chicago Press, 1960), and Alpheus Mason, *The Supreme Court from Taft to Warren* (Baton Rouge: Louisiana State University Press, 1958).

[25] The best summaries of this shift from radical collectivism in literature to a more individualistic tone are given in Daniel Aaron, *Writers on the Left* (New York: Harcourt, Brace & World, 1961), and Walter B. Rideout, *The Radical Novel in the United States* (Cambridge: Harvard University Press, 1956).

[26] Erskine Caldwell and Margaret Bourke White, *Say, Is This The U.S.A.?* (New York: Duell, Sloan & Pearce, 1941); *You Have Seen Their Faces* (New York: Modern Age, 1937). The novelist James Agee, in collaboration with photographer Walker Evans, produced a far more sensitive, beautifully constructed, but less widely read documentary account of poor Southern whites in *Let Us Now Praise Famous Men* (Boston: Houghton, Mifflin Company, 1941).

[27] Agar and Tate, *Who Owns America?*, p. 271.

[28] Joseph E. Baker and Paul Robert Beath, "Regionalism: Pro and Con," *Saturday Review of Literature*, 15 (November 28, 1936), pp. 3–4.

[29] *Ibid.*, p. 3.

[30] Henry Seidel Canby, *American Memoir* (Boston: Houghton, Mifflin Company, 1947).

[31] Wallace Stegner, et al., *Four Portraits and One Subject: Bernard De Voto* (Boston: Houghton, Mifflin Company, 1963).

³² Henry Seidel Canby, "Literature and the Planned State," *Saturday Review of Literature*, 16 (August 4, 1934), p. 30.

³³ Bernard De Voto, "A Primer for Intellectuals," *Saturday Review of Literature*, 9 (April 22, 1933), p. 545; "The Importance of Pareto," *Saturday Review of Literature*, 12 (May 25, 1935), p. 11. Included with De Voto's article in 1935 were three other discussions of Pareto's work, distinctly less praiseful than De Voto's: Lawrence J. Henderson, "Pareto's Science of Society," pp. 3–4; Arthur Livingston, "Vilfredo Pareto: A Biographical Portrait," p. 12; Benedetto Croce, "The Validity of Pareto's Theories," pp. 12–13. De Voto wrote at greater length in "Sentiment and the Social Order," *Harper's*, 167 (October, 1933), pp. 569–81. The Pareto revival reached its peak in 1935. That year an edition of his *The Mind and Society* was completed by Livingston; and Henderson published his major analysis, *Pareto's General Sociology: A Physiologist's Interpretation* (Cambridge, Mass.: Harvard University Press, 1935).

³⁴ Ralph Borsodi, *The Distribution Age. A Study of the Economy of Modern Distribution* (New York: D. Appleton & Co., 1927), p. 320.

³⁵ Borsodi, *This Ugly Civilization* (New York: Simon and Schuster, 1929), p. 204.

PART III: Chapter 2

³⁶ Kallen's major early writings on cultural pluralism were collected in *Culture and Democracy in the United States* (New York: Boni and Liveright, 1924).

³⁷ Edward A. Ross, "Old World in the New," *Nation*, 100 (February 18–25, 1915), pp. 190–94, 217–20.

³⁸ Horace Kallen, "Democracy vs. the Melting Pot," *Nation*, 100 (February 18–25, 1915), p. 220.

³⁹ *Ibid.*, p. 217.

⁴⁰ *Ibid.*, p. 220.

⁴¹ In addition to *Culture and Democracy* Kallen wrote several pieces urging cultural pluralism and economic democracy. Among the most important were the book *Education, The Machine, The Worker* (New York: New Republic, Inc., 1925) and articles: "Humanism and the Industrial Age," *New Republic*, 33 (January 10–24, 1923), pp. 168–71, 191–93, 219–21; "Roots of Anti-Semitism," *Nation*, 116 (February 28, 1923), pp. 240–42; "Arts Under a Dictatorship," *Saturday Review of Literature*, 5 (December 29, 1928), pp. 549–51; "Fear, Freedom and Mass," *American Mercury*, 18 (November, 1929), pp. 281–92.

⁴² Kallen's principal works on cooperatism during the thirties were: *Individualism: An American Way of Life* (New York: Liveright, 1933), *A Free Society* (New York: Robert O. Ballou, 1934), *The Decline and Rise of the Consumer* (New York: Appleton-Century-Crofts, 1936), and "Philosophical and Ethical Aspects of Consumer Cooperation," *Annals of the American Academy of Political and Social Science* (May, 1937), pp. 38–45. An even stronger influence on his thought than the Scandinavian cooperatives was the Rochdale Consumer Plan.

⁴³ Carey McWilliams, *Louis Adamic and Shadow-America* (Los Angeles: Arthur Whipple, 1935), pp. 53–54.

⁴⁴ Louis Adamic, "Land of Promise," *Harper's*, 163 (October, 1931), pp. 619–20.

⁴⁵ McWilliams, *Louis Adamic and Shadow-America*, p. 41.

⁴⁶ *Ibid.*, p. 100.

⁴⁷ Adamic, "Thirty Million New Americans," *Harper's*, 169 (November, 1934), p. 692.

[48] Adamic, "Alien Baiters," *Harper's*, 173 (November, 1936), p. 572.

[49] Some of the more notable persons on the editorial board were Nicholas Kelly, Sigurd J. Anresen, Ida Tarbell, Langston Hughes, Van Wyck Brooks, and Pearl Buck.

[50] Adamic, *A Nation of Nations* (New York: Harper, 1945), p. 7. Adamic was not able to carry out the project completely. The four volumes that were finished were *From Many Lands* (New York: Harper, 1940), *Two-Way Passage* (New York: Harper, 1941), *What's Your Name?* (New York: Harper, 1942), and *A Nation of Nations*. Adamic planned a fifth volume, to be titled *Plymouth Rock and Ellis Island*, which was scheduled to be published in 1947 or 1948 but which never appeared.

[51] William Allen White, "Adamic's America," *Saturday Review of Literature*, 18 (May 28, 1938), p. 5.

[52] Louis Adamic, "Muscular Novel of Immigrant Life," review of Pietro di Donato, *Christ in Concrete*, *Saturday Review of Literature*, 20 (August 26, 1939), p. 5; "American Humanity on Parade," review of Benjamin Appel, *The People Talk*, *Saturday Review of Literature*, 22 (June 8, 1940), p. 5.

[53] Louis Adamic, "Thirty Million New Americans," *Harper's*, 169 (November, 1934), p. 692.

[54] Eric Goldman, "Ancestors for Everybody," *New Republic*, 113 (November 19, 1945), p. 5.

PART III: Chapter 3

[55] Max Lerner, "The Supreme Court and American Capitalism," *Yale Law Journal*, 42 (1933), pp. 688 ff, reprinted in Robert G. McCloskey, ed., *Essays in Constitutional Law* (New York: Knopf, 1957), pp. 107–44. Edwin Corwin, *The Twilight of the Supreme Court* (New Haven: Yale University Press, 1934). Robert K. Carr, *Democracy and the Supreme Court* (Norman, Oklahoma: University of Oklahoma Press, 1936).

[56] A good summary of support and opposition given to Roosevelt's proposal is given in Joseph Alsop and Turner Catledge, *The 168 Days* (New York: Doubleday, Doran, 1938). The most cogent arguments offered to defend Roosevelt's position are in Robert H. Jackson, *The Struggle for Judicial Supremacy* (New York: Knopf, 1941).

[57] Irving Howe and Lewis Coser, *The American Communist Party* (Boston: Beacon Press, 1957), pp. 300 ff.

[58] *Ibid.*, p. 296.

[59] *Ibid.*, p. 315.

[60] Howe and Coser in *The American Communist Party* tend toward the general view that the Popular Front represented a great advance for the Communists. Agreement is recorded by James Oneal and G. A. Werner, *American Communism* (New York: E. P. Dutton & Co., 1947). The first, and highly influential, popularization of that view appeared in the book by the disillusioned ex-Communist Eugene Lyons, *The Red Decade* (Indianapolis: Bobbs Merrill, 1941). More recently Frank Warren in *Liberals and Communism* (Bloomington, Ind.: Indiana University Press, 1966) has charged that the liberals' lack of a firm ideology obliged them to defer to the Communists after their penchant for cooperative action brought them into the Popular Front. But independent liberals, if they lacked ideology, tended to have definite programs and beliefs.

[61] James Farrell, "The End of a Literary Decade," *American Mercury*, 48 (December, 1939), p. 409.

[62] *Ibid.*, p. 413.

[63] MacLeish, "Ars Poetic," from *Streets in the Moon* (1926), reprinted in *Collected Poems, 1917–1952* (Boston: Houghton, Mifflin, 1952), p. 40.

[64] MacLeish, "American Letter," from *New Found Land* (1930), reprinted in *Collected Poems*, p. 65.

[65] MacLeish, "The Fourteenth Amendment," *Fortune*, 5 (June, 1932), pp. 52 ff.

[66] MacLeish, "The Grasslands," *Fortune*, 12 (November, 1935), pp. 59–67 ff. In an interview with this writer MacLeish declared that the eyewitness research he did for this article impressed him more than any other single incident with the desperate plight of many Americans during the Depression.

[67] MacLeish, "The Social Cant," *New Republic*, 73 (December 21, 1932), pp. 156–57.

[68] MacLeish, "Machines and the Future," *Nation*, 136 (February 8, 1933), pp. 140–42; "Preface to an American Manifesto," *Forum*, 91 (April, 1934), pp. 195–98; review of Frank Arkright, *The A B C of Technocracy*, *Saturday Review*, 9 (January 14, 1933), pp. 373–74; review of Howard Scott, *Introduction to Technocracy*, *Saturday Review*, 9 (January 28, 1933), p. 400.

[69] MacLeish, "Lines for an Interment," review of Lawrence Stallings, ed., *The First World War*, *New Republic*, 76 (September 20, 1933), pp. 159–60.

[70] MacLeish, "Preface to an American Manifesto," *Forum*, 91 (April, 1934), p. 195.

[71] *Ibid.*, pp. 195–98.

[72] Van Wyck Brooks, *Days of the Phoenix. The Nineteen-Twenties I Remember* (New York: F. P. Dutton, 1957), Chapter 2, "The Newness."

[73] Frank contributed to the most important study of Stieglitz: Waldo Frank, Dorothy Norman, Paul Rosenfeld and Harold Rugg, eds., *America and Alfred Stieglitz. A Collective Portrait* (New York: The Literary Guild, 1934). The tone of the many contributors was almost uniformly praiseful.

[74] Waldo Frank, *Our America* (New York: Boni and Liveright, 1919), p. 20.

[75] *Ibid.*, pp. 27–28.

[76] *Ibid.*, p. 28.

[77] Bittner, *The Novels of Waldo Frank*, pp. 56–60. Gorham B. Munson, *Waldo Frank: A Study* (New York: Boni and Liveright, 1923), pp. 77–86.

[78] *The Dark Mother* (1920); *City Block* (1922); *Rahab* (1922); *Holiday* (1924); *Chalk Face* (1925).

[79] Waldo Frank, *The Rediscovery of America* (New York: Charles Scribner's, 1929), p. 235.

[80] Sidney Hook, "The Non-Sense of the Whole," *Modern Quarterly*, 5 (1931), pp. 504–13. Frank rebutted Hook in the same issue, pp. 514–16.

[81] *Ibid.*, p. 516.

[82] Frank, *The Rediscovery of America*, pp. 258 ff.
258 ff.

[83] Frank, "Why Should the Jews Survive?" *New Republic*, 77 (December 13, 1933), pp. 121–25.

[84] Frank, *Our America*, pp. 82–83.

[85] *Ibid.*, p. 124.

[86] *Ibid.*, p. 121.

[87] Frank, Foreword to André Malraux, *Days of Wrath* (New York: Random House, 1936), pp. xi–xii.

PART III: Chapter 4

[88] Agar, "The War Is Worth Fighting," *American Mercury*, 51 (December, 1940),

pp. 401–7; "Who Are the Appeasers?" *The Nation*, 152 (March 22, 1941), pp. 316–18.

[89] Agar, *A Time for Greatness* (Boston: Little, Brown, 1942), p. 15.

[90] *Ibid.*, p. 169.

[91] Odum, *American Social Problems* (New York: Henry Holt, 1939), p. 133.

[92] *Ibid.*, p. 143. The fear of the irrational, which was markedly on the increase at the time Odum was writing, was excellently summarized and analyzed in Erich Fromm, *Escape from Freedom* (New York: Farrar and Rinehart, 1941).

[93] Odum, *American Social Problems*, p. 287.

[94] *Ibid.*, p. 296.

[95] *Ibid.*, p. 297.

[96] *Ibid.*, p. 298.

[97] *Ibid.*, p. 300.

[98] *Ibid.*, p. 406.

[99] Odum, *The Way of the South* (New York: Macmillan, 1947), p. 335.

[100] William Allen White made the position of the Committee to Defend America clear in a letter to Roy Howard of the Scripps-Howard newspaper chain on December 20, 1940. Quoted in Walter Johnson, *The Battle Against Isolation* (Chicago: University of Chicago Press, 1944), pp. 181–82.

[101] Poll taken by *Fortune* in May, 1940, cited in William L. Langer and S. Everett Gleason, *The Challenge to Isolation* (New York: Harper's, 1952).

[102] Johnson, *The Battle Against Isolation*, pp. 114–17.

[103] *Ibid.*, p. 115.

[104] *Ibid.*, pp. 223–27. The aims of the Fight for Freedom Committee were announced in the New York *Times*, April 20, 1941.

[105] MacLeish, *A Time to Speak* (Boston: Houghton, Mifflin, 1941), p. 99.

[106] MacLeish, *The Fall of the City* (New York: Farrar & Rinehart, 1937), p. 32.

[107] MacLeish, "The Irresponsibles," *The Nation*, 150 (May 18, 1940), pp. 618–23.

[108] *Ibid.*, pp. 116–17.

[109] Stephen Vincent Benét, review in *Books* (May 11, 1941), p. 2; Reinhold Niebuhr, review in *The Nation*, 152 (April 26, 1941), p. 506.

[110] Malcolm Cowley, "Poets and Prophets," review of MacLeish, *A Time to Speak*, *New Republic*, 104 (May 5, 1941), p. 640.

[111] Max Lerner, et al., "On 'The Irresponsibles,'" *The Nation*, 150 (June 1, 1940), pp. 678–82.

[112] Burton Rascoe, "The Tough-Muscle Boys of Literature," *American Mercury*, 51 (November, 1940), pp. 369–74. Mary Colum, "The Double Men of Criticism," *American Mercury*, 52 (June, 1941), pp. 762–68.

[113] Max Lerner, et al., "On 'The Irresponsibles,'" p. 680.

[114] Frank, "Our Guilt in Fascism," *New Republic*, 102 (May 6, 1940), p. 605.

[115] *Ibid.*, p. 608.

[116] Frank, *Chart for Rough Water* (New York: Doubleday, Doran, 1940), p. 23.

[117] *Ibid.*, pp. 152–53.

[118] *Ibid.*, pp. 164–66.

PART IV: Chapter 1

[1] Mumford, "The City," in Harold E. Stearns, ed., *Civilization in the United States* (New York: Harcourt, Brace, 1922), pp. 3–20.

[2] Mumford, *The Story of Utopias* (New York: Boni and Liveright, 1922), pp. 25–26.

[3] *Ibid.*, p. 108.

4 *Ibid.*, p. 113.
5 *Ibid.*, p. 173.
6 *Ibid.*, pp. 244–45.
7 Walter Lippmann, *Public Opinion* (New York: Macmillan, 1922), p. 15.
8 *Ibid.*, p. 25.
9 Mumford, *The Story of Utopias*, p. 296.
10 Mumford, *Sticks and Stones* (New York: Boni and Liveright, 1927), p. 1. The story of the Regional Planning Association of America is told admirably in Roy Lubove, *Community Planning in the 1920's: The Contribution of the Regional Planning Association of America*. (University of Pittsburgh Press, 1963).
11 *Ibid.*, p. 3.
12 *Ibid.*, p. 37.
13 *Ibid.*, p. 124.
14 *Ibid.*, pp. 124–25.
15 *Ibid.*, p. 128.
16 *Ibid.*, p. 147.
17 *Ibid.*, p. 150.
18 *Ibid.*, pp. 175–76.
19 *Ibid.*, p. 196.
20 *Ibid.*, p. 206.
21 *Ibid.*, p. 227.
22 Mumford, *The Golden Day* (New York: Boni and Liveright, 1926), pp. 19–20.
23 *Ibid.*, p. 91.
24 *Ibid.*, p. 108.
25 *Ibid.*, p. 191.
26 *Ibid.*, p. 136.
27 *Ibid.*, p. 166.
28 *Ibid.*, p. 243.
29 *Ibid.*, pp. 243–44.
30 *Ibid.*, p. 238.
31 *Ibid.*, p. 256.
32 *Ibid.*, p. 256.
33 *Ibid.*, pp. 256–57.
34 *Ibid.*, p. 262.
35 *Ibid.*, p. 258.
36 Horace Kallen, *Education, The Machine, The Worker* (New York: New Republic, Inc., 1925).
37 Mumford discussed the evolution of his view toward technology in the preface he wrote in 1955 for *Sticks and Stones* (New York: Boni and Liveright, 1924). Mumford's admiration for Geddes was not matched by a personal affinity between the two men. As Mumford, often edgy in his contacts with people, expressed it, "our rhythms of work and thought were entirely different, and I couldn't bear to be talked at for hours at a time." Quoted in Philip Boardman, *Patrick Geddes: Maker of the Future*. (Chapel Hill: University of North Carolina, 1944), p. 412.
38 Mumford, *The Brown Decades* (New York: Dover, 1931), p. 5.
39 Quoted in Ralph L. Rusk, *The Life of Ralph Waldo Emerson* (New York: Columbia University Press, 1949), p. 289. F. O. Matthiessen in his classic work *American Renaissance* (New York: Oxford University Press, 1941) indicates clearly the emphasis on art in Emerson's organic principle. See: Book One, Chapter IV, "The Organic Principle," pp. 133–66. Two pieces in the collection of essays about Emerson edited by Milton R. Konvitz and Stephen E. Whicher, *Emerson* (New

Jersey: Prentice Hall, 1962), show with useful clarity Emerson's views toward society and the organic principle. See, on Emerson's aloofness from collective social action, Daniel Aaron, "Emerson and the Progressive Tradition," pp. 85–99; on his organic views, Norman Foerster, "Emerson and the Organic Principle in Art," pp. 108–20. The suspicion of Emerson and his like-minded contemporaries toward technology is well described in Leo Marx, *The Machine in the Garden* (New York: Oxford, 1964), especially in Chapter 4, "The Machine."

[40] Mumford, *The Brown Decades*, pp. 268–69.

[41] *Ibid.*, pp. 273–83.

PART IV: Chapter 2

[42] Mumford, "What I Believe," *Living Philosophies* XIV, *Forum* (November, 1930), p. 263.

[43] Mumford, *Technics and Civilization* (New York: Harcourt Brace, 1934), pp. 46–47.

[44] *Ibid.*, p. 51.

[45] *Ibid.*, p. 25.

[46] *Ibid.*, p. 112.

[47] *Ibid.*, p. 195.

[48] *Ibid.*, p. 324.

[49] *Ibid.*, p. 354.

[50] *Ibid.*, p. 216.

[51] *Ibid.*, p. 259.

[52] *Ibid.*, p. 292.

[53] *Ibid.*, pp. 266–67.

[54] *Ibid.*, p. 297.

[55] *Ibid.*, pp. 402–4.

[56] *Ibid.*, p. 405.

[57] *Ibid.*, p. 409.

[58] *Ibid.*, p. 417.

[59] *Ibid.*, p. 421.

[60] *Ibid.*, p. 429.

[61] Mumford, *The Culture of Cities* (New York: Harcourt, Brace, 1938), Chapter II, "Court, Parade, and Capital," pp. 73–142; Chapter III, "The Insensate Industrial Town," pp. 143–222.

[62] *Ibid.*, p. 278.

[63] *Ibid.*, p. 349.

[64] *Ibid.*, p. 206.

[65] *Ibid.*, p. 371.

[66] *Ibid.*, p. 361.

[67] Interview between the author and Archibald MacLeish in Conway, Massachusetts, September, 1964.

[68] Mumford, "A Challenge to American Intellectuals," *Modern Quarterly*, 5 (1931), pp. 407–10.

[69] A good example of the Marxians' disdain of Brooks is provided by Bernard Smith in "The Liberals Grow Old," *Saturday Review of Literature*, 10 (December 30, 1933), pp. 377–78.

[70] Mumford, "What Has 1932 Done for Literature?" *Atlantic*, 150 (December, 1932), pp. 761–67. Mumford's championing of Brooks may well have been related to his concern for his friend's fragile health. Brooks recovered from mental illness in 1931, and his *The Life of Emerson* (1932) expressed that new health in its praise

of the Concord sage. Earlier Brooks had described Emerson and other American writers as captives of narrow Puritanism. Henceforth he was to stress the unique virtues to be found within the American heritage. Mumford wished to protect Brooks' hard-won optimism from discouraging attacks.

71 Mumford, "Roosevelt and Public Works," *New Republic*, 76 (October 11, 1933), pp. 243–44.

72 Mumford, "On the Road to Collectivism," *New Republic*, 81 (February 6, 1935), pp. 361–62.

73 Mumford, "A Letter to the President," *New Republic*, 89 (December 30, 1936), p. 264.

74 Mumford, "The Menace to the American Promise," *New Republic*, 101 (November 8, 1939), pp. 64–65.

75 Mumford, "Notes on Germany," *New Republic*, 72 (October 26, 1932), pp. 279–81.

76 Mumford, "On the Road to Collectivism," p. 362.

77 Mumford, "Call to Arms," *New Republic*, 95 (May 18, 1938), pp. 39–42. An interesting rebuttal was presented in the same issue by the editors, who felt non-intercourse to be impractical and the use of force, generally, to be reprehensible. Another rejoinder appeared in the *American Mercury*, a journal that was especially active in opposing interventionism: Albert J. Nock, "The State of the Union," *American Mercury*, 44 (August, 1938), pp. 467–72. Nock, a noted Jeffersonian conservative, opposed interventionism as a means of unduly increasing the power of the government over individuals.

78 Mumford, *Men Must Act* (New York: Harcourt, Brace, 1939), p. 8.

79 *Ibid.*, p. 99.

80 Mumford, "On the Road to Collectivism," p. 361.

81 Mumford, *Men Must Act*, p. 177. Mumford's proposals were influentially seconded by the prominent leftist critic Max Lerner in *Ideas Are Weapons* (New York: Viking Press, 1939) and *It Is Later Than You Think: The Need for a Militant Democracy* (New York: Viking Press, 1939).

82 Mumford, *Men Must Act*, pp. 141–42.

83 Jerome Frank, *Save America First* (New York: Harper's Brothers, 1938); Stuart Chase, *The New Western Front* (New York: Harcourt, Brace, 1939); George Soule, "If Germany Wins," *New Republic*, 102 (April 22, 1940), pp. 525–26; "Is This a World Revolution?" *New Republic*, 102 (June 24, 1940), pp. 845–46.

84 Mumford, "America at Armageddon," *Current History*, 50 (March, 1939), pp. 24–25. Mumford's concept is similar to that expressed by TVA Director David Lilienthal in his famous book, *TVA: Democracy on the March* (New York: Harper, 1944).

85 Mumford, "Menace to the American Promise," p. 65.

86 Mumford, "The Corruption of Liberalism," *New Republic*, 102 (April 29, 1940), p. 572.

87 Mumford's sharpest attack on Americans' lack of moral fiber was made in "The Passive Barbarian," *Atlantic*, 166 (September, 1940), pp. 274–76.

88 Mumford, "The Corruption of Liberalism," p. 573.

89 Herbert Agar, et al., *World-Wide Civil War*, Freedom House Pamphlet (1941).

90 Mumford, *Faith for Living*, p. 105.

91 *Ibid.*, p. 195.

92 *Ibid.*, p. 195.

93 *Ibid.*, p. 292.

94 *Ibid.*, p. 331.

PART V: Chapter 1

[1] "Toward a New Party," *Common Sense*, 3 (December, 1934), p. 2.
[2] "How Shall I Vote?" *Common Sense*, 5 (October, 1936), pp. 3–4 ff.
[3] "Not a Labor Party," *Common Sense*, 5 (December, 1936), pp. 3–5.
[4] *Ibid.*, p. 4.
[5] *Annals of the American Academy of Political and Social Science*, "Consumer Cooperation," (May, 1937).
[6] F. Jay Taylor, *The United States and the Spanish Civil War* (New York: Bookman Associates, 1956). Allen Guttmann, *The Wound in the Heart* (New York: The Free Press of Glencoe, 1962).
[7] Guttmann, *The Wound in the Heart*, pp. 115–21.
[8] *Ibid.*, pp. 29–51.
[9] A perceptive account of Frank's adventure in Spain is given in William Bittner, *The Novels of Waldo Frank* (Philadelphia: University of Pennsylvania Press, 1955). Bittner's judgment of Frank's deep emotional involvement in the Spanish War was confirmed in an interview between Mr. Frank and the author in New York in August, 1964. For examples of *Common Sense*'s attitude, see: "Guns and Butter" (January, 1939), pp. 3–5; G. F. Eliot, "What Cost National Defense?" (February, 1939), pp. 8–10; "War Over What?" (May, 1939), pp. 16–17; "What Are They Fighting For?" (November, 1939), pp. 16–17; Carleton Beals, "The Defense of the Americas" (December, 1940), pp. 9–12.
[10] In his rather discouraged résumé of the state of affairs in sociology at the end of the decade, Robert Lynd repeated his urgings for radical change. At that point he did not so much foresee Fascism as the result of inaction, but rather expected that stagnation would fix the country in a condition of permanent depression. Robert Lynd, *Knowledge for What?* (Princeton: Princeton University Press, 1939), pp. 202–50.
[11] See, for example: Carmen Haider, *Do We Want Fascism?* (New York: The John Day Company, 1934); Henry Seidel Canby, "Literature in a Planned State," *Saturday Review of Literature*, 11 (August 4, 1934), pp. 29–30; Raymond Gram Swing, *Forerunners of American Fascism* (New York: J. Messner, 1935); Lewis Corey, *The Crisis of the Middle Class* (New York: Covici Friede, 1935); Ernest K. Lindley, *Half Way with Roosevelt and Norman Thomas; After the New Deal, What?* (New York: Viking Press, 1936).
[12] See, for example: Stanley High, *Roosevelt—and Then?* (New York: Harper, 1937); Gilbert Seldes, *Your Money and Your Life* (New York: Whittlesey, 1938); Marquis Childs, *This Is Democracy* (New Haven: Yale University Press, 1938); David Cushman Coyle, *Roads to a New America* (Boston: Little, Brown, 1938); Arthur N. Holcombe, *The Middle Classes in American Politics*.

PART V: Chapter 2

[13] Alfred Korzybski, *Science and Sanity* (Lancaster, Pennsylvania: The Science Press Printing Co., 1933). C. K. Ogden and I. A. Richards, *The Meaning of Meaning* (New York: Harcourt, Brace, 1936).
[14] Chase, review of Thurman Arnold, *Symbols of Government* in *Common Sense*, 5 (April, 1936); "The Tyranny of Words," *Harper's*, 175 (November, 1937), pp. 175 ff; "Word-Trouble Among the Economists," *Harper's*, 176 (December, 1937), pp. 48–58.
[15] Chase, *The Tyranny of Words* (New York: Harcourt, Brace, 1938), p. 3.

16 *Ibid.*, p. 6.

17 *Ibid.*, p. 18. The widely held concept of the mind as a switchboard came under increasing attack in the period following *The Tyranny of Words*. That concept, with its mechanistic implications, did not fit well with the growing stress on evanescent, often irrational bases of human thought. For a masterful early analysis of the issue in behalf of the later view, see: Susanne K. Langer, *Philosophy in a New Key* (Harvard University Press, 1942).

18 The works of Hogben and Bridgman that influenced Chase most were: Lancelot Hogben, *Mathematics for the Millions* (New York: W. W. Norton, 1937); *The Retreat from Reason* (London: Watts & Co., 1937); P. W. Bridgman, *The Logic of Modern Physics* (New York: Macmillan, 1932).

19 Chase, *The Tyranny of Words*, p. 208.

20 *Ibid.*, p. 221.

21 *Ibid.*, p. 112.

22 *Ibid.*, p. 113.

23 *Ibid.*, p. 113.

24 *Ibid.*, pp. 115–16.

25 *Ibid.*, p. 178.

26 *Ibid.*, p. 135.

27 *Ibid.*, pp. 27–28.

28 *Ibid.*, p. 198.

29 *Ibid.*, p. 199.

30 *Ibid.*, p. 304.

31 *Ibid.*, p. 304.

32 Chase, "Civilization in Our Keeping?" *Common Sense*, 8 (August, 1939), p. 5.

33 Chase, *Keeping the Peace*, pamphlet for the Keep America Out of War Congress (New York, 1940).

34 Chase, *The New Western Front* (New York: Harcourt, Brace, 1939), p. 13.

35 *Ibid.*, p. 45.

36 *Ibid.*, p. 51.

37 *Ibid.*, p. 173.

38 Chase, "If You Were President," *New Republic*, 103 (July 15, 1940), pp. 73–76.

39 Chase, *What Kind of War?* pamphlet for the Post War World Council. Chase wrote a series of short studies for the Twentieth Century Fund under the general title, *Guide Line to America's Future* (New York: Twentieth Century Fund, 1942–1946): Vol. 1, *The Road We Are Traveling* (1942); Vol. 2, *Goals for America* (1942); Vol. 3, *Where's The Money Coming From?* (1943); Vol. 4, *Democracy Under Pressure* (1945); Vol. 5, *Tomorrow's Trade* (1945); Vol. 6, *For This We Fought* (1946).

40 Chase, *What Kind of War?*

41 George Soule, "Does Socialism Work?" *New Republic*, 85 (February 5, 1936), pp. 356–59.

42 Soule, "The Next Four Years," *New Republic*, 90 (March 10, 1937), p. 130.

43 Soule, *The Future of Liberty* (New York: Macmillan, 1936), p. 30.

44 Soule, *An Economic Constitution for Democracy* (New Haven: Yale University Press, 1939), p. 101.

45 *Ibid.*, pp. 14–15.

46 Soule, "If Germany Wins," *New Republic*, 102 (April 22, 1940), p. 526.

47 Soule, "Bases of Foreign Policy," *New Republic*, 103 (August 19, 1940), pp. 233–35.

48 *Ibid.*, p. 235.

[49] Soule, "Is This a World Revolution?" *New Republic*, 102 (June 24, 1940), p. 846.

[50] *Ibid.*, p. 846.

[51] Soule, *An Economic Constitution for Democracy*; "Toward a Planned Society," *New Republic*, 101 (November 8, 1939), pp. 29–32.

[52] Soule, "Is This a World Revolution?" p. 846.

[53] Alfred Bingham, "The New Deal Has a Future," *Common Sense*, 8 (August, 1939), p. 6.

[54] *Ibid.*, p. 7.

[55] *Ibid.*, p. 7.

[56] *Ibid.*, p. 9.

[57] Seven Harvard and Tufts Economists, *An Economic Program for American Democracy* (New York: Vanguard Press, 1938), p. ix.

[58] *Ibid.*, pp. 88–91.

[59] Bingham, "The New Deal Has a Future," p. 8.

[60] Bingham, *The Techniques of Democracy* (New York: Duell, Sloan and Pearce, 1942), p. 82.

[61] Bingham, *The Practice of Idealism* (New York: Duell, Sloan and Pearce, 1944), p. 84.

[62] John Dewey, "Liberalism and Equality," *Social Frontier*, 2 (January, 1936), pp. 105–6.

[63] Dewey, "Liberalism and Civil Liberties," *Social Frontier*, 2 (February, 1936), p. 137.

[64] *Ibid.*, p. 138.

[65] An interesting account of the refusal of Charles Beard and Carl Becker to serve on the commission—a refusal that was likely typical in its reasoning of many liberals—is given in Harold Kirker and Burleigh Taylor Wilkins, "Beard, Becker and the Trotsky Inquiry," *American Quarterly*, 13 (Winter, 1961), pp. 516–25.

[66] The members of the commission at the completion of the investigation were John Dewey, chairman; John Chamberlain; Wendelin Thomas; Carlo Tresca; Francisco Zamora; Suzanne La Follette, secretary; John F. Finerty, counsel. Carleton Beals resigned during the investigation because of a disagreement with Dewey's procedure. See: Commission of Inquiry, *Not Guilty* (New York: Harper, 1938).

[67] Commission of Inquiry, *The Case of Leon Trotsky* (New York: Harper, 1937); *Not Guilty*.

[68] Commission of Inquiry, *Not Guilty*, p. 5.

[69] Dewey, "Means and Ends," *New International* (August, 1938); Interview with Agnes Meyer, "Significance of the Trotsky Trial," *International Conciliation*, 337 (February, 1938), pp. 53–60.

[70] Dewey, "No Matter What Happens—Stay Out," *Common Sense*, 8 (March, 1939), p. 11.

[71] Dewey, "The Basis for Hope," *Common Sense*, 8 (December, 1939), p. 9.

[72] *Ibid.*, p. 10.

[73] In the collection of Dewey's writings, Joseph Ratner, ed., *Intelligence in the Modern World* (New York: Random House, 1939), a long discussion of Dewey's work with Salmon O. Levinson in behalf of the Kellogg-Briand Pact and international peace is included (pp. 525–66), indicating the nature of Dewey's antiwar feelings stemming from the First World War experience.

[74] *Ibid.*, pp. 431–32.

[75] Dewey, "What I Believe," *Forum*, 38 (March, 1939), pp. 176–82, quoted in Gail Kennedy, ed., *Pragmatism and American Culture* (Boston: Heath, 1950), p. 31.

[76] Dewey, *Freedom and Culture* (New York: Putnam's, 1939), pp. 7–8.

[77] *Ibid.*, p. 18. Dewey had affirmed that preference for the proofs offered by the anthropologists over those devised by psychologists several years earlier in *Human Nature and Conduct* (New York: Henry Holt, 1922).

[78] Dewey, *Freedom and Culture*, p. 35.

[79] *Ibid.*, p. 131.

[80] *Ibid.*, p. 41.

[81] *Ibid.*, p. 94.

[82] *Ibid.*, p. 96.

[83] *Ibid.*, p. 170.

[84] *Ibid.*, pp. 171–72.

[85] *Ibid.*, p. 176.

AFTERMATH

[1] In an unsigned review of *Men Must Act* the *Partisan Review* accused Mumford of advocating a policy of mobilization that would lead to Fascism. The situation reminded the reviewer of Huey Long's classic description of how easy it would be to institute Fascism by claiming to be interested in running a crusade against it. "However good the intentions of the war party and its liberal politicians," the review concluded, "I think it unlikely, once war has introduced dictatorship, that our rulers will be able to afford the luxury of a return to democratic government." *Partisan Review*, VI (Spring, 1939), p.12.

[2] *Partisan Review*, IX (March–April, 1942).

[3] James Agee, "Pseudo-Folk," *Partisan Review*, XI (Spring, 1944), p. 221.

[4] *Partisan Review*, XI (Fall, 1944), p. 488. Lionel Trilling's novel, *The Middle of the Journey* (New York: Viking, 1947) pursued the theme of despair into the postwar period.

[5] An excellent illustration of the romantic view toward World War II, as expressed at that time and in retrospect, is provided by James MacGregor Burns's admiring study, *Roosevelt: The Soldier of Freedom* (New York: Harcourt, Brace, Jovanovich, 1970).

[6] Quoted in Stuart Chase, "Where's the Money Coming From? Problems of Postwar Finance" (Pamphlet of the Twentieth Century Fund, 1943), p. 22.

[7] *Ibid.*, p. 129.

[8] George Soule, *The Strength of Nations. A Study in Social Theory* (New York: Macmillan, 1942), p. 252.

[9] See, for example, Horace Kallen, "National Solidarity and the Jewish Minority," *Annals* of the American Academy of Political and Social Science, CCXXIII (September, 1942), pp. 17–28; and "Jewry Must Wait," *Saturday Review* (March 8, 1947), pp. 25 ff.

[10] Adamic, "Death in Front of the Church," *Harper's* CLXXXVII (September, 1943), pp. 365–75.

[11] Adamic did not carry out the project completely. The volumes that were finished were: *From Many Lands* (New York: Harper, 1940); *What's a Name?* (New York: Harper, 1942); and *Nation of Nations* (New York: Harper, 1945). Adamic planned a fifth volume to be titled *Plymouth Rock and Ellis Island*, which was scheduled for 1947 or 1948 but never appeared.

[12] Archibald MacLeish, *A Time to Act* (Boston: Houghton, Mifflin, 1943).

[13] Howard Odum, *The Way of the South* (New York: Macmillan, 1947).

[14] Mumford, *City Development. Studies in Disintegration and Renewal* (New York: Harcourt, Brace and Co., 1945), pp. 167–68.

[15] Granville Hicks, "The Fighting Decade," *Saturday Review*, XXII (July 6, 1940), pp. 3–5 ff.

[16] Max Lerner to Hadley Cantrill, December 19, 1941, Lerner ms. (Yale).

[17] Chase, *Some Things Worth Knowing. A Generalist's Guide to Useful Knowledge* (New York: Harper, 1958). Taking advantage of the missed guess to illustrate his favorite theory that institutions, not natural law, determine economics, Chase stated that "no better illustration could be given of the fact that behavior governs economics, or that modern money is highly elastic" (p. 182).

[18] David Potter, *People of Plenty. Economic Abundance and the American Character* (University of Chicago Press, 1954). David Riesman, with Reuel Denney and Nathan Glazer, *The Lonely Crowd* (Yale University Press, 1950). Daniel Boorstin, both historian and social critic, has been the most throughgoing in drawing historical conclusions to match the postwar emphasis on consumption. Boorstin considers the interdependency formed by rising consumer desires to have been the key to America's unique pattern of community development. See Daniel Boorstin, *The Americans: The Colonial Experience* (New York: Random House, 1958).

[19] Lewis Mumford, *The City in History. Its Origins, Its Transformations, and Its Prospects* (New York: Harcourt, Brace & World, 1961), p. 432. Mumford concentrated on the significance of the machine and its modern destructiveness in *The Myth of the Machine. Technics and Human Development* (New York: Harcourt, Brace & World, 1966). The menacing shape of the Pentagon occupies the center of his sequel to that study, *The Pentagon of Power* (Harcourt, Brace, Jovanovich, 1970).

[20] Mumford, "Apology to Henry Adams," *Virginia Quarterly Review*, XXXVIII (Winter, 1962), pp. 196–217. In a review of his *Technics and Civilization*, twenty-five years after its first appearance, Mumford emphasized how development of the destructive potential of atomic energy had undermined the optimism he had held in the thirties for technology and industry. Before World War II he had not been able to face the ugly possibilities. After Hiroshima there was no choice. Mumford, "An Appraisal of Lewis Mumford's 'Technics and Civilization,'" *Daedalus*, LXXXVIII (Summer, 1959), pp. 527–36.

[21] Mumford, *The Myth of the Machine*, p. 12.

[22] *Ibid.*, p. 70.

[23] *Ibid.*, p. 76.

[24] Waldo Frank, "Introduction" (1947) to a new edition of *The Rediscovery of America* and *A Chart for Rough Water* (New York: Doubleday, 1947), pp. xii–xiii.

[25] Quoted in June Bingham, *Courage to Change. An Introduction to the Life and Thought of Reinhold Niebuhr* (New York: Charles Scribner's Sons, 1961), p. 335.

[26] Donald Meyer, *The Protestant Search for Political Realism, 1919–1941* (Berkeley: University of California Press, 1960), pp. 404–5.

[27] The Progressive Party deserves some further attention as part of the undercurrent of dissatisfaction with the cold war that is again surfacing. Existing studies, even when sympathetic, tend to see it as a hapless aberration. See: Karl Schmidt, *Henry Wallace: Quixotic Crusader* (Syracuse University Press, 1960) and the discussion in David A. Shannon, *The Decline of American Communism* (New York: Harcourt, Brace, 1959). Sardonic William Hesseltine dismissed the Progressives, along with other third parties in American history, on the eve of election in *The Rise and Fall of Third Parties* (Washington: Public Affairs Press, 1948). By contrast, third-party enthusiasts in earlier and more optimistic times felt that voting for what seems right has its own intrinsic rewards and that "wild-eyed" third-party programs have a way of making their way into polity despite the defeats of the

parties that sponsored them. A rereading of the American Socialist platform of 1912, the Populist platform of 1892, and the *Communist Manifesto* of 1848 should be enough to make that point. Farm radical Oscar Ameringer expressed old-style third-party convictions in 1940, the year Henry Wallace was elected Vice President. "By the time the election of 1940 rolled around," Ameringer recalled, "my experience . . . had taught me the rule of never voting for a Presidential candidate who had the slightest chance of election. The ballot is too precious lightly to be thrown away on candidates selected and financed by the 'angels' and archangels of the two historic old parties which have managed my adopted country into the condition it is in today." From which stemmed Ameringer's first political law: "Politics is the art by which politicians obtain campaign contributions from the rich and votes from the poor on the pretext of protecting each from the other." Ameringer, *If You Don't Weaken*, pp. 156–57, 393. A forthcoming study of the Progressive campaign of 1948 by Norman Markowitz will add a perspective more positively attuned to Wallace and third parties than has been customary since 1948.

[28] Adamic was cited by the House Un-American Activities Committee several times for alleged Communistic activities. See: New York *Times*, June 26, 1949. Adamic also became embroiled with the ex-Communists turned informants, Louis Budenz and Elizabeth Bentley. See: Budenz, *This Is My Story* (New York: McGraw-Hill, 1947), p. 187; and Bentley, *Out of Bondage* (New York: Devin-Adair, 1951), p. 208.

[29] "Adamic Murdered?" *Newsweek*, XXXVIII (September 17, 1951), pp. 20–21.

[30] Carey McWilliams, "Louis Adamic, American," *Nation*, CLXXIII (September 22, 1951), pp. 203–32. Conservatives tended to disagree on the suicide verdict, claiming that the Communists had murdered Adamic and that his friends refused to accept the fact because of their chronic "softness on Communism." See: Ralph De Toledano, *Lament for a Generation* (New York: Farrar, Straus and Cudahy, 1960), Chapter 7, "No Sound of Trumpets."

[31] David Cushman Coyle, *Day of Judgment. The Economic and Political Challenge to the West* (New York: Harper & Bros., 1949).

[32] Arthur M. Schlesinger, Jr., *The Vital Center* (Boston: Houghton, Mifflin, 1949), p. 37.

[33] Archibald MacLeish, *JB, A Play in Verse* (Boston: Houghton, Mifflin, 1958).

[34] Mumford to Brooks, January 6, 1951, reprinted in Robert Spiller, ed., *The Van Wyck Brooks-Lewis Mumford Letters* (New York: F. P. Dutton, 1970), p. 350.

[35] The scattered ideas and evidence of these rebels are starting to be gathered. Especially successful is Theodore Roszak, *The Making of a Counter Culture. Reflections on the Technocratic Society and Its Youthful Opposition* (New York: Doubleday, 1969). For a lucid summary of the culture being countered see Ronald Berman, *America in the Sixties. An Intellectual History* (New York: The Free Press, 1968).

[36] John Dewey, "Wallace vs. a New Party," *New Leader*, XXXI (October 30, 1948), pp. 1 ff.

[37] Dewey, *German Philosophy and Politics*. (New York: G. P. Putnam's, 1942), p. 47.

[38] Dewey, "Challenge to Liberal Thought," *Fortune*, XXX (August, 1944), p. 184.

[39] Dewey to Robert V. Daniels (1947), "Letters of John Dewey to Robert V. Daniels, 1946–1950," *Journal of the History of Ideas*, XX (October–December, 1959), p. 571.

[40] Dewey, "Liberating the Social Scientist. A Plea to Unshackle the Study of Man," *Commentary*, IV (October, 1947), pp. 379–80.

41 The concept of the Soviet Union as a marginal menace recurred often in Chase's writings and was a crucial postwar restatement of his old optimism that kept him from joining the cold warriors. See: Chase, "Will Communism Conquer the World? A Balance Sheet" (New York: Sidney Hillman Foundation Reprint, undated); "Nineteen Propositions about Communism," *Saturday Review*, XXXV (April 5, 1952), pp. 20–21. Chase's perspective on the Soviet Union and on national priorities led him to favor substantial disarmament and to oppose confrontation politics. He criticized President Kennedy's ultimatum to Russia to remove her missiles from Cuba as overly bellicose, as well as frightened, in "Two Worlds," *Bulletin of the Atomic Scientists*, XIX (June, 1963), pp. 18–20.

42 Chase, *A Generation of Industrial Peace* (Standard Oil Co., N.J.: 1947), p. 55.

43 Stuart Chase, with Marian Tyler Chase, *Roads to Agreement. Successful Methods in the Science of Human Relations* (New York: Harper's, 1951), p. 171.

44 Eduard C. Lindemann, *Social Discovery; an Approach to the Study of Functional Groups* (New York: Republic Publishing Co., 1924), with an introduction by Herbert Croly; *The Democratic Man; Selected Writings*, Robert Gessner, ed. (Boston: Beacon Press, 1956).

45 Chase, *Roads to Agreement*, p. 239.

46 The dilemma of managers trying to retain paternal control over workers and belief in their own innate superiority, while promoting the ideal of cooperation, is cogently explored in Reinhard Bendix, *Work and Authority in Industry. Ideologies of Management in the Course of Industrialization* (New York: John Wiley & Sons, 1956), Chapter 5, "The American Experience." Bendix's study moved to the forefront of growing concern at that time over the place of the managerial class in American life. William H. Whyte examined communication between workers and managers some years earlier and concluded in *Is Anybody Listening?* (New York: Simon and Schuster, 1952) that management was little inclined to base any of its decisions on what it heard from the workers. Whyte followed that study with *The Organization Man* (New York: Simon and Schuster, 1956), the most popular book on the subject and one which found corporate life troubled by conformism and lack of a sense of humane purpose. Max Lerner used what he had learned from Thorstein Veblen for a corollary discussion of how businessmen and technicians fit together in *America as a Civilization* (New York: Simon and Schuster, 1957), "The Culture of Science and the Machine."

The mood of the sixties stemmed from these doubting studies. See, on the side of parody, C. Northcote Parkinson, *Parkinson's Law and Other Studies in Administration* (Boston: Houghton, Mifflin, 1957); John K. Galbraith, *The McLandress Dimension* (Boston: Houghton, Mifflin, 1963); and Stanley M. Herman, *The People Specialists* (New York: A. A. Knopf, 1968). The move toward Marxism and rage was most importantly furthered by Paul Baran and Paul Sweezy, *Monopoly Capital* (New York: Monthly Review Press, 1966) and the several books of Herbert Marcuse, especially *One Dimensional Man* (Boston: Beacon, 1964) and *Essay on Liberation* (Boston: Beacon, 1969).

47 Edward Dahlberg, *Epitaphs of Our Times* (New York: George Braziller, 1967), p. 193. Originally a proletarian novelist, author of *Bottom Dogs* (1930) and *From Flushing to Calvary* (1932), Dahlberg later rejected Communism and modern mechanized society and adopted a neo-Biblical style of social criticism. The publication of his autobiography, *Because I Was Flesh* (New York: New Directions, 1963), established him as an important retrospective critic of the thirties. A collection of his essays, *Alms for Oblivion* (University of Minnesota Press, 1964), and his letters gathered in *Epitaphs of Our Times*, extended his commentary.

[48] The idea that the present system must first be cleared away before concepts of a new community might be clearly formulated had become commonplace by 1970. More confident than Goodman of youth's capacity to carry out wisely such a dual project were Margaret Mead, *Culture and Commitment* (Garden City, New York: American Museum of Natural History, 1970) and Charles Reich, *The Greening of America* (New York: Random, 1970). John Aldridge countered in *In the Country of the Young* (New York: Harper's Magazine Press, 1970) with a judgment that youthful militance was the expression of a generation that had been spoiled by affluence and was demanding to have satisfactions given to it, not the opportunity to carry out hard and constructive work of its own. Reich's proposal for a peaceable revolution duplicates Edward Bellamy's optimism in *Looking Backward*. Reich dismisses signs of a repressive oligarchy in America as illusory, insisting that the time is ripe for citizens to revolutionize their lives by simply withdrawing their support from a system that would then collapse emptily. In *Looking Backward* the narrator Julian West, awakening in 1988 after a hundred-year sleep, asks his host about the revolution that produced Utopia. "'Such a stupendous change as you describe . . . did not, of course, take place without great bloodshed and terrible convulsions.'

"'On the contrary,' replied Doctor Leete, 'there was absolutely no violence. . . . The Change had been long foreseen. Public opinion had become fully ripe for it, and the whole mass of the people was behind it. There was no more possibility of opposing it by force than by argument.'" *Looking Backward* (New York: New American Library, 1960), p. 54.

Bibliographical Note

Writing about such a recent period as the 1930's is an equivocal affair. One has a certain feeling of at-homeness there, a link by experience or word of mouth and a familiarity with the general social issues. Recent printed materials are abundant. Moreover, many veterans of the 1930's are still with us and willing to share their memories and perceptions. My work benefited from interview with several persons who are mentioned in the acknowledgments.

On the other hand, the very nearness of the 1930's makes that decade more remote in certain ways than earlier periods whose records are less diffuse, and often more completely catalogued, and whose inhabitants are no longer able to dispute the order visited upon them by biographers and historians. Also, no one has yet drawn together the detail of the 1930's into a general cultural history. The dense surface of those years is only now being chiseled into a number of shapes, most of them defined by the influence of the New Deal.

My subject presented a challenge of special importance for research into the 1930's. Most of the people I have studied remained a significant distance from the centers of power. Reformers who are willing thus to advocate ideas that do not stand a good chance for immediate application are apt to be rather stoic or abstract. They defer their hopes to the future or else simply dare to act on what seems right, regardless of the odds. Such independent people do not tend toward large popular organizations. Under the circumstances I saw my task as essentially one of gathering into descriptive groups those people who had been scattered in their lives but kindred in their thinking. Readers should be alert to the possibilities of typological fallacies in my selection and use of data, though I meant my labels to serve merely as conveniences for tracing historical patterns of movement, like bands on the legs of migrating birds. Having tagged certain representative persons, I read virtually all they had written during the 1930's and much of what they wrote at other times and of what has been written about them.

Because I was primarily concerned with thought bearing upon public issues, most of my research dealt with printed social criticism. But more private sources proved valuable as well, mostly for biographical insights, since one's utterances are never without personal coloration. Edward Norman's papers in the custody of his son, Andrew, gave useful information about the consumer cooperative movement and the attempts during the 1930's to find a home for Jewish refugees. The Thomas Amlie papers at the University of Wisconsin provided extensive information on the progressive farm-labor movement. And letters to a wide variety of people commenting on the state of society and the arts are to be found in the Max Lerner and Alfred Stieglitz correspondences at Yale and in the letters of John Dewey at Columbia. In addition to my own interviews I found the holdings of the Columbia Oral History Projects useful, even though most of the transcripts are still being withheld from public view. Interviews of particular interest included:

Maxwell Anderson	Members of the Civil Liberties
Louis Bean	Commission of 1939, convened
John Dewey	by Senator Robert La Follette, Jr.
Robert L. Duffus	A. J. Muste
Mordecai Ezekiel	Upton Sinclair
Gardner Jackson	John Spargo
Alvin Johnson	Gerard Swope
William Heard Kilpatrick	Ordway Tead
Rexford Tugwell	Norman Thomas

For their rare and often ephemeral materials, the Labadie Collection of radical writings in Michigan, the Tamiment Institute in New York City, and the pamphlet collection of the New York Public Library were especially important places to visit.

Many works bear usefully on the development of American thought before the 1930's. Robert Wiebe in *The Search for Order*, 1877–1920 (New York: Hill and Wang, 1967) analyzes the growing desire for organizational principles to adjust society to a new world. Henry May's *The End of American Innocence* (New York: Knopf, 1959) examines the rebelliousness attendant on such a felt need for change, and Morton White's *Social Thought in America* (New York: Viking, 1949) describes the simultaneous "revolt against formalism" in the higher realms of intellect. The penchant for progressive change from the 1890's onward persuaded Richard Hofstadter to label his shrewd overview of the period *The Age of Reform* (New York: Knopf, 1955). Eric Goldman's *Rendezvous with Destiny* (New York: Knopf, 1952) surveys the age perceptively with a similar sense of its reformist "destiny." Christopher Lasch explores the psychological matrix of that reformist thought in *The New Radicalism* (New York: Knopf, 1965). An earlier study of motives that still bears consideration is John Chamberlain's *Farewell to Reform* (New York: John Day, 1932). Chamberlain's analysis of the inherent insufficiencies of liberal reformism, when it would not agree to scrap the capitalist system, gave useful support to the Marxian left.

Historians have approached the 1930's largely through the New Deal. Although no general cultural history of the period exists, there are important insights into the era in the fine, dramatic story of *The Age of Roosevelt*, by Arthur M. Schlesinger, Jr., 3 vols. (Boston: Houghton Mifflin, 1957–60) and in the unusually thoroughgoing one-volume study by William Leuchtenburg of *Franklin D. Roosevelt and the New Deal* (New York: Harper, 1963). Statements by New Dealers are well represented in Howard Zinn's *New Deal Thought* (Indianapolis: Bobbs-Merrill, 1966), and Zinn's introduction is a lucid, succinct interpretation from the present-day left. From an independently radical perspective Matthew Josephson's *Infidel in the Temple* (New

York: Knopf, 1967), an autobiographical sequence to his remembrances of the 1920's, *Life Among the Surrealists* (New York: Knopf, 1962), offers perceptive, and often amusing, commentary on the mood of the Depression years. Links between the planning conceptions of the pragmatic rationalists and the development of planning and administrative thought within government service are indicated by Barry Karl in *Executive Reorganization and Reform in the New Deal* (Cambridge, Mass.: Harvard, 1963). Karl notes affinities in thought and action on socioeconomic issues between certain governmental bureaus and such independent reformist agencies as the National Bureau of Economic Research and Brookings Institution. Helping form the nexus was the reformist social science developed since the turn of the century at the University of Chicago, Columbia University, and the New School for Social Research by such giants as John Dewey, Thorstein Veblen, Charles Merriam, and Wesley Clair Mitchell. The writings of Rexford Tugwell from the early 1920's onward further illuminate the ground stretching from one edge of the New Deal toward more systematic concepts of reform.

A shrewd appraisal of the cultural tenor of the 1930's is contained in Warren Susman's essay, "The Thirties," in Stanley Coben and Lorman Ratner, *The Development of an American Culture*. Its conclusion that the period was less preoccupied with ideological commitment than most accounts suggest balances it well against the article by William Phillips on the Marxist fervor of those years, "What Happened in the Thirties" (*Commentary*, XXXIV [September 1962], pp. 204–12). On a larger scale Daniel Aaron in *Writers on the Left* (New York: Harcourt, 1962) has incisively chronicled the thought of the left. And Harvey Swados in his anthology *The American Writer and the Great Depression* (Indianapolis: Bobbs-Merrill, 1966), has incorporated some of the best writing produced in that period from all standpoints.

The two major figures of this story, John Dewey and Lewis Mumford, wrote extensively during exceptionally long careers. The bibliography compiled by Milton Thomas is thorough both for Dewey's own writings and for writing about him. No such handy reference exists for Mumford, who is still producing at an impressive rate.

The essentials of Dewey's social criticism are contained in *Reconstruction in Philosophy* (New York: Holt, 1920); *The Public and Its Problems* (New York: Holt, 1927); *Individualism New and Old* (New York: Minton, Balch, 1930), and *Liberalism and Social Action* (New York: Putnam, 1935). Joseph Ratner's compilation of Dewey's writings, *Intelligence in the Modern World* (New York: Random House, 1939), is an admirably condensed guide to the major dimensions of Dewey's philosophic and humanist thought.

Mumford's historical viewpoint on the society of Emerson, Thoreau, Whitman, Melville, and the other giants of the mid-nineteenth century to whom Mumford long professed a moral and intellectual debt is expressed in *The Golden Day* (New York: Boni and Liveright, 1924). Mumford's *Technics and Civilization* (New York: Harcourt, 1934) was a landmark in his ensuing effort to relate man's organic character to the history of his technology. *Men Must Act* (New York: Harcourt, 1939) displays Mumford's humanism in vehement opposition to Fascism, and *Values for Survival* (New York: Harcourt, 1946) reiterates that spirit in a perceptive appraisal of the possibilities for life in the post-World War II world. *The City in History, Its Origins, Its Transportations, Its Prospects* (New York: Harcourt, 1961) and *The Myth of the Machine* (New York: Harcourt, 1966, 1970, 2 vols.) continue Mumford's examination of technology in a broad sweep of cultural history that decries the blight materialism and war has laid upon the human spirit.

Stuart Chase was a leader among pragmatic rationalists in taking up the cause of rational efficiency from Thorstein Veblen. His *The Challenge of Waste* (New York: Macmillan, 1926) is an enduring example of that concern. *A New Deal* (New York: Macmillan, 1932) remains the best guide to Chase's reformist approach to the Depression. And his post-World War II outlook is captured in *The Proper Study of Mankind* (New York: Harper, 1948), in which he surveys the advances made by the social sciences.

George Soule in *The Intellectual and the Labor Movement* (New York: League for Industrial Democracy, 1923) indicates the nature of the conscientious drive for reform that early possessed him. His *A Planned Society* (New York: Macmillan, 1934) and *The Coming American Revolution* (New York: Macmillan, 1934) were major essays in planning during the 1930's. And *A Time for Living* (New York: Viking, 1955) contains a partly philosophic, partly economic appraisal of the possibilities of post-World War II society.

A Challenge to the New Deal (New York: Falcon, 1934), which Alfred Bingham edited with Selden Rodman, is revealing of the left liberal critique of politics at the start of the 1930's. Bingham's *Insurgent America* (New York: W. W. Norton, 1935) develops his central theory of a rising middle-class militancy. And his *Techniques of Democracy* (New York: Duell, Sloan and Pearce, 1942) outlines ideas for reform action attuned to a close examination of basic American social institutions. Although Bingham virtually ceased his writing career with *Techniques*, he continued to hold to the point of view and the means of action presented there.

Lewis Lorwin's *Time for Planning* (New York: Harper, 1945), gathering the threads of his planning theories after the tests of the 1930's, is the best guide to his pragmatic rationalist thought. Charles Beard's introduction to Bury's *Idea of Progress* (New York: Macmillan, 1932) is a useful, succinct key to his view of planned progress. Carl Becker in *Progress and Power* (Palo Alto, Calif.: Stanford Press, 1936) and *New Liberties for Old* (New Haven: Yale Press, 1941) explains his uneasy outlook on social and technical organization at greater length.

A fuller introduction to pragmatic rationalism can be gained by looking at the writings of others mentioned in the text, especially David Cushman Coyle, John Commons, Paul Douglas, Arthur Holcombe, Robert Lynd, Robert MacIver, Wesley Mitchell, and Ordway Tead.

Horace Kallen became the prime publicist of cultural pluralism with his essay "Democracy vs. the Melting Pot" (*Nation*, 100 [February 18–25, 1915], pp. 190–94, 217–20), written in response to the racism in Edward A. Ross' discussion of immigration, *The Old World in the New* (New York: The Century Co., 1914). Kallen's fully developed thoughts on the subject, not essentially different from his judgments of 1915, are contained in *Cultural Pluralism and the American Idea* (Philadelphia:

University of Pennsylvania Press, 1956). His interest in the economic and industrial means for orchestrating diverse society is best presented in *Education, The Machine, The Worker* (New York: New Republic, Inc., 1925) and "Philosophic and Ethical Aspects of Consumer Cooperation" (*Annals of the American Academy of Political and Social Science*, 191 [May, 1937], 38–45). The former book expressed Kallen's hopes for an industrial democracy along the lines espoused by such labor union reformers as Morris Hillquit and Sidney Hillman. The latter article promoted consumer cooperation at a time when that cause had gained greater currency. Louis Adamic's cultural pluralism, the fruit of a self-taught journalist's unusually keen observations of human types, was less systematic than the thought of the trained moral philosopher, Kallen. Adamic's judgments, scattered through a wide variety of reportage, were probably best summarized in *A Nation of Nations* (New York: Harper, 1944).

Waldo Frank significantly furthered the search for a Great Tradition in *Our America* (New York: Boni and Liveright, 1919) and *The Rediscovery of America* (New York: Scribner, 1929). At the start of the next decade his *Chart for Rough Water* (New York: Doubleday Doran, 1940) applied his moral values to the coming struggle against Fascism. Archibald MacLeish's "The Irresponsibles" (*Nation*, 150 [May 18, 1940], pp. 618–23) was a more widely noted appeal to traditional values, angled from a more exclusive interest in the American case. MacLeish's views on the needs of the spirit during the Depression were well expressed in *America Was Promises* (New York: Duell, Sloan and Pearce, 1939) and in several of his poems brought together in *Collected Poems, 1917–1952* (Boston: Houghton Mifflin, 1958).

The distributist and regionalist arguments bearing on usable tradition can be fruitfully approached through the manifesto of Herbert Agar and Allen Tate's *Who Owns America?* (Boston: Houghton Mifflin, 1936) and Herbert Odum's massive compilation, *Southern Regions of the United States* (Chapel Hill: University of North Carolina Press, 1936).

The liberal traditionalist vision affected many other persons in varying degrees. In exploring the wider dimensions one could usefully begin with the writings of Van Wyck Brooks, Edward Dahlberg, Robert Hutchins, and Gorham Munson.

Economic thought has, of course, played a vast role in reform. One would be wise to begin an assessment with Joseph Dorman's *The Economic Mind in American Civilization*, Vols. 3–5 (New York: Viking, 1949–59). Dorfman's biography of Thorstein Veblen is also the best introduction to that controversial social critic whose influence on many independent liberals was crucial. Lewis Corey's *The Decline of American Capitalism* (New York: Covici, Friede, 1934) and *The Crisis of the Middle Class* (New York: Covici, Friede, 1935) ably advanced the Marxian critique that was a formidable rival and sometime ally to independent liberalism. And Lawrence Dennis' *Is Capitalism Doomed?* (New York: Harper, 1932) and *The Coming American Fascism* (New York: Harper, 1936) created a stir with their shrewd expositions of Fascist economics. For an able description of the flagging Socialist cause after World War I see James Weinstein, *The Decline of Socialism, 1912–1925* (New York and London: Monthly Review Press, 1967). Countering Weinstein's gloomy tale of Socialism's political ebb is Joseph Schumpeter's equally gloomy prediction in *Capitalism,*

Socialism and Democracy (New York: Harper, 1942) that Socialist economics are destined to take over the Western democracies.

During the confused times after World War II many writings have offered illuminating reflections on independent liberalism. Daniel Bell's *The End of Ideology* (New York: Free Press, 1960) describes "the exhaustion of political ideas" that characterized the 1950's. Ronald Berman's *America in the Sixties: An Intellectual History* (New York: Free Press, 1968) charts the revival of political activism and ideology. Herbert Marcuse's writings, especially *One Dimensional Man* (Boston: Beacon, 1964) and *An Essay on Liberation* (Boston: Beacon, 1969), comprise the most telling neo-Marxist analysis. At the far end of the ideological scale from Marcuse's sometimes abrasive concept of a unitary state are the anarchist critiques of Paul Goodman and Robert Paul Wolff. Theodore Roszak in *The Making of a Counter-Culture* (Garden City: Doubleday, 1969) discusses radical dissociation from all political systems and the prevailing social norms. And, more recently, Charles Reich in *The Greening of America: The Coming of a New Consciousness and the Rebirth of a Future* (New York: Random, 1970) has offered an ecstatic vision, provocative if not entirely plausible, of a new world yet to come.

Index

313